THE NEGLECTED HARDY

THE NEGLECTED HARDY

Thomas Hardy's Lesser Novels

Richard H. Taylor

First published 1982 by
THE MACMILLAN PRESS LTD
London and Basingstoke
Companies and representatives
throughout the world

ISBN 0 333 31051 9

Printed in Hong Kong

To all my former students and colleagues
in the Department of English at Stockwell College,
with thanks for their good friendship

Contents

Prefatory Note

'And did it hold your interest?' Hardy asked Virginia Woolf of *The Mayor of Casterbridge*. To the novelist that is the first criterion of judgement, and if Hardy had asked me the same question of the lesser novels the answer would have been a distinct affirmative. For this book has been inspired by the enjoyment of reading *all* Hardy's novels and by the belief that those which are less highly esteemed are nevertheless both interesting and rewarding. At a time when studies of Hardy's major fiction continue to proliferate at an astonishing rate, the critical focus should surely be shifted for once to the lesser novels, in which I suspect there is a growing interest. And it is this regard for some often neglected works that I hope to stimulate.

I have always been encouraged in this enterprise by my wife Pamela, whose enthusiasm and bright good spirits and humour are invaluable; my first and greatest acknowledgement of thanks must always go to her. In writing about Hardy's lesser novels I have enjoyed the immense benefit of the wisdom, advice and friendship of Professor Kenneth J. Fielding and Mr T.R.M. Creighton, of the Department of English Literature, University of Edinburgh, as well as the great pleasure of working with them. I thank Kenneth Fielding and Tom Creighton warmly for their continuing interest and generosity.

I wish to thank the Trustees of the Thomas Hardy Memorial Collection in the Dorset County Museum for their kind permission to quote from materials in the Hardy Collection. And I would like to thank Hardy friends and scholars who encouraged me to publish my studies of these lesser novels, including Dr James Gibson, Professor Ian Gregor and Dr Frank Pinion, as well as those other Hardy enthusiasts who responded so kindly to the original draft of Chapter 4, which in a slightly different form constituted a lecture I delivered on 14 August 1978 at the Summer School organised at Weymouth by the Thomas Hardy Society.

At The Macmillan Press Miss Julia Tame and Mr T.M. Farmiloe have been a constant support and courteously helpful at every stage of planning and production, and I offer them my gratitude for all their efforts. I have enjoyed working with them and Ms Susan Metham, Mr Keith Walker and Mr Timothy Fox, whom I thank for their care and thoroughness in seeing the book through the press. Mr Roger Peers, Curator of the Dorset County Museum, has continued to be remarkably good-humoured and helpful during my researches there, and he has clearly infected his fine staff with these same qualities. And, more locally, I am grateful to Mrs Carol Fox for binding my typescript before publication, and to Miss Linda Valenti, a student whose enthusiasm for the lesser novels while writing a dissertation which I supervised had the timely effect of limiting any procrastination over finishing my own study!

Over a number of years and in different institutions in Britain and Canada I have been exceptionally fortunate in my students, with whom it has always been a delight to explore Hardy's prose and poetry. Most recently this has been at Stockwell College, a constituent college of the University of London Institute of Education. Stockwell College has long enjoyed Hardy connections: Hardy's cousin Tryphena Sparks was one of its students in 1870–1 (graduating in the first class) and Hardy himself visited the college in June 1891 (an occasion recalled in the *Life*). But Stockwell College finally closes its doors on 31 August 1980, so I dedicate this book to my Stockwell College students and colleagues. I am thinking of each one of those students, too numerous to mention individually but all remembered, with their keenness and humour and conviviality. The good friendship that can arise from close working is something that I am happy to have shared and to continue to share with them and with my colleagues. Among the latter I would like to make particular mention of Michael Blake, Jean Cardy, Mike Cooper, Bob Dixon, John Elwell, Dorothy Gulliver, Audrey Insch, Colin Mortimer, Johanna Thorpe and Joan Walmsley, for all of whom I shall always have a special affection and regard, the warmth of their friendship being more than I can tell.

June 1980   R.H.T.

Abbreviations

The following abbreviations are used throughout to identify frequently cited texts:

L	Florence Emily Hardy, *The Life of Thomas Hardy* (1962)
Collected Letters	R.L. Purdy and Michael Millgate (eds), *The Collected Letters of Thomas Hardy*, I (1978)
Literary Notes	L.A. Björk (ed.), *The Literary Notes of Thomas Hardy*, I (1974)
One Rare Fair Woman	Evelyn Hardy and F.B. Pinion (eds), *One Rare Fair Woman: Thomas Hardy's Letters to Florence Henniker 1893–1922* (1972)
Personal Notebooks	Richard H. Taylor (ed.), *The Personal Notebooks of Thomas Hardy* (1979)
Personal Writings	Harold Orel (ed.), *Thomas Hardy's Personal Writings* (1966)
Purdy	Richard L. Purdy, *Thomas Hardy: A Bibliographical Study* (1954)

DCM indicates the Dorset County Museum.

1 Introduction

Hardy's lesser novels have been consistently undervalued and, though no revaluative process could elevate them to the stature of the major works, they deserve a fuller and more sympathetic reading than they have conventionally been accorded. The great novels of character and environment have cast them into shadow so that they have remained dustily elusive of serious critical examination. Yet they are worth reading and, now that at last they are available for the first time in paperback and therefore within reach of a wider audience, new readers may see that even Hardy's 'worst' novel (if such an epithet can ever be objectively applied to a work of literature) does not need any strenuous apology. And, as Edmund Gosse wrote, 'The worst chapter of *The Hand of Ethelberta* is recognisable, in a moment, as written by the author of the best chapter in *The Return of the Native*.'[1]

We can see at once what he means: that a common quality informs Hardy's whole *œuvre*, the least fortunate aspects of the lesser novels as well as the most imposing features of those most highly esteemed, with a stamp of greatness. Hardy never wrote a 'bad' novel. Among the fourteen that he wrote his range is considerable, his materials and methods are diverse and his idiosyncratic experiments are often bold, but there is no failure. This may not be the conventional view, but only a reading of Hardy's work as a whole can reveal the unity and consistency of his art and his fictive world. But it is not a consistency of the kind sometimes alleged and often sought. Criticism, both individual and cumulative, has tried to define Hardy's achievement more exactly than he would have wished. His 'unadjusted impressions'[2] have been knitted together into fabrics that quite often do not in any real sense exist. The network is more complex than some

1

such studies allow and less ingenious than others predicate. 'The mission of poetry', Hardy said, 'is to record impressions, not convictions' (*L*, 377), and this stands for all his art. This is not to say that Hardy is detached or that conviction is absent: like the real firmness of Anne Garland in *The Trumpet-Major*, conviction is there, 'often unperceived at first, as the speck of colour lurks unperceived in the heart of the palest parsley flower'. But Hardy's conviction is not set out in the form of convictions, and the distinction is important. This makes him hard to pin down and define, and impossible to 'explain' in any simplistic way, but the response that his work provokes is all the more rewarding for its denial of ready definition.

It is not surprising that Hardy resists classification, either in mode or literary tradition. He is like no other novelist, and no other novelist is like him. It is not new to say that it is the unusual way in which the individual impress of Hardy's mind is made present in his work that makes it distinctive, but it is this which gives inescapable unity to all his writing. Whether or not he is consistent in his ideas is a red herring: few people are, and consistency is not necessarily a virtue. It matters more that he is consistent in his art, that *The Hand of Ethelberta*, whatever its rank as a novel, can be recognised as the work of a great writer. In view of the obvious homology of all his novels it is a typical oddity of Hardy's experience that he should be seen as notoriously uneven.

His reputation as one of the greatest novelists in the English language is based upon seven remarkable novels, only half his output of fiction; the reputation of few other modern novelists of comparable status rests on such a proportion of their work. We are left with the question: what are we to say of the other seven novels? They are traditionally regarded as minor works, as experiments and mistakes, and as being comparatively unimportant. The critical lines have been sharply drawn and without significant dissent. If a graph were mounted to show the critical acceptability of Hardy's successive novels a curious pattern of peaks and valleys would emerge, and not only at the beginning of his career. After *Far from the Madding Crowd* he wrote *The Hand of Ethelberta*; after *The Return of the Native* came *The Trumpet-Major*, *A Laodicean* and *Two on a Tower*; after three major novels, which included *The Mayor of Casterbridge* and *Tess*, he wrote *The Well-Beloved*. Either Hardy is an author of greater flexibility than the standard account suggests or the quality of his writing is oddly variable: there is some truth in each of these contentions.

The distinctions were not so finely drawn when the novels appeared. *A Pair of Blue Eyes* could be seen in 1873 as the work of a man of genius and *A Laodicean*, now regarded as his worst novel, could be highly commended in 1881. In 1890 *The Mayor of Casterbridge* could be found less perfect in its proportions than *A Pair of Blue Eyes*. Some of these verdicts may now seem eccentric, and changes in sensibility and fashion as well as critical judgement have diminished the stature of several novels since then; but even in 1906, when *The Pocket Thomas Hardy*[3] was published, with selections from his prose and verse, the most numerous extracts (after *Tess* and *Far from the Madding Crowd*) came from *Desperate Remedies* and *A Pair of Blue Eyes*. The present modest estimation of these novels cannot be attributed only to changes in taste; nor can critical wrongheadedness be blamed, though the impression sometimes remains that the lesser novels have been read very perfunctorily. It is partly due to the remarkable qualities of the more successful novels, which have demanded and sustained extensive critical exploration and which can fairly be said to contain the centre of Hardy's achievement in prose. They represent such a major corpus of work that the remaining novels have almost inevitably been cast as a sub-group.

This derogation invites a new reading. It is surely wrong to isolate the lesser novels as separate and distinct, as aberrations and failures. They play an essential part in the dynamic process of the development of Hardy's fiction, and each stage of his career contributes to the integrity of the whole. To exclude the seven less successful novels is to distort his career and to disguise the interpenetrating unities of his fiction. Yet it is hard to approach them without prejudice, to escape the sometimes extreme and emotive critical language which has been applied to them (they have been called 'execrable', 'nonsense' and 'trash'), and to set aside the established value-judgements which may intervene between the reader and his direct engagement with the text. It may be useful, therefore, to see these novels as being different rather than inferior and to seek their peculiar and individual qualities. In this study I am deliberately reversing the traditional order of priority and inverting the usual pattern of criticism of the novels. Because these works are more substantial

than the term implies, the comparative adjective 'minor' is
abjured in favour of calling them 'lesser' novels; a nicety
perhaps, but one meant to escape the more pejorative assumptions that I believe attach to 'minor', and yet to acknowledge
that these fictions have peculiar weaknesses as well as peculiar
strengths and that an attempt has to be made to discover what
distinguishes them from the major novels. The chapters that
follow have been motivated and sustained by the enjoyment of
reading these lesser novels and the belief that they are of unique
interest to all those who value Hardy's fiction.

Since there is no doubt that the circumstances of composition
and publication had an important bearing on each of Hardy's
novels, the first part of each of the following chapters sets the
novel in question in its context in Hardy's life and career and
examines the novel's progress from genesis to publication. For
the same reason contemporary criticism is invoked, since each
novel's reception can be seen to have influenced Hardy's
development.

Hardy's fiction has inspired a massive body of criticism and
analysis, almost all of which has been devoted to the major
novels. It often seems doubtful whether anything new remains to
be said, though from time to time distinctive new readings and
surveys emerge to surprise and delight (such as John Bayley's
urbane and subtle study, *An Essay on Hardy*, in 1978). But it is fair
to say that analysis of the major fiction has otherwise probably
reached a point of diminishing returns. And through a century of
critical endeavour certain preconceptions about Hardy's writing
have, at various stages, hardened into myth: that he is a gloomy
pessimist, a disciple of Schopenhauer, a topographical novelist, a
bucolic antiquarian, the chronicler of agricultural decline, the
author by chance of a few good poems, even that he is the author
by chance of a few good novels. Of course he is much more than
any of these things. It is one of the most unfortunate legends,
that Hardy's lesser novels are such failures that they are scarcely
worth reading, that the present study seeks to disprove. Several
questions are borne in mind throughout. What value can we set
upon each of these lesser novels? What do they contribute to the
Hardy canon as a whole and what is their relationship to the
better-known novels? What themes or other characteristics do
they have in common and what can we learn from them about
Hardy and the development of his art?

Conclusions are offered in a series of individual case studies which seek to discover the nature of each novel's deficiencies and (in so far as such things are discoverable) the circumstances which may have contributed to their lesser stature, and to validate what is good in them. What emerges is the way in which the lesser novels successively contribute to what I called earlier the interpenetrating unities of his fiction and, I believe, a vindication of my initial claim that Hardy never wrote a bad novel. The author's poetic description of 'Our Old Friend Dualism' seems an apt account of Hardy himself as he finally emerges from this extended discussion: 'All hail to him, the Protean! A tough old chap is he.' There is a resilience about these neglected novels as well as their author. For in their unexpected, unusual and sometimes remarkable range, written under the direction of a Protean intellect, there can be no doubt that they offer what Hardy regarded as the proper end of reading fiction for readers rightly intent upon 'getting good out of novels': 'intellectual or moral profit to active and undulled spirits'.[4]

This study does not propose a radical reappraisal of the comparative rankings of Hardy's novels, nor does it pretend to be a definitive study of these lesser works, but it does aim to be a contribution towards their rehabilitation. George Steiner once proposed an unexceptionable criterion for literary criticism: 'Criticism should open more books than it closes.' If this study proves a book-opener it will have served its purpose. For the ulterior motive of this discussion is to encourage readers to dust down and recover these neglected works from the critical attic to which they have been consigned, and consequently to discover and enjoy the individual delights which they have to offer.

2 'Well, that's a rum story': *Desperate Remedies* (1871)

1

Desperate Remedies, Hardy's first published novel, is an unlikely progenitor of a career that later included *The Mayor of Casterbridge* and *Tess of the d'Urbervilles*. It is a thriller, a Victorian sensation novel written at the end of a decade during which the most popular novels included *The Woman in White* (1860) and *The Moonstone* (1868), both by Wilkie Collins, whose sensational influence is shot through Hardy's novel.[1] *Desperate Remedies* is an unusual first novel in so far as it is not, in the context of the author's *œuvre*, as *The Pickwick Papers* is to Dickens, as *Mary Barton* is to Mrs Gaskell, or as *Scenes of Clerical Life* is to George Eliot. But it is emphatically not the false start that it is often claimed to be. Partly the product of chance advice, partly a pot-boiler, it is flawed but idiosyncratic. *Desperate Remedies* is a better novel, and one more characteristic of Hardy, than has been generally supposed, and hardly deserves the low critical status to which it has been assigned.

By the time it was written Hardy had been chastened by the rejection of his first novel, a sweeping socialistic satire called *The Poor Man and the Lady*, which would have introduced him even more curiously. The influences which helped to shape it were not those that inform *Desperate Remedies* but, rather, Hardy's passionate hatred of social injustice, and the reading which encouraged and fortified this animus. In 1863 Hardy commended Thackeray to his sister, describing him as 'considered to be the greatest novelist of the day – looking at novel writing of the highest kind as a perfect and truthful representation of actual life – which is no doubt the proper view to take' (*L*, 40). *Desperate Remedies* is a different matter and in it the regard for realism implicit in this respect for Thackeray is swept away by the impulse to write a different kind of novel. But in 1865 Hardy was sending his sister

6

Trollope's *Barchester Towers* and recommending Bulwer-Lytton's *Pelham*, another novel concerned with social and political life. In 1868 he was still 'reading Browning and Thackeray' (*L*, 57) and, as he read them, writing out *The Poor Man and the Lady*. He was attempting to achieve realism after the manner of Thackeray and on Thackeray's social level, though he later admitted how naïve this realism was in circumstantial detail, and trying to write with 'the affected simplicity' of Defoe's style (*L*, 61). This too is abandoned in *Desperate Remedies*, though the novel inherits Defoe's minute precision of detail and chronology, his empirical or (in Ian Watt's term) 'formal' realism. But the radicalism which had motivated *The Poor Man and the Lady* has had to be laid aside entirely.

Hardy began his first novel at Bockhampton in late summer 1867 and made his fair copy between 16 January and 9 June 1868. He had worked in London for five years but on account of weakening health in the city, where 'his languor increased month by month', had returned to work for a period with his old architectural instructor, John Hicks, in Dorchester. It was in this mood of discontent and urban *ennui* that *The Poor Man and the Lady* was conceived. His manuscript revealed no lack of confidence in attacking London society and his own lack of immediate experience therein did not restrain him. There is a telling thought among his 'Notes of 1866–67': 'The defects of a class are more perceptible to the class immediately below it than to itself.' (*L*, 55) But what Hardy had supposed to be satiric realism turned out to be unacceptable caricature. In a remarkably buoyant letter submitting his novel to Alexander Macmillan on 25 July 1868 Hardy claimed that his 'utterances of strong feeling' against 'the upper classes of society' had been 'inserted edgewise so to say; half concealed beneath ambiguous expressions'.[2] Yet the satire seemed to its few readers oppressive and ill-informed.

In the absence of the manuscript (Hardy told Vere Collins in 1921 that he had 'got rid of it' when moving), or more evidence than exists in the various fragments which are located in revised forms elsewhere in Hardy's fiction, the novel can only be judged by the story 'An Indiscretion in the Life of an Heiress', into which a decade later Hardy distilled all that remained of the original novel, and through the contemporary reactions of those who read it – Alexander Macmillan and John Morley, Frederick

Chapman and George Meredith. Macmillan sent Hardy a long letter on 10 August, criticising in detail the excesses and 'fatal drawbacks' of the novel: Hardy is found guilty of 'the wholesale blackening of a class' without intimate knowledge of it and without allowing the redeeming features granted it by Thackeray who, Macmillan tells Hardy, 'meant fun'. By contrast, Hardy is said to 'mean mischief'. His 'black wash will not be recognised as anything more than ignorant misrepresentation'; yet much of the writing is admirable, a scene in Rotten Row is praised, and the publisher sees Hardy as a writer 'of, at least potentially, considerable mark, of power and purpose'. His reader John Morley, while thinking the story too much 'like a clever lad's dream', describes the work as 'a very curious and original performance'.[3] But the book was found unsuitable for Macmillan's list, passed on to Chapman and Hall on 8 December but rejected by them also on 8 February 1869 (unless Hardy would guarantee £20 against loss). In the following month Frederick Chapman called Hardy in to meet the reader who had read the manuscript. Unknown to Hardy, this was George Meredith, whose advice to the young author not to 'nail his colours to the mast' (*L*, 61) so uncompromisingly in a first book led Hardy to withdraw his manuscript. It was Meredith's further advice that Hardy should attempt a more complicated plot that impelled him to write *Desperate Remedies*.

Some of the defects of this sensation novel derive from the sequence of events that led to its genesis. His trials over *The Poor Man and the Lady* set the pattern for Hardy's difficulties in dealing with publishers over many years, difficulties which could not fail to have a serious effect on the manner and direction of his fiction. Hardy's immediate problem lay in trying to write a novel acceptable to Macmillan, and he had already been reproved for the subversiveness of *The Poor Man and the Lady*, in which his views had been 'obviously those of a young man with a passion for reforming the world' (*L*, 61). To read the correspondence between Hardy and Alexander Macmillan is moving and disturbing. A much tighter rein was imposed on Hardy than on Dickens in *The Pickwick Papers* or Mrs Gaskell in *Mary Barton*: Macmillan would probably have wanted the vulgarism of the former tamed and the revolutionary character of the latter softened before he would risk them. *Desperate Remedies* was written, in a further attempt to please him, between autumn

1869 and (apart from the last four chapters) March 1870, and submitted to Macmillan on 5 March. But the publisher wrote back on 4 April rejecting the novel as being 'of far too sensational an order for us to think of publishing.'[4] John Morley discovered in the book '*power* – at present of a violent and undisciplined kind', but he was shocked by its central incident:

> But the story is ruined by the disgusting and absurd outrage which is the key to its mystery. The violation of a young lady at an evening party, and the subsequent birth of a child, is too abominable to be tolerated as a central incident from which the action of the story is to move.[5]

We cannot assess the fairness of Morley's judgement, since Hardy edited this incident out of the story. Yet it is precisely from some such event that Hardy's subject develops in both *The Poor Man* and *Desperate Remedies*, and even in the limited circles of Macmillan, Morley or the reviewer for the *Spectator* (who also took great offence at the published novel), women could be violated and have children; the passions of the past could not be dispelled by the respectable face-savers of the present. It is even less acceptable to find Macmillan, writing about *The Poor Man*, lecturing Hardy with Grundyan logic so extraordinary as to be almost comic:

> *Romeo and Juliet* and *Hamlet* have many unnatural scenes, but Shakespeare put them in foreign countries, and took the stories from old books. When he was nearer home and his own time you don't find such things in his writing.

D. H. Lawrence's similar experience with a publisher 45 years later begs the same question about some publishers' sensibilities: 'William Heinemann said he thought *Sons and Lovers* the dirtiest book he had ever read. I should not have thought the deceased gentleman's reading had been so circumspectly narrow.'[6] In both of Hardy's novels he was feeling his way to something difficult and disturbing but he was doubtfully helped by all the well-meant advice he received. And it was only after Hardy had contributed £75 towards its expenses that *Desperate Remedies* was eventually published, by the less-reputable house of William Tinsley,[7] on 25 March 1871.

2

'Now isn't that an odd story?'
'It is, indeed,' Cytherea murmured. 'Very, very strange.'

Hardy's first published novel is distinguished by its oddity. Inspired by Meredith's advice, but against his own judgement, to write the kind of novel he had never intended, the young author produced what one of his characters calls 'a rum story'. And it is in the rumness and oddity that much of the work's curious power, as well as its weakness, is found. In *Desperate Remedies* Hardy renounces his early emulation of Thackeray. In the terms of David Masson's mid-century review of *Pendennis* and *David Copperfield*,[8] Hardy's novel represents a shift from the real (as represented by Thackeray) to the ideal (in the mode of Dickens), but it is the Wilkie Collins strain of idealism that it inherits. The sensation novel, in the hands of Collins and Charles Reade and others, had flourished in the preceding decade; when *Desperate Remedies* appeared in 1871 the genre was still alive but flagging. Among novels published in this year was *Not Wooed, But Won* by James Payn, an imitator of Reade and Collins; Reade's *A Terrible Temptation* appeared, a sensational, semi-autobiographical, social reform novel; Collins himself had moved on to propaganda fiction – *Poor Miss Finch* is about a blind girl who marries a man whose treatment for epilepsy has made him turn blue, still a sensational enough premise. But the year in which Hardy made his first appearance also included new work from three major novelists. George Meredith, whose advice had inspired the form of Hardy's novel, himself produced a story with a plot, the romantic comedy *Harry Richmond*. Nearing the end of her career, George Eliot was publishing in 5s. parts her most ambitious work, *Middlemarch*. But Hardy's comparative insignificance in this overlap of literary generations is sharply emphasised by his financial arrangements. While Hardy was having to pay £75 to have his novel published by Tinsley, Trollope's *Ralph the Heir* appeared. Trollope received £2,500 for what he called 'one of the worst novels I have written'.[9] Although written in a popular genre, Hardy's novel, which according to the conventions of the day was published anonymously, stood little chance of commercial success in comparison with such established names. Unsurprisingly it was remaindered, and Hardy made an overall loss of £15. 7s. 5d.

The balance sheet reveals nothing of the novel's unusual range of properties, which suggests influences and capabilities extending far beyond the stock of the sensation novel. *Desperate Remedies* has a lively assortment of ingredients: it includes a murder, a dramatic fire, ghostly apparitions, wailings in the night, a suicide, a mysterious disease, false and confused identities, a fight, philosophical reflections, extensive literary allusions, a Byronic and Mephistophelian villain, a love story, farce and an apparently Lesbian incident. The tone varies from comedy to tragedy, from the light and flippant to the gruesome and macabre, from fixation upon things ephemeral to the intimation of things eternal and universal. It is a remarkable range. But of course the total fusion of these disparate elements is scarcely possible and Hardy's handling of his material is sometimes tentative: in the 1889 Prefatory Note Hardy tells us that he was 'feeling his way to a method'. But despite subsequent disclaimers – he called it a 'melodramatic novel ... the unfortunate consequence of Meredith's advice "to write a story with a plot"' (*L*, 64) – he was satisfied enough to have it reissued many times, deeming it 'extremely clever' (*L*, 85) and 'not unworthy of a little longer preservation' (Prefatory Note).

The tentativeness of the work is shrewdly concealed in Hardy's apt classification of it in 1912 as a 'Novel of Ingenuity'. Ingenious it is, and the facility with which Hardy handles the complex structure is astonishing. Intricate mechanisms are invoked to engineer the ambitious plot – such as the arrangement of three observers simultaneously yet secretly watching Manston's attempt to bury his wife's body, and watching each other – and Hardy adheres to a minute chronological verisimilitude. Individual sections describe periods of widely varying duration, ranging from eighteen years (Chapter 1, Part 2) to half an hour (Chapter 19, Part 5, and elsewhere). Hardy's architectonic skill is self-evident, yet the conventions of the genre permit the creaking of joints in the plot: that Hardy is aware of coincidences that might elsewhere seem wilfully implausible is implied in suggestive phrases about 'the farce of an accidental meeting' or 'the strange confluence of circumstances'. The novel's epigraph, from Scott, shows that as early as 1871 Hardy was quite clear about the mode of his fiction:

> Though an unconnected course of adventure is what most
> frequently occurs in nature, yet the province of the romance-
> writer being artificial, there is more required from him than a
> mere compliance with the simplicity of reality.

This anticipates Hardy's later advocacy of licensed exaggeration
and idealisation at the expense of realism or naturalism, which
places him firmly outside the objective tradition of, for example,
Flaubert (whose *Madame Bovary* had appeared in 1857 and
Sentimental Education in 1869), and aligns him with the more
flexible aesthetic of Dickens. There is nothing tentative about
Hardy's adoption of the romance mode: fiction, he wrote later,
must always be more than 'a precise transcript of ordinary life'
(July 1881; *L*, 150). So Hardy's adoption of the sensation genre
for *Desperate Remedies* is consistent with this. The sensation novel
endeavours to escape the limitations of realism while often
exploiting aspects of it, such as exactness of plot. The ballad, the
popular drama, the Gothic novel, the Newgate novel, the fiction
of the working man – these all deal with fictions that are not in
the least like Henry James's, and that like the sensation novel are
perhaps more popular at a time when there are no positive
beliefs. But although they are not written within the conventions
of the educated middle class of the latter half of the nineteenth
century, they do correspond to inner experience.

In this respect *Desperate Remedies* is congeneric with Hardy's
later fiction, for in a very real sense he remained a sensation
novelist throughout his career. Seventeen years after the publication of *Desperate Remedies* he noted:

> January 14 [1888]. A 'sensation-novel' is possible in which the
> sensationalism is not casualty, but evolution; not physical, but
> psychical.... The difference between the latter kind of novel
> and the novel of physical sensationalism – i.e. personal
> adventure, etc. – is this: that whereas in the physical the
> adventure itself is the subject of interest, the psychical results
> being passed over as commonplace, in the psychical the
> casualty or adventure is held to be of intrinsic interest, but the
> effect upon the faculties is the important matter to be
> depicted. (*L*, 204)

This is vital to the proper understanding of Hardy's fiction.

Thus defined, every one of his novels is a sensation novel: the 'effect upon the faculties' (of the characters) is always the most important interest, even in *Desperate Remedies*, which relies more on external event than most of the others. It is in Hardy's concern with the 'psychical results' of the adventures which he depicts that his real *vraisemblance* lies. He becomes increasingly an inward artist, celebrating individual lives; the real drama becomes cerebral. But this alone does not make a novel for Hardy, whose disdain for Henry James's 'ponderously warm manner of saying nothing in infinite sentences' (*L*, 181) comes as no surprise. Fiction, he says, must first of all tell a striking but believable story: 'human nature must never be made abnormal, which is introducing incredibility. The uncommonness must be in the events, not in the characters.' (July 1881; *L*, 150) A sensation novel may also violate realism in order to express something important. It frees the writer from the need to be respectable; he does not have to keep to the drawing-room or drawing-room subjects. That it is about violence, is sensational in its treatment of sex, is not in its disfavour; that it has to treat these themes in a merely sensational or even absurd manner is its misfortune. But some of its qualities lie on the surface and some lie below it. *Desperate Remedies*, though a novel of physical adventure, is more than what Hardy calls 'a novel of physical sensationalism', and the distinction is important. The 'psychical' interest is predominant and an intense psychological pressure operates not far below the surface.

Desperate Remedies also has affinities with the Victorian popular theatre. Hardy's description of the novel as 'melodramatic' aligns it with such influential plays as *Sweeney Todd* (1842), any of the numerous versions of *Maria Marten*, or Dion Boucicault's adaptations of French melodrama. Such plays sought to thrill their audiences by using various conventional devices; improbability mattered little and their subject-matter might include the supernatural or demonic. The conflict between good and evil was usually wrought between an implacably evil villain and a strikingly virtuous heroine, and sensationalism of incident was heightened by unsubtle, forceful acting. Unlike Hardy's refinement of the technique of the stage, the form itself was unsophisticated and the characters mere stereotypes. The 'mystery, entanglement, surprise, and moral obliquity' (Prefatory Note) of *Desperate Remedies* are also enlivened by properties of the Gothic romance. Hardy writes approvingly elsewhere of Mrs Radcliffe, and as a boy revelled in the novels of Harrison Ainsworth, but the Gothic is fundamental to his creative imagination. The setting is generically conventional: rushing waterfall, howling dogs, the death-rattle and, powerfully, the 'general unearthly weirdness' of the crashing storm as Manston plays the organ for Cytherea. But Hardy simultaneously exposes the artifice of the Gothic suggestiveness, as Jane Austen does in *Northanger Abbey*: ''Tis jest the house for a nice ghastly hair-on-end story,' says the coachman.

In writing this novel of 'purely artistic purpose' and more complicated plot, Hardy had shown his readiness to take advice with great humility and had displayed eagerness to aim at a specific market. But Meredith had not advised Hardy to write a thriller. This decision was entirely his own and calculated 'to attract public attention at all hazards' (*L*, 85). And the novel did win a good measure of critical attention, in which recognition of Hardy's distinct abilities was tempered with severe reservations. *Desperate Remedies* was seen as having 'considerable artistic power' (*Athenaeum*, 1 April 1871), a plot 'worked out with abundant skill' (*Saturday Review*, 30 September 1871), and as a novel displaying 'talent of a remarkable kind' (*Spectator*, 22 April 1871). The *Athenaeum* and the *Saturday Review* noticed the affinity with George Eliot, and all praised the rustics. But what drew down the wrath of the critics was its coarseness and the supposed moral outrage of Miss Aldclyffe's having borne an illegitimate child. This had already caused Macmillan to reject the book. The *Athenaeum* found that 'certain expressions' were 'remarkably coarse', but the most oppressively severe review appeared in the *Spectator* and this, in its own words, set out 'to warn ... readers against this book'.[10] Again an ironic circularity in Hardy's career is suggested: it was on similar grounds that later reviewers set out to 'warn against' *Jude the Obscure*.

The constant sexual pressure in *Desperate Remedies*, on and below the surface, is unusual in kind and intensity, and exceptional even in a sensation novel, and its manifestations are not always conventional. Both Miss Aldclyffe and Cytherea have suggestively Freudian dreams. Time and his scythe set upon Miss Aldclyffe: 'he seized me, took a piece of me only ... I can't bear to think of it.' Cytherea, who has already revealed herself as something of a masochist 'with a wayward pleasure in giving herself misery', has an odd dream of being 'whipped with dry bones, suspended on strings', and the perpetrator's form is Manston's. The narrative is full of sexual insistence. Cytherea twice feels, with a mixture of sensations, Manston pressing against her dress; Miss Aldclyffe articulates neurotic sexual views; Cytherea is seen admiring 'her own magnificent resources in face and bosom' reflected in a mirror; the older lady is seen undressing, and there is a certain sensuousness in the description. The most unexpected sexual manifestation is the ambivalent relationship between the two women. It is not clear whether Hardy realised that he was portraying an apparently Lesbian attachment; on the whole it seems likely that he did not understand the full implications of his narrative. Miss Aldclyffe's characteristics are pervasively masculine: she has 'a severity about the lower outlines of the face which give a masculine cast to this portion of her countenance'; she is 'as jealous as any man' about Cytherea, whom she holds 'almost as a lover'; 'Cythie,' she implores elsewhere, 'don't let any man stand between us. O, I can't bear that!'; when she weeps, 'the weeping of such a nature [is] as harrowing as the weeping of a man.' After her earliest interview with Cytherea, Miss Aldclyffe yields to sensuous reflections: 'It is almost worth while to be bored with instructing her in order to have a creature who could glide round my luxurious indolent body in that manner ... I warrant how light her fingers are upon one's head and neck.'

All this reaches its climax in the scene between the two women in bed:

> The instant they were in bed Miss Aldclyffe freed herself from the last remnant of restraint. She flung her arms round the young girl, and pressed her gently to her heart.
> 'Now kiss me,' she said.

She then variously describes herself as 'an ill-tempered woman ... half out of my mind ... a very fool ... a wicked old sinner', and demands that Cytherea kiss her more heartily while her own kisses are 'given as if in the outburst of strong feelings, long checked, and yearning for something to love and be loved by in return'.[11] An even stranger emotion emerges as Miss Aldclyffe reveals embittered cynicism about men. When told of Springrove she speaks 'in jealous and gloomy accents', reproaching

Cytherea for having been 'sullied by a man's lips'. Men, she says, make 'a regular highway' of girls' lips:

> 'I – an old fool – have been sipping at your mouth as if it were honey ... a minute ago, and you seemed to me like a fresh spring meadow – now you seem a dusty highway.'

This anticipates Knight's equally unbalanced reaction in *A Pair of Blue Eyes* upon his discovery that Elfride has been kissed before: 'And he used to kiss you ... I *hate* the fact that you have been caressed before; yes, hate it!' Miss Aldclyffe is a victim of severe emotional repression and her outbursts are classic instances of frustrated sexuality: in this she establishes a character typology principally found in the lesser novels. The entire episode is powerful however interpreted, both physically and psychically suggestive. It could have been the most controversial of all Hardy's presentations of sexuality; that it provoked no outcry perhaps signifies the comparative innocence of the sensation-novel-reading public of 1871. But it is small wonder that the critics, who may have been less oblivious of the implications of the situation than the author himself, were startled.[12]

The intensity of the relationships in *Desperate Remedies* distinguishes it from the usual sensation novel. Hardy's characters transcend the flat stereotypes of melodrama, though their roles are traditional. Miss Aldclyffe is the mysterious lady of the manor, Cytherea and Edward are the innocent heroine and heroic saviour, Manston is the villainous anti-hero. Hardy wrote of them in a letter:

> The characters were, to myself, mere puppets or pegs to weave the work upon – without reality or character enough in them to warrant their being denounced for want of moral attributes – the villain being in fact just about as human as the giants slain by Jack, and capable of corrupting to the same degree.[13]

But, like many of Hardy's self-defensive statements, this has to be read with caution: the context shows Hardy's claim to be a defence against imputations of immorality, made by the critic of the *Spectator*. The suggestion that Manston is inhuman is simply disingenuous. The characters are types but this need not undermine their realism: D. H. Lawrence writes of the white, black and red qualities of the characters as if this gives a definitive account of their reality,[14] yet this simplicity of design is exactly what Hardy avoids. It is one of the unusual attributes of *Desperate Remedies* that the characters do not simply conform to their linear functions but become beings of some psychological complexity, unusual but real, though this sets up one of the tensions which ultimately weaken the novel. Their realism seems sometimes at odds with the form and, conversely, the melodramatic framework tends to dissipate the effectiveness of their dramatic relationship. And eventually the characters have to submit to their conventional roles: Hardy is unable to follow his own imaginative prescription for their destiny since he is limited by what may happen in the kind of novel he has chosen to write.

Yet Hardy establishes his characters with great vigour. Miss Aldclyffe, her thwarted emotions exercising intense psychological pressures within her, is drawn on a grand scale. She is not just 'red and black': a genuine and strong affection underlies the violent physicality of her ambivalent relationship with Cytherea, and her crime (in aiding Manston) is pathetically human, the action which a mother might take, through love and misguided loyalty, for an errant son. Early disappointments have shaped an embittered tyrant, and here a stereotype would end, but Hardy shows that her immoral efforts are disarmingly directed by the pursuit of a 'sweet dream'. Even in this attempt to achieve vicarious satisfaction of her own thwarted love she is acutely aware of the effects of her action upon others. Though single-minded, she is not mean: in deceiving Springrove about Cytherea's affections, at Manston's instigation, she 'descended to an action the meanness of which haunted her to her dying hour'. All the extremes of her behaviour are summarised, almost expiated, in her death-bed declaration: 'to die unloved is more than I can bear!'

The social mask is intermittently stripped from Miss Aldclyffe to reveal the woman within, a victim of social and sexual taboos. The portrayal of Cytherea is of the reverse pattern: she is too young to have any significant social *persona*, so her inner life is made more prominent from the beginning and she enjoys a complexity denied the conventional heroine. She is Hardy's first flirt, vain enough to know her physical attractions and to enjoy a *frisson* of satisfaction even at Manston's unwelcome attentions.

Volubly jealous of Adelaide Hinton's engagement to Springrove ('My nature is capable of more, far more, intense feeling than hers!'), she is equally prepared to indulge in the 'pleasure of re-creating defunct agonies, and lacerating herself with them now and then' if the affection she demands is not immediately forthcoming. Animal passion and this masochistic tendency alternate in Cytherea, and the latter dictates her submission to marriage with Manston because of her concern for, and feeling of duty towards, Owen. But her complex and resilient sexuality confounds the traditionally simple and virtually asexual role of the naïve young heroine, and makes it possible that even this surrender will not be for Cytherea a wholly unpleasurable experience. Edward Springrove, the young architect and poet and cynic, is Cytherea's rescuer, but he is much nearer to the conventional figure, insipid and dull, acquiescent in his fate and as drably functional as Cytherea's pompous brother, Owen. These dim figures are redeemed by the appearance among the lesser characters of the splendid Richard Crickett, the parish clerk, 'a kind of Bowdlerized rake', a man who swallows nothing as if it were a great deal. With his cries of 'Dang my old sides!', he is the ubiquitous village gossip and the leader of the rustic comedy of manners. The rustics' dispensation of bucolic wisdom, a Greek choric commentary in Barnes-like Wessex vernacular, establishes a distinctive tradition in Hardy's fiction as surely as it enriches this unusual sensation novel.

Although Cytherea's is the pivotal role, the dominating character is Aeneas Manston, the evil genius of the story. Too often curtly dismissed by critics in phrases like 'most outrageous' or 'wholly absurd', Manston is an impressive creation. He is, to be sure, 'a voluptuary with activity; which is a very bad form of man'; he exhibits a hot, animal passion; he emanates a Mephistophelian aura; he murders his wife, though indeliberate-ly, and has to engage in the deceit which culminates in his discovery. Manston is the agent of the 'desperate remedies' of the title:

> Diseases desperate grown
> By desperate appliance are relieved,
> Or not at all.
> (*Hamlet*: the King, IV, 3, 9–11)

He shares the dilemma of the King in *Hamlet*, and in the title is a clue to the outcome of the plot. And yet it is only at the end of the book that he sheds his complexity and degenerates into the black villain. He is a victim of social misfortune, and extenuating circumstances are offered for his villainy; as the offspring of an unhappy and unsatisfactory relationship, 'farmed out' as an orphan, his life cannot have been a happy one. Though he is a hot voluptuary he has to repress his desires, so it is no surprise that he is

> of a nature to kick against the pricks; the last man in the world to put up with a position because it seemed to be his destiny to do so; one who took upon himself to resist fate with the vindictive determination of a Theomachist.

It is of such material that Hardy later moulds tragic heroes, yet Manston is denied any such dignity by the demands of the sensation genre. But his violent nature is tempered with gentleness, and he is not without 'a sense of morality' in his relationship with Cytherea. It is neither an outrageous nor an absurd figure who reflects on the little creatures sporting in the rainwater-butt, after his rejection by Cytherea:

> Staves of sunlight slanted down through the still pool, lighting it up with wonderful distinctness. Hundreds of thousands of minute living creatures sported and tumbled in its depth with every contortion that gaiety could suggest; perfectly happy, though consisting only of a head, or a tail, or at most a head and a tail, and all doomed to die within the twenty-four hours.

And who then observes, with reasonable logic: 'Damn my position! Why shouldn't I be happy through my little day too?' This pained exclamation, which accompanies Manston's pathetic philosophical insight, finds its logical culmination in his suicide note, and its moving conclusion:

> I am now about to enter on my normal condition. For people are almost always in their graves. When we survey the long race of men, it is strange and still more strange to find that they are mainly dead men, who have scarcely ever been otherwise.

Manston is the first of Hardy's characters to suffer the
Schopenhauerean will-not-to-live, and his death has a pathos
not entirely dispelled by the summary conclusion of melodrama.
His quietistic abandonment of the will prefigures the submission
of Hardy's most complete characters, Henchard, Tess and Jude,
and after a series of conventionally macabre doings he is in his
'Last Words' rescued once again from the strait-jacket of the
stereotype. This 'black' character, externally a melodramatic
villain as evil as Webster's Bosola, of whom he is reminiscent,
thus ends his unrewarding life with what appears to be an
invocation of Petronius: *abiit ad plures*.[15]

Desperate Remedies establishes character typologies which run,
without major variation, throughout Hardy's fourteen novels.
Cytherea has immediate successors in Fancy Day and Elfride
Swancourt, and establishes a type evident in Thomasin, Anne
Garland, Grace Melbury and Marty South. Cytherea is said to
possess 'Arcadian innocence'; Grace and Giles, fifteen years
later, are described as 'Arcadian innocents' (*The Woodlanders*,
Chapter 38). Miss Aldclyffe has affinities with Lady Viviette
Constantine and Mrs Charmond, since all are grand ladies who
are brought down, but especially with Mrs Charmond. Both
inherit social rank by chance, not birth; both are haughty,
impetuous, handsome; both lay plots and plans and die seeing
these in ruins. Manston is surely the first of Hardy's 'Mephistophelian Visitants', though he is not formally enrolled in J. O.
Bailey's famous 'series of invaders ... all presented in a
background of suggestions that they are preternatural'.[16] Manston inaugurates the tradition which includes Elizabeth
Endorfield, Sergeant Troy, Diggory Venn, William Dare,
Baron Von Xanten, Donald Farfrae and Dr Fitzpiers.[17]
These typologies anticipate the later novels where, freed
from the restrictions of the sensation novel and in the
more expansive settings congenial to Hardy's imagination, the
same character types can generate more powerful dramatic
tensions.

It is not only in the evolution of character that *Desperate
Remedies* anticipates Hardy's later fiction. The narrative is often
enriched by curious and memorably vivid images, characteristic
of Hardy's mature work. In the home of Mrs Higgins, gin-
besotted and living in desperate circumstances, there is an
almost surrealist description of a clock:

Against the wall a Dutch clock was fixed out of level, and
ticked wildly in longs and shorts, its entrails hanging down
beneath its white face and wiry hands, like the faeces of a
Harpy.

The recurrent emphasis on pictorial and aural detail later
becomes a habitual feature of Hardy's novels, and the indebted-
ness to the Dutch painters acknowledged in the sub-title of his
next fiction, *Under the Greenwood Tree* ('A Rural Painting of the
Dutch School'), is evident here too. The natural descriptions
also possess qualities of the late Turner, so much admired by
Hardy: 'The light so intensified the colours that they seemed to
stand above the surface of the earth and float in mid-air like an
exhalation of red.' Even in his first novel Hardy does not want to
see 'the original realities, as optical effects ... [but] the deeper
reality underlying the scenic' (notebook, January 1887; *L*, 185).
Elsewhere he praises Turner's painting of 'light modified by
objects' and his presentation thus of 'a landscape *plus* a man's
soul' (notebook, 9 January 1889; *L*, 216). Hardy had earlier been
attracted by the same element of 'human connection' to
Hobbema's paintings, where he admires the artist's 'infusing
emotion into the baldest external objects either by the presence
of a human figure among them, or by mark of some human
connection with them' (notebook, 22 April 1878; *L*, 120). None
of Hardy's landscape paintings in the novels is gratuitous and all
are associative. His modulation of colour, here as later, is vital:
the orange tint added to the vivid purple of the heather, soon to
be succeeded by brown after its bloom is over; the red and blue
of the sky, the light green ferns and the dark green holly. The
pictorial intensity of Hardy's use of colour is almost Pre-
Raphaelite in its precision. But it is when a human figure is
introduced among these colours that the effect is striking and
symbolic, as in the first encounter between Cytherea and Miss
Aldclyffe, even though this takes place indoors:

>   The direct blaze of the afternoon sun, partly refracted
> through the crimson curtains of the window, and heightened
> by reflections from the crimson-flock paper which covered the
> walls, and a carpet on the floor of the same tint, shone with a
> burning glow round the form of a lady standing close to
> Cytherea's front with the door in her hand. The stranger

appeared to the maiden's eyes – fresh from the blue gloom, and assisted by an imagination fresh from nature – like a tall black figure standing in the midst of fire.

Cytherea herself had earlier been introduced as 'an exceptional young maiden who glowed amid the dulness like a single bright-red poppy in a field of brown stubble'. The countryman's eye, the technical skill and perspective of the draughtsman and Hardy's own 'idiosyncratic mode of regard' (*L*, 225) combine to account for the author's early command of visual devices. Aural observation is equally important and often evokes tension: the waterfall, the pumping-engine, the howling dogs and the death-rattle; the thunder and the organ music in and around the manor house; the flapping of the flames as the inn burns down; the rustling of Anne Seaway's dress and the mysterious sounds of Manston in the out-house, making his macabre arrangements for the disposal of Eunice's body. Most congenial to Hardy are the secret and distinctive sounds recognised by the countryman, such as Manston's identification of the fields which he crosses in darkness by the sounds which different crops make under his boots.

Already implicit in the natural environment is the animistic empathy between man and nature which in later novels becomes thematically prominent. The suggestion that human emotion and external surroundings are conterminous recurs throughout, usually in a sinister tone. Manston wanders through dense woods in which trees are 'stretching out their boughs like hairy arms' and where he begins to feel at one with this dismal place: 'The scene, from its striking and emphatic loneliness, began to grow congenial to his mood.' There is something premonitory about the smacking of the trees, 'like a man playing castanets or shaking dice', during the night before Cytherea's marriage to Manston. The elements seem to be sentient – 'the weather seemed in flat contradiction of the whole proceeding' – and Cytherea is 'as cold as the air surrounding her'. Eventually, as the various observers watch each other and Manston as he attempts to bury the body, a climactic anthropomorphic image unites the humans with their temporal and spatial surroundings: 'Intentness pervaded everything; Night herself seemed to have become a watcher.' Yet the empathy implicit in all this is not, in contrast to the famous 'Unfulfilled Intention' passage in *The*

Woodlanders (Chapter 17), linked with any larger philosophical speculation. There is indeed no schematic philosophical structure to the novel, in common with all Hardy's fictions, though there is a speculative and inconclusive arbitration between deterministic notions and the operation of chance. The latter is said to be the architect of all the amazing coincidences in *Desperate Remedies*: Cytherea says that

> two disconnected events will fall strangely together by chance, and people scarcely notice the fact beyond saying, 'Oddly enough, it happened that so and so were the same,' and so on. But when three such events coincide without any apparent reason for the coincidence, it seems as if there must be invisible means at work.

This is almost the Immanent Will; there is a pattern, and there are moments of insight into existence. Manston experiences such a moment as he observes all the different persons about their business on the Strand:

> Each and all were alike in this one respect, that they followed a solitary trail like the interwoven threads which form a banner, and all were equally unconscious of the significant whole they collectively showed forth.

The metaphor of the threads both recalls Carlyle's organic filaments, binding nature and man together in one garment of God, and anticipates D. H. Lawrence's observation that 'in the immediate present there is no perfection, no consummation, nothing finished. The strands are all flying, quivering, intermingling into the web.'[18] The apparent lack of society – the crowds which flow, like Eliot's over London Bridge, with each individual insensible of the others – should not obscure the 'significant whole' which Hardy identifies. But where Lawrence would say that there is still hope for each of the solitary trails according to the individual's ambitions and energies, for Hardy the pattern of existence seems fixed, if not yet by such a concept as the Immanent Will, at least by an invisible and incontrovertible working of chance and coincidence. Chance is already shown to be envisaged by man in anthropomorphic terms:

Reasoning worldliness, especially when allied with sensuous-ness, cannot repress on some extreme occasions the human instinct to pour out the soul to some Being or Personality, who in frigid moments is dismissed with the title of Chance, or at most Law.

And it is the same projected Being who later makes Manston feel like a madman: 'Providence, whom I had just thanked, seemed a mocking tormentor laughing at me.'
   The most deterministic notion contained in the novel is the idea of death as a fixed point towards which we advance in ignorance. Farmer Springrove ruminates to Farmer Baker:

Ah, Baker, we say sudden death, don't we? But there's no difference in their nature between sudden death and death of any other sort. There's no such thing as a random snapping off of what was laid down to last longer. We only suddenly light upon an end – thoughtfully formed as any other – which has been existing at that very same point from the beginning, though unseen by us to be so soon.

Death is seen by Manston as man's 'normal condition'; Cytherea and Miss Aldclyffe both, separately, experience a death-wish, but only Manston withdraws into quietism. He desires not only to abjure sentience, to withdraw from consciousness and very existence to a condition which is somehow more natural than life itself (as in the poem 'The Aërolite': 'Maybe now/Normal unwareness waits rebirth'), but also the obliteration of all memory of his ever having existed.[19] Manston's desire to be one of the 'dead men, who have scarcely ever been otherwise', as he enters upon this 'normal condition', shares the impulse found in 'Tess's Lament':

I cannot bear my fate as writ,
   I'd have my life unbe;
Would turn my memory to a blot,
Make every relic of me rot,
My doings be as they were not,
   And gone all trace of me!

The tentative philosophical elements in *Desperate Remedies* suggest that Hardy is also 'feeling his way' to the tragic vision which dominates his best work. But while their presence reveals a thoughtfulness rare in the sensation novel, they are not consistently enough invoked to inform the story with a compulsive sense of fate.

Although *Desperate Remedies* is a novel with a story rather than a theme, and Hardy submitted to write it 'quite against his natural grain' (*L*, 85), some fundamental emotional concerns of the author cannot be subdued. *The Poor Man and the Lady* had been impelled by social radicalism. Social satire and overt protest is not to be found in *Desperate Remedies*, but the author has again 'inserted edgewise' his sentiments on matters he cared about: pressures of social institutions, the marriage contract and social stratification. Cytherea submits to her duty to society, but she protests about having to subject her happiness to 'the benefit of the many'. Even the pity of others, if they observe her self-immolation, is quite inadequate. They will not realise that

> what to them is but a thought, easily held in these two words of pity, 'Poor girl!' was a whole life to me; as full of hours, minutes, and peculiar minutes, of hopes and dreads, smiles, whisperings, tears, as theirs.

Miss Aldclyffe's unhappiness also derives from social insistences about marriage. Hardy's attitude to love is already gently cynical but, long before his own embittering experiences with Emma, he is openly scornful of the marital contract. On the Strand there are 'lost women of miserable repute looking as happy as the days are long; wives, happy by assumption, looking careworn and miserable'. A harrowing picture of married life is drawn:

> Of all the ingenious and cruel satires that from the beginning till now have been stuck like knives into woman-kind, surely there is none so lacerating to them, and to us who love them, as the trite old fact, that the most wretched of men can, in the twinkling of an eye, find a wife ready to be more wretched still for the sake of his company.

The other causes of wretchedness obliquely challenged are the injustice of the class system, and the concomitant poverty, both of which lie at the root of the difficulties of Owen, Cytherea and Springrove. But the poor eventually inherit Knapwater House in a foretaste of social movements later found in *The Hand of Ethelberta* and *A Laodicean*. Springrove is an architect but scorns the methods of advancement in his profession:

> worldly advantage from an art doesn't depend upon mastering it ... [but upon] a certain kind of energy which men with any fondness for art possess very seldom indeed – an earnestness in making acquaintances, and a love for using them.[20]

Such remarks may reflect Hardy's bitterness over his early inability to be published, and there are traces of the young radical's contempt for the closeness of artistic circles in London. His attitudes softened when, in later years, he transcended social barriers to be accepted, like his creation Jocelyn Pierston, as a cultural celebrity. But his awareness of social division is acute: Springrove, like Hardy educated above what the author calls 'the farming grade', surprises Miss Aldclyffe with 'all a developed man's unorthodox opinion about the subordination of classes'.[21] Poverty inspires some bitter rustic dialogue and Cytherea articulates the age-old and poignant lament of the unemployed:

> 'We can put up with being poor,' she said, 'If they only give us work to do ... Yes, we desire as a blessing what was given us as a curse, and even that is denied.'

The impulse to disturb operates forcefully but irregularly. Hardy's humane indignation cannot be contained by the restrictions of the form, but its effectiveness is dissipated by its lack of connection with the story. The 'edgewise' social concerns are superfluous to the objectives of a sensation novel, and their inclusion helps to make it an odd one.

Without such qualities, however, *Desperate Remedies* could have remained a novel of action, but action to no purpose outside the plot itself. This is what worries D. H. Lawrence:

> In *Desperate Remedies*, there are scarcely any people at all, particularly when the plot is working. The tiresome part

about Hardy is that, so often, he will neither write a morality play nor a novel. The people of the first book, as far as the plot is concerned, are not people: they are the heroine, faultless and white; the hero, with a small spot on his whiteness; the villainess, red and black, but more red than black; the villain, black and red; the Murderer, aided by the Adulteress, obtains power over the Virgin, who, rescued at the last moment by the Virgin Knight, evades the evil clutch. Then the Murderer, overtaken by vengeance, is put to death, whilst Divine Justice descends upon the Adulteress. Then the Virgin unites with the Virgin Knight, and receives Divine blessing.

That is a morality play, and if the morality were vigorous and original, all well and good. But, between-whiles, we see that the Virgin is being played by a nice, rather ordinary girl.[22]

This recognises the archetypal basis of the novel, though it is hard to agree that Hardy should be blamed for not producing an 'original' morality when he is restricted by the conventions of the thriller. There is insufficient latitude in the form for the tendencies of mind that later produced remarkably original moral stories. And Lawrence's simplification, entirely accurate in isolating the functions of the characters, fails to allow for their individualised qualities; and Cytherea is more than 'a nice, rather ordinary girl'. The physical-psychical balance is well maintained, and when the latter does give way it is the price Hardy has to pay for wishing to attract public attention 'at all hazards'.

Desperate Remedies is finally unsatisfying because of the conflicting demands of the sensation novel and Hardy's inchoate but distinctive vision. The result is a series of unconnected strands. No individual character arrests Hardy's imagination to become the focal point of the reader's concern, and the episodic quality of the structure inevitably flaws the novel. The social commitment is extraneous to the story; philosophical ideas are fragmentary; visual devices and images, individually acute, are not systematically incorporated. But these characteristics combine to make *Desperate Remedies* 'rum', 'odd' and 'very strange' as well as exciting, and more than the light-weight pot-boiler it has usually been taken to be. Hardy was later to find the 'method' for incorporating the rum and odd as one of his unique strengths.

The idiosyncratic impress of Hardy's mind is always felt in this unusual first novel. Though it may not have set Hardy's standards, it set his course and inaugurated a literary career which, in prose and verse, was to last for another 57 years. Farmer Baker's words to Farmer Springrove give us a fitting proleptic epigraph to the career on which Hardy now embarked:

Why should we not stand still, says I to myself, and fling a quiet eye upon the Whys and Wherefores, before the end o' it all, and we go down into the mouldering-place, and are forgotten?

3 Finding a method: *A Pair of Blue Eyes* (1873)

1

In the summer of 1871 Hardy was already sketching in outline his fourth novel, under the provisional title of 'A Winning Tongue Had He'. Of three novels he had written, one had been abandoned on the advice of publishers and readers, another had been published in March of the same year, and a third was now being considered by Alexander Macmillan. The pressures of getting published inevitably influenced the young author's artistic decisions, and Hardy's uncertainty of direction is shown in the diverse qualities of his early novels. *The Poor Man and the Lady* had been a social satire thought to have missed its mark; *Desperate Remedies* was a sensation novel; and in *Under the Greenwood Tree* Hardy had changed direction again and written a pastoral romance. He was feeling his way to a method, as he put it, and *A Pair of Blue Eyes*, as the new novel was at last entitled, proved to be more than another interesting change. This time the influence of the three earlier works could be seen as Hardy tried to co-ordinate his best effects. It is a bridge between Hardy's period of initial experimentation and what is generally seen as his mature work. Yet the first distinction between *A Pair of Blue Eyes* and its predecessors is a circumstantial one: it was the first of Hardy's novels that was not specifically devised for publication by Macmillan. Hardy's determination to be accepted by this publisher, presumably inspired by the fact that Macmillan was the most distinguished and successful publishing house of the time, had shown itself from the beginning. Hardy was rebuffed three times, however, and it was not until 1887 that Macmillan and Co. finally published the first edition of a novel by Hardy: it was *The Woodlanders*, his eleventh.

To set the new novel in its context we need to return to Hardy's dealings with Macmillan over his first manuscript.

After receiving Alexander Macmillan's long letter of 10 August 1868 about *The Poor Man and the Lady*, Hardy waited for a month and then wrote again to the publisher, with great humility:

> I have become anxious to hear from you again. As the days go on, and you do not write, and my production begins to assume that small and unimportant shape everything one does assumes as the time and mood in which one did it recedes from the present, I almost feel that I don't care what happens to the book, as long as something happens ...
>
> I wonder if your friend meant the building up of a story, and not English composition, when he said I must study composition. Since my letter, I have been hunting up matter for another tale, which would consist entirely of rural scenes and humble life, but I have not courage to go on with it till something comes of the first.[1]

Charles Morgan records Hardy's postscript and adds a comment of his own:

> 'Would you mind suggesting,' Hardy added, 'the sort of story you think I could do best, or any literary work I should do well to go on upon?' That was Alexander's reward for having written as he did.[2]

But the book was rejected in December 1868 and Macmillan also refused *Desperate Remedies* in April 1870. In a third attempt to please Macmillan, on 7 August 1871, Hardy sent the manuscript of *Under the Greenwood Tree*, with a covering letter describing the modest aims of his story of rural life and indicating the favourable aspects of the reviews of his recently published novel which had encouraged him to develop his rustic characters.

It must have been grindingly disheartening for Hardy to receive a reply from Malcolm Macmillan expressing his father's unawareness that *Desperate Remedies* had been published; and with some restraint Hardy notes, in a letter enclosing his press-cuttings on 17 August, that 'the novel was *Desperate Remedies* and the MS. was submitted to you in the first place.'[3] He goes on to remark that 'upon the whole a pastoral story would be the *safest* venture', still trying to satisfy Macmillan; and, with minor reservations, the story did appeal to their reader John Morley.

Alexander Macmillan himself eventually rejected the novel on 18 October 1871, for whereas *Desperate Remedies* had been 'of far too sensational an order', *Under the Greenwood Tree* was 'very slight and rather unexciting'!⁴ It is not surprising that after this, in his evident failure to please Macmillan one way or another, Hardy says that he 'threw the MS. into a box with his old poems, being quite sick of all such', and told Emma Gifford that 'he had banished novel-writing for ever' (*L*, 86). His despair recalled that provoked by Macmillan's letter about *The Poor Man* over three years earlier.

Hardy's account, however, does not tell the whole truth, since he wrote to Tinsley on 20 October, presumably on receipt of Macmillan's letter of 18 October. In this letter the story which was to become *A Pair of Blue Eyes* is first mentioned:

> Early in the summer I began, and nearly finished, a little rural story [*Under the Greenwood Tree*], but owing to the representation of critic-friends who were taken with D. R., I relinquished that and have proceeded a little way with another, the essence of which is plot, *without crime* – but on the plan of D. R. The result of the first venture [*Desperate Remedies*] would of course influence me in choosing which to work up with the most care.⁵

Hardy had not 'nearly finished' and 'relinquished' *Under the Greenwood Tree* but had completed it some months earlier, submitted it to Macmillan in early August, and had presumably received the letter of rejection the previous day. All these facts he omits. In any case Tinsley appears to have ignored the implications of Hardy's remarks, replying on 23 October in a letter confined to details of the sales of *Desperate Remedies*. But he did ask for the rural story the following spring, and *Under the Greenwood Tree* was published in June 1872. Its reviews prompted Tinsley to request a serial for *Tinsleys' Magazine*, to begin in the September issue (published 15 August). This was on 24 July, and Hardy began writing on 27 July. He had only 'roughly noted down the opening chapters and general outline' one year before; so 'the writing it out connectedly must have been done very rapidly' and, although this was the first time that Hardy had written a serial, the first instalment was delivered 'in an incredibly quick time' (*L*, 90–1). This was literally true: the first five chapters, not begun until 27 July, were in print and published on 15 August. The serial version appeared in *Tinsleys' Magazine* from September 1872 to July 1873; the novel (with some alterations to the opening chapter) was published, with Hardy's name on the title-page for the first time, under the same title of *A Pair of Blue Eyes*, in May 1873.[6]

2

The strength of *Under the Greenwood Tree* had been defined by its limitations: modest in scope, careful in execution, it is as nearly faultless a novel as Hardy ever produced. But this limited perfection was the prelude to attempting a more ambitious work, a deeper psychic account of individual experience. Hardy now wrote his first moral drama about love and its consequences; a novel in which for the first time Hardy's tragic vision, already implicit in *Desperate Remedies*, emerges amid more complex ironies than he had yet attempted. The critical reception of *A Pair of Blue Eyes* gave it a higher place than it has been able to sustain,[7] and the reviewer in the *Pall Mall Gazette* (25 October 1873) was emphatic:

> We are very careful how we use the word 'genius'; but we have no hesitation in saying of the author of *A Pair of Blue Eyes* and *Under the Greenwood Tree* that he is distinctly a man of genius.
> But the author whom we are now praising is young; and that fact is visible in his work. If he has growth in him, he will be heard of to his own great advantage by-and-by.

A Pair of Blue Eyes was also highly esteemed by some of Hardy's contemporaries, notably Coventry Patmore and Tennyson. Patmore in a letter 'regretted at almost every page that such unequalled beauty and power should not have assured themselves the immortality which would have been impressed upon them by the form of verse' (*L*, 104–5). Patmore's widow wrote to Hardy on 14 March 1899, telling him that for over twenty years her husband had had the novel read aloud to him: 'Each time he felt the same shock of surprise and pleasure at its consummate art and pathos.' (*L*, 302) In 1880 Tennyson told Hardy that he liked *A Pair of Blue Eyes* the best of all his novels (*L*, 137).

Perhaps the fact that it was so highly regarded by the Victorians contains a clue to its diminished popularity today. Its tone seems to locate it more obstinately in its own age, and it lacks the ambitious moral investigation that makes *The Mayor of Casterbridge, Tess* and *Jude,* despite their settings, modern and universal. It is Victorian in the sense that it is concerned with time and class and men and women whose sexual feelings are deeply constrained by convention, and its story moves well within the bounds of Victorian propriety (Hardy had been well chastened by Alexander Macmillan). But its 'consummate art' is poetic, and perhaps the inherent pathos finds the twentieth-century sensibility less responsive. Patmore was right: *A Pair of Blue Eyes* might have made an impressive narrative poem – it has all the ingredients for that popular Victorian form – especially in the hands of its admirer, Tennyson. Hardy classified the novel among the 'Romances and Fantasies', 'as if to suggest its visionary nature' (*L*, 73); the setting is, for him, 'pre-eminently ... the region of dream and mystery' (Preface). But it is the resonance of Hardy's tragic and ironic poetry that is also felt, sometimes unexpectedly, as the tone of the novel alters: the light and comic story becomes a serious moral drama when Knight is introduced, and it ends in tragedy. If Hardy's best novels possess a unique poetic grandeur, being 'that kind of imaginative writing which lies nearest to the epic, dramatic, or narrative master-pieces of the past',[8] *A Pair of Blue Eyes* is no less obviously the work of a poet who happened to write novels, as he later described himself, rather than of a novelist who wrote poems. The chapter-heading quotations of poetry underscore the novel's tone; Hardy seems to be postulating readers who are poetically aware and responsive, and designing a romanticism and legend-ary setting to appeal to their sensibilities as well as to satisfy his own. Perhaps it is because some of the assumptions implicit in this are no longer true that the novel fails to satisfy contemporary taste.

Some of the novel's defects are more objectively identifiable, and the circumstances of composition were surely influential. The novel suffers, as Hardy admits in the 1912 Preface, 'an immaturity ... in its workmanship'. Hurried along by the printers, Hardy had to draw more extensively on his own recent emotional history than he might otherwise have done, a process encouraged by his writing much of the novel at St Juliot, where he had met Emma Gifford the previous summer. When he began he had not conceived an ending, he says, nor even decided what the later chapters were to be about. As a result there is a lack of balance: almost all the action is compressed into the second half of the novel, and Knight, though a central character, does not appear until the book is one-third through. There is then an abrupt acceleration of the action. And again Hardy salvaged portions of *The Poor Man*, notably the Rotten Row scenes in Chapter 14, which are powerful but which do not neatly blend with the rest of the story. This patchwork quality and the author's initial uncertainty of direction limits the novel's effectiveness.

How far Hardy was aiming at an inconsistency of mood is not clear. Variations of tone are sought in his poetry, comic interludes relieve the dramatic tensions of his major novels, and the mode of *A Pair of Blue Eyes* is tragi-comedy. Sometimes the inconsistency makes a piquant irony: Parson Swancourt is introduced as a buffoonish, Dickensian character; quite suddenly he ceases to be comically pretentious and becomes a harsh and disagreeable snob; later still, on the sea passage, he reverts to his earlier role. But elsewhere the inconsistency makes it hard for the reader to 'catch the vision which the writer has in his eye'.[9] What do we make of the scene in which Stephen and Elfride sit in the churchyard after Stephen has revealed to her his social origins, and she is answering his questions about the 'sweetheart' who had loved her 'very much' twelve months earlier?

> 'Where is he now?' he continued to Elfride.
> 'Here.'
> 'Here! What do you mean by that?'
> 'I mean that he is here.'
> 'Where here?'
> 'Under us. He is under this tomb. He is dead, and we are sitting on his grave.'
> 'Elfie,' said the young man, standing up and looking at the tomb, 'how odd and sad that revelation seems! It quite depresses me for the moment.'

Two dramatic revelations have been made, the social and personal standing of the relationship has been altered and potential unhappiness is implied; yet the scene is faintly ridiculous. And in a parallel scene later Elfride is again in the church, this time with Knight, and in process of confession now about Smith *and* Jethway:

> 'Did you say you were sitting on that tomb?' [Knight] asked moodily.
> 'Yes; and it was true.'
> 'Then how, in the name of Heaven, can a man sit upon his own tomb?'
> 'That was another man. Forgive me, Harry, won't you?'
> 'What, a lover in the tomb and a lover on it?'
> 'O – O – yes!'

Both passages are oddly equivocal: we are unsure how serious an appeal to our sympathies is being made, and our uncertainty about whether the ironies are comic or tragic weakens the effectiveness of either possibility. The final sequence is also equivocal. David Cecil suggests that the 'tragic irony appears as a practical joke on the part of the author: it is not consistent with the atmosphere of tense emotion which should colour the scene.'[10] The tragic *dénouement*, Elfride's death, seems incongruous after the comic description of Smith and Knight on their embarrassed train journey to Elfride's home. That Elfride and her coffin have shared their journey to Camelton seems calculated to give an ironic shock, but the narrative verges on black comedy. Perhaps Hardy is aiming for incongruity, for something true to experience, a coincidence of events which expresses precisely the diverse aspects of life which are ironic, but in technique and intention he seems unsure.

Yet the *dénouement* is not, as some critics have alleged, entirely unprepared for. Proleptic images and hints lay a series of clues. There has been much talk about (and there have been meetings among) tombs, and we learn that even in Elfride's childhood Martin Cannister used to amuse her with tales of corpses dug up in the course of his work. There are more specific clues about her fate too. As early as Chapter 5 she says:

> They have taken it into their heads lately to call me 'little mamma', because I am very fond of them, and wore a dress the other day something like one of Lady Luxellian's.

She utters a vague death-wish at St Launce's Station (Chapter 12) which foreshadows her final rail journey, and in Chapter 26 Simeon relates the tale of the first Lady Elfride, her grand-mother, who 'died at her first groaning, and her husband – who was as tender-hearted a man as ever eat meat, and would have died for her – went wild in his mind, and broke his heart.' And in Chapter 3 Elfride sings in a tender *diminuendo*:

> O Love, who bewailest
>> The frailty of all things here,
> Why choose you the frailest
>> For your cradle, your home, and your bier!

All this calls into question Hardy's claim that at the beginning he had 'shaped nothing of what the later chapters were to be like' (*L*, 91). He may mean that he had an ending in mind but was uncertain how to get there. But proleptic clues are schematically incorporated into the serial version too, and the final impression, in details of plot rather than overall balance, is of careful planning.[11] The experience of writing 'a story with a plot' more than two years earlier must have provided a good training. Following the intricate entanglements of *Desperate Remedies* and the simplicity of *Under the Greenwood Tree* Hardy strikes a new balance between ingenuity and straightforwardness of plot which is much closer to his characteristic production. But it is in Hardy's control of irony that maturing craftsmanship is re-vealed. *A Pair of Blue Eyes* contains a striking exercise in modulated parallelism, which lends a plausible resonance to the author's ironic vision and anticipates the system of balancing and recurrent motifs in Hardy's later novels. It is here that the organising principle of the story is to be found.

The most basic symmetries are those centring upon Elfride, since she is the pivot of the plot. Three men (Jethway, Smith and Knight) are successively slighted by her, and all arrive at exactly the same spot in the churchyard: Jethway in his tomb, Smith and Knight in turn above it. The owner of the pair of blue eyes ruins the men's aspirations unthinkingly rather than by design. The parallel relationships with Elfride of Smith and Knight are precise down to topographical detail, and in their similarity reveal much about Elfride's personality. The chess scenes are both analogous and symbolic. In the first Elfride has the upper hand over the inexperienced Stephen and sympathetically allows him to win, a gesture much resented on its discovery. In the second the situation is ironically reversed: Knight now has command over Elfride, causing her to be neurotically distressed ('O, the difference between Elfride's condition of mind now, and when she purposely made blunders that Stephen Smith might win!') and 'full of mortification at being beaten'. Now Knight exercises a patronising charity, to which she reacts as violently as Stephen had to hers. The traditional sexual symbolism of the game is implicit, and these episodes point the change in Elfride's fortunes.

Elfride conceals details of her past from Knight just as she had from Stephen. The burden of confession accumulates to her disadvantage as she now has *two* former sweethearts to reveal to the astonished Knight. On each confessional occasion she rides to her destination on horseback and the man walks on foot, an arrangement of which Elfride is conscious. On the second occasion the narrator conveys her thoughts: 'A duplicate of her original arrangement with Stephen. Some fatality must be hanging over her head.' To extract early compliments from each man Elfride adopts a coy and teasing mood, both times enjoying as truth what she knows to be flattery. Her success in inspiring the compliments is born respectively of Smith's exasperation and Knight's infatuation. Immediately following each of these light, coquettish moods the crucial episodes concerning the earrings occur, each time consequent upon a kiss. On the first occasion Elfride again has the upper hand over Stephen, being able to chide him for failing in his sentinel duty in respect of her earrings. The second time the earring is revealed as the instrument of her undoing with Knight: there is a hint of this in her indiscreet statement, 'Ah, we must be careful! I lost the other earring doing like this.'

Later an even more unfortunate parallel for Elfride is that Knight and herself are kissing in the same seat that she had earlier shared with Smith, and just as she had *lost* the earring with him she now *finds* it with Knight:

Only for a few minutes during the day did the sun light the alcove to its innermost rifts and slits, but these were the minutes now, and its level rays did Elfride the good or evil turn of revealing the lost ornament.

This seems less gratuitously coincidental than it might seem
since it is incorporated within the structure of parallelism;
coincidence is dramatically invoked as an instrument of irony.[12]
Among other telling parallels of circumstance the most ironic are
those involved in the grave-vault scenes. It is in the first of these
that the three main protagonists, themselves the subjects of
many symmetrically organised experiences known only to Elfride, meet together. This is a heavily ironic convergence of
hitherto parallel lines, severely uncomfortable for Elfride and
Stephen, which becomes more impressive in the light of other
associations which are revealed then or later. In the vault is the
coffin of Lady Elfride Kingsmore, Elfride's grandmother, who is
a spiritual antecedent too in that she ran away to marry against
her parents' wishes. The occasion for the opening of the vault is
the death of Lady Luxellian who, like Elfride herself later, had
been socially elevated to become Lord Luxellian's wife. The next
scene in the vault occurs after the death of Elfride herself as the
second Lady Luxellian. Once again the three of them, Elfride,
Smith and Knight, are united in the vault:

> Knight and Stephen advanced to where they once stood
> beside Elfride on the day all three had met there, before she
> had herself gone down into silence like her ancestors, and shut
> her bright blue eyes for ever.

It is a moving scene. Despite the equivocally comic events which
precede it, in these final paragraphs all the intricately wrought
and interconnected parallels concentrate upon the now pathetic
Elfride in her coffin, and the double and treble ironies resound as
Smith and Knight make their slow retreat down the still valley to
Castle Boterel.

In addition to this display of controlled parallelism Hardy
makes another vital advance in *A Pair of Blue Eyes*: the tension of
external adventure becomes much more dependent upon its
psychical importance. The novel is not free of traces of *Desperate
Remedies*-type sensationalism – Knight's discovery of the dead
Widow Jethway is a somewhat crudely administered shock – but
elsewhere the excitement is both physical and psychical, as in
Elfride's fall from the tower or in the tense games of chess. The

most exceptional and literal suspense is found in Chapters 21 and 22 as Henry Knight hangs precariously on the Cliff without a Name. It is not only physically exciting but exploits the intellectual sensations of evolution and mortality, of man thrown against nature and of the ineluctability of time: it is a measure of Hardy's growing commitment to the novel as a vehicle for ideas as well as entertainment. The incident itself may well originate in part in a childhood experience of Emma Gifford, which she records in *Some Recollections*:

> I often dream of the dangerous pathways over cliffs and rocks leading to spots almost inaccessible. Once I hung over the 'devil's hole' by a tuft of grass whilst my schoolfellow shouted to a mussel-seeking man far below, who rushed up the steep ascent and rescued me.[13]

Emma is likely to have told Hardy about this during their courtship, when he was writing *A Pair of Blue Eyes*; this part of the novel appears to have been written at St Juliot, and the Cliff without a Name is based upon Beeny Cliff. But it is the imaginative transformation that makes the episode memorable. Knight, 'in the presence of a personalized loneliness', is shown as man faced blankly with the indifference of Nature and with no human intermediary. To the suffering eye Nature seems to be a capricious creature, and Knight is pitted against her:

> She is read as a person with a curious temper; as one who does not scatter kindnesses and cruelties alternately, impartially, and in order, but heartless severities or overwhelming generosities in lawless caprice.

At such moments man seems to be a pawn in her hand as she exercises her 'feline fun' as 'a foretaste of her pleasure in swallowing the victim'. But this is a good example of Hardy's making clear that the anthropomorphic delusion is man's own. The rain which pours down on Knight is not, in his subjective view, casual or indifferent, but a 'cosmic agency, active, lashing, eager for conquest'. Even the sun, usually a caressing symbol of harmony and love, takes on a new aspect in a brilliant image: 'a splotch of vermilion red upon a leaden ground – a red face looking on with a drunken leer'.

Before the sun appears, however, Knight has experienced one

of the most awesome panoramas ever afforded one of Hardy's characters, a vision of the entire evolutionary process; this is mature writing and the work of a poet. Knight, in his awful predicament, reclines 'hand in hand with the world in its infancy' as he sees the imbedded Trilobite before him: 'separated by millions of years in their lives, Knight and this underling seemed to have met in their place of death.' The vision inspired in Knight by this insensate creature, one of man's earliest progenitors, realises the implications of the opening lines in Blake's 'Auguries of Innocence':

> To see a World in a Grain of Sand,
> And a Heaven in a Wild Flower,
> Hold Infinity in the palm of your hand
> And Eternity in an hour.

The compression of an immensity of Time is described in a fine passage:

> Time closed up like a fan before him. He saw himself at one extremity of the years, face to face with the beginning and all the intermediate centuries simultaneously. Fierce men, clothed in the hides of beasts, and carrying, for defence and attack, huge clubs and pointed spears, rose from the rock, like the phantoms before the doomed Macbeth. They lived in hollows, woods, and mud-huts – perhaps in caves of the neighbouring rocks. Behind them stood an earlier band. No man was there. Huge elephantine forms, the mastodon, the hippopotamus, the tapir, antelopes of monstrous size, the megatherium, and the myledon – all, for the moment, in juxtaposition. Further back, and overlapped by these, were perched huge-billed birds and swinish creatures as large as horses. Still more shadowy were the sinister crocodilian outlines – alligators and other uncouth shapes, culminating in the colossal lizard, the iguanadon. Folded behind were dragon forms and clouds of flying reptiles: still underneath were fishy beings of lower development; and so on, till the lifetime scenes of the fossil confronting him were a present and modern condition of things. These images passed before Knight's inner eye in less than half a minute, and he was again considering the actual present. Was he to die?

This vision of the vastness of the world's history lends a pathetic resonance to Knight's subjective question. In the event, he is not to die. Though 'inexorable circumstance only tries to prevent what intelligence attempts', human ingenuity outwits pitiless nature, and Elfride's rescue of Knight represents the victory of intelligence over the force of circumstance.

A Pair of Blue Eyes is Hardy's most serious novel so far, the first coherent attempt tentatively to define a reading of life. In Knight's experience Hardy expounds his own view that nature is indifferent to man's interests, but makes it clear that it is a neutrality often as frightening as active hostility would be. And in his presentation, for the first time in his fiction, of the apparently systematic direction of events to a tragic conclusion by circumstance, Hardy's view of the patterning of men's lives is emerging; at the same time, a more thorough moral exploration of their reactions is being begun. In a preface superseded in 1895 and omitted from all subsequent editions, Hardy says of his characters:

> Their course of thought and action under the circumstances which surround them is shown to be ... sometimes right, and sometimes wrong. Right or wrong, their conduct ... directs the course ... of the story.[14]

Tension is generated by individual conduct and choice, and this time Hardy lets his characters meet their fate without concession to the sensibilities of readers who would wish to see a happy ending. Elfride triumphs briefly over circumstance in rescuing Knight, but she is eventually overwhelmed. Ominously, as Hardy's outlook begins to assume its characteristic cast, what had been 'Time, the Improver' in *Desperate Remedies* has now become 'Time the Cynic'.

The author's seriousness is not dissipated but enhanced by his personal engagement with the experiences of his protagonists. Biographical influences are directly at work as Hardy's own Cornish romance occasions the scenes, and to some extent the characters, of the novel, though he carefully and fairly disparages any idea that it is autobiography (*L*, 73–4). But he does say that his architectural expedition to St Juliot and his meeting with Emma Gifford account for the basic situation. Elfride's appearance, horsemanship and literary impulses at least are based on Emma, the early part of the novel is very much in the

mood of 'When I set out for Lyonnesse', and there is more of
Hardy in Stephen than he cares to admit. His claim that Stephen
is based on a fellow-pupil at John Hicks's architectural practice
(*L*, 73) is unconvincing. Like Hardy, Stephen is a stonemason's
son who goes to London as an apprentice architect, learning his
'gentlemanliness by going to the galleries of theatres, and
watching stage drawing-room manners'; Stephen's father, rather
than being based on 'a mason in Hardy's father's employ' (*L*,
73), shares the author's father's quiet and retiring nature; and
Mrs Smith's 'sound common sense' and gentle ambition mirror
qualities of Hardy's mother, Jemima. Hardy admits that 'Henry
Knight the reviewer ... was really much more like Thomas
Hardy' (*L*, 74), though the character seems to compound the
author and his literary mentor, Horace Moule. Here Knight
seems very much like Hardy:

> Knight certainly did not mind being frank with her. Instances
> of this trait in men who are not without feeling, but are
> reticent from habit, may be recalled by all of us. When they
> find a listener who can by no possibility make use of them,
> rival them, or condemn them, reserved and even suspicious
> men of the world become frank, keenly enjoying the inner side
> of their frankness.

But his characteristics are predominantly those of Moule, also a
reviewer and as revered by Hardy as Knight is by Stephen, and
a man who felt his life to have been a failure and who was
similarly sexually inhibited.[15]

These influences are unimportant as autobiography and
irrelevant to textual criticism; it would be quite wrong to regard
any part of the novel as a literal transcript of Hardy's experience.
But the unusually urgent pressures of serialisation here reveal
more clearly than usual an intrinsic part of Hardy's method, the
importation of features of his own personality into one or more of
the characters who are acting out his preoccupations. This is
neither narrowly autobiographical nor basically unusual: au-
thors invariably write from within their own psychical history.
In 1879 Hardy noted Arnold's quotation, in his essay on Heine,
from Goethe: 'as man must live from within outwards, so the
artist must work from within outwards, seeing that make what
contortions he will, he can only bring to light his own individu-

ality.'[16] Yet in Hardy this often represents a deeper emotional investment. Hardy's fictional world is deliberately circumscribed because 'the domestic emotions have throbbed in Wessex nooks with as much intensity as in the palaces of Europe, and ... [there is] quite enough human nature in Wessex for one man's literary purpose.'[17] It is his psychical knowledge of Wessex that animates the novels, and his ability to enter into the experience, individuality and human nature of the inhabitants, because he is one of them, that enables Hardy to describe 'from within outwards' their lives and the injustices and circumstances which tacitly conspire against them.

In the process Hardy's vision of a world that is socially inequitable is brought to light, and social divisiveness and snobbery furnish an urgent theme. Hardy's indignation at the slighting of a master-mason's profession is less than impersonal, and he subtly records the intricate ways and degrees of snobbery. Lord Luxellian, despite his rank, is no snob; but the pretentious and socially indeterminate Parson Swancourt is both a theoretical snob in his own study and an active one in the outer world, peremptorily crushing the happiness of Elfride and Stephen. At the same time, to satisfy his own pretensions, he is prepared to 'marry money' in the unbeguiling form of Charlotte Troyton. He confuses money with rank yet shows how one can purchase the other, in essence if not in title. But the social strata are finely distinguished and Mrs Smith, while resenting the Swancourts' snobbery, ironically displays her own:

> ... she's not a bit too high for you, or you too low for her. See how careful I am to keep myself up. I'm sure I never stop for more than a minute together to talk to any journeymen people; and I never invite anybody to our party o' Christmases who are not in business for themselves.

Class division, nevertheless, is the barrier that the young architect cannot surmount, and it is a problem exacerbated by the urban community. John Smith's respected standing as the village artificer in stone would be lost in a town where, because of 'the beach-pebble attrition with his kind only to be experienced in large towns', he would find that 'the unit Self [is metamorphosed] into a fraction of the unit Class.' In town Mr Smith would be assimilated into the 'Humanity Show' which is seen incongruously through Knight's windows, in such close proximity to Bede's Inn, which faces on to a street of wealth and respectability. This ironic contrast is pictorially vivid:

> Crowds – mostly of women – were surging, bustling, and pacing up and down. Gaslights glared from butchers' stalls, illuminating the lumps of flesh to splotches of orange and vermilion, like the wild colourings of Turner's later pictures, whilst this purl and babble of tongues of every pitch and mood was to this human wild-wood what the ripple of a brook is to the natural forest.

The sense of community is discerned as keenly here as in the country, and the town is judged by the condition of the people in it. This recalls Manston's view of humanity on the Strand, each person following a 'solitary trail' and unaware of the 'significant whole' to which he belongs. It is a mode of existence inimical to Hardy's conception of the fulfilled man, and this scene, with its further implication of 'Nature, red in tooth and claw' in urban disguise, is more memorable than the satirical scenes in Hyde Park in Chapter 15. Illustrative as they are of metropolitan social pretension and of fatuous etiquette –

> 'My dear, you mustn't say "gentlemen" nowadays,' her stepmother answered in the tones of arch concern that so well became her ugliness. 'We have handed over "gentlemen" to the lower middle class, where the word is still to be heard at tradesmen's balls and provincial tea-parties, I believe.'

– they are obviously lifted from *The Poor Man* and not properly integrated into this novel.

More of Hardy's feelings are brought out 'from within outwards' in a number of wry comments on the art of fiction and, especially, in reflections on Knight's reviewing activities and his review of Elfride's romance in particular. Hardy almost parodies his own reviewers and attributes to his characters attitudes which are demonstrably his own. Hardy as well as Parson Swancourt is 'tickled with a sort of bucolic humour at the idea of criticizing the critic' when he makes the minister remark that 'critics go on writing, and are never corrected or argued with, and therefore are never improved.' The offending review of

Elfride's novel is largely a compound of reviews of Hardy's earlier novels, particularly *Desperate. Remedies*. Elfride's dejection is similar to Hardy's when he read the *Spectator* review in 1871, and like her creator she is attacked for 'wearisome details in modern social scenery, analyses of uninteresting character, [and] the unnatural unfoldings of a sensational plot'. Knight's remark in his review that 'the bait is so palpably artificial that the most credulous gudgeon turns away' was, ironically, to be echoed by real reviewers throughout Hardy's career as a novelist. Even the commendations of Elfride's book recall the approval of Hardy's homely pictures of rural simplicity:

> We are far from altogether disparaging the author's powers. She has a certain versatility that enables her to use with effect a style of narration peculiar to herself, which may be called a murmuring of delicate emotional trifles, the particular gift of those to whom the social sympathies of a peaceful time are as daily food. Hence, where matters of domestic experience, and the natural touches which make people real, can be introduced without anachronisms too striking, she is occasionally felicitous; and upon the whole we feel justified in saying that the book will bear looking into for the sake of those portions which have nothing whatever to do with the plot.

Implied in this parody is the measure of Hardy's seriousness about his art and some bitterness about his early experiences. *Under the Greenwood Tree* had been written partly to satisfy the delicate tastes of Macmillan and to avoid the strictures accorded *Desperate Remedies* while developing those bucolic aspects which had won approbation. But this was hardly the limit of Hardy's literary ambition, and he may well have resented having to subdue essential interests to 'those portions which have nothing whatever to do with the plot', as he made clear after *Far from the Madding Crowd*. Perhaps the most pregnant remark is Knight's, though Hardy later learned its truth more bitterly than he could have anticipated: 'It requires a judicious omission of your real thoughts to make a novel popular.'

Hardy's real thoughts are not omitted from *A Pair of Blue Eyes*; for the first time they are emerging coherently. So too is the texture of his style, but here distracting qualities persist. The self-conscious erudition of *Desperate Remedies*, largely absent from

Under the Greenwood Tree, reappears. The first two pages yield two allusions to Shakespeare, one to Wordsworth, and one each to the 'Madonna Della Sedia', Rubens and Correggio. Later, in one chapter Stephen is likened to a little-known bust of Nollekens, while elsewhere Elfride must have 'her head thrown sideways in the Greuze attitude'. The reader is doubtfully helped by learning, for example, that 'Mrs Smith threw in her sentiments between the acts, as Coryphaeus of the tragedy.' Elsewhere he is confronted with 'a dull parallelepipedon'. Another distracting exercise of Hardy's pedantry occurs in his description of Knight's ordeal on the cliff face as the author inserts not only the height of the cliff (650 feet) but a curious catalogue of the heights of other cliffs:

> That is to say, it is nearly three times the height of Flamborough, half as high again as the South Foreland, a hundred feet higher than Beachy Head – the loftiest promontory on the east or south side of this island – twice the height of St Aldhelm's, thrice as high as the Lizard, and just double the height of St Bee's. One sea-board point on the western coast is known to surpass it in altitude, but only by a few feet. This is Great Orme's Head, in Caernarvonshire.

The author leaves Knight and Elfride perilously suspended on the cliff face while he indulges this finicking altitudinary survey. Hardy's prose style too can disturb and puzzle the reader with ambivalently comic sentences like this: 'Stephen was now a richer man than heretofore, standing on his own bottom; and the definite position in which he had rooted himself nullified old local distinctions.'

Yet these convolutions of style are not confined to the novels of modest reputation but persist throughout Hardy's career. Two years after this novel he noted:

> Read again Addison, Macaulay, Newman, Sterne, Defoe, Lamb, Gibbon, Burke, *Times* leaders, etc., in a study of style. Am more and more confirmed in an idea I have long held, as a matter of common sense, long before I thought of an old aphorism bearing on the subject: 'Ars est celare artem.' The whole secret of a living style and the difference between it and a dead style, lies in not having too much style – being, in fact,

a little careless, or rather seeming to be, here and there. (*L*, 105)

Ironically enough Hardy comes close to defining his problem: 'Art', he says, 'is to conceal art,' yet his own style rarely does this. His prose seems quite the opposite of careless, and at its weakest it is much too curiously and carefully involved. But this failure to conceal art is so idiosyncratic that it almost ceases to be a problem, and Hardy's contortions of language are so profuse that they begin to 'sound right'; and we can agree with Pascal that 'when one finds a natural style, one is amazed and delighted, for where one expected to see an author, one discovers a man.'[18] And it is this informing presence of the man that eventually ensures that, for all its blemishes, Hardy's is a 'living style'. The passing deficiencies of Hardy's writing are more than redeemed when he is at his best, as in his description of the first scene in the vault. This is a picture as harshly branded on the consciousness of the reader as it is upon the memories of the characters, with its Turneresque use of colour and light, and it conveys acutely the unease and embarrassment of two of the participants and the unwary composure of the third:

Stephen briefly assented, and there was a silence. The blackened coffins were now revealed more clearly than at first, the whitened walls and arches throwing them forward in strong relief. It was a scene which was remembered by all three as an indelible mark in their history. Knight, with an abstracted face, was standing between his companions, though a little in advance of them, Elfride being on his right hand, and Stephen Smith on his left. The white daylight on his right side gleamed faintly in, and was toned to a blueness by contrast with the yellow rays from the candle against the wall. Elfride timidly shrinking back, and nearest the entrance, received most of the light therefrom, whilst Stephen was entirely in candlelight, and to him the spot of outer sky visible above the steps was as a steely blue patch, and nothing more.

And in this novel the vivid imagery of natural phenomena attains a new sharpness, both tactile (the rain-drops 'stuck into [Knight's] flesh like cold needles') and visual (a young cedar 'shot its pointed head across the horizon, piercing the firmamental lustre like a sting'). Hardy's vision of nature transcends the conventional pastoral. Another memorable cameo, using the term advisedly, is the 'strongly illuminated picture' which Stephen sees, when Elfride and Knight are in the summerhouse, with all the minute detail of a September evening:

> The light gave birth to dancing leaf-shadows, stem-shadows, lustrous streaks, dots, sparkles, and threads of silver sheen of all imaginable variety and transience. It awakened gnats, which flew towards it, revealed shiny gossamer threads, disturbed earthworms.

This is the detail known only to the countryman who sees 'into the life of things'. Modulation of colour and light lends visual intensity throughout, but the landscape is increasingly becoming the objective correlative of the characters' state of mind, as in Knight's reaction to Elfride's confession about her journey to London with Stephen:

> The scene was engraved for years on the retina of Knight's eye: the dead and brown stubble, the weeds among it, the distant belt of the beeches shutting out the view of the house, the leaves of which were now red and sick to death.

This psychical inter-relationship between people and environment hints at a new maturity in character-drawing too. Appropriately enough, in this first novel in which all the main protagonists are thwarted by disappointment in a circumstantially inclement universe, the characters are psychologically real enough for the reader to care about their fate. In the abandoned preface quoted earlier Hardy says:

> In some of my former novels the object proposed has been to trace the influence of circumstances upon character. In the present story I have reversed the process. The attempt made here is to trace the influence of character upon circumstances.[19]

The same aim later motivates *The Mayor of Casterbridge*, but in this early novel there is only submission. The human concern of the story is the gradual disintegration of Elfride and Knight; Elfride, as Lawrence says, is the 'poor innocent victim of a passion not vital enough to overthrow the most banal conventional ideas.'[20] She goes to her death for this moral inaction, while Knight becomes broken-spirited as a result of his own lack of reason, drifting through Europe without even the methodical supports of his earlier existence. He is equally responsible for his fate, and the situation he finds himself in at the end is of his own making. The germ of their respective failures is gradually advanced upon the reader as the complexity of their personalities is revealed with a new confidence by Hardy. Like his later tragic figures they are shown to be vulnerable and bound to fail, not only repressed by contemporary social customs but by their own submission to 'circumstances'. There emerges an engaging and sympathetic picture of what life is like for those who are borne down by it.

Elfride is compared to Miranda, and the story tells how she copes with her brave new world of experience. As the tale develops a subtle shift in authorial attitude towards her is engineered as she is gradually transformed from a vain coquette into a young woman falling helplessly short of Knight's impossible standards. Hardy's first three heroines can be seen as the same character passing through different stages of experience. Elfride does not have either Cytherea's marriage, one of undispelled promise, or Fancy's, which is faintly qualified by the existence of the 'secret she would never tell'; instead she marries neither of her two sweethearts but a pallid substitute, and soon afterwards goes to her death. She is the first heroine to realise her tragic potential. Beautiful, intelligent, resourceful and vain, Elfride is a flirt who readily plays 'La Belle Dame sans merci'. Her claim that she 'never [encouraged Jethway] by word, look or sign', vouchsafed to Smith and Knight in turn, is not persuasive, but her retribution is always disproportionate: her offence against Felix is hardly of the enormity implied by Mrs Jethway. Yet she is by no means free of blame. In her vacillation over the runaway marriage Elfride anticipates the moral failure of nerve which agitates Sue Bridehead, and which eventually precipitates her own end. And though we soon learn that Elfride 'had such a superlative capacity for being wounded that little hits struck hard,' the narrator adds many chapters later that 'Elfride's capacity for being wounded was only surpassed by her capacity for healing, which rightly or wrongly is by some considered an index of transientness of feeling in general.'

Hardy is no longer telling but showing, so the reader is left to judge. Nine months later, with Smith in Bombay, she has exercised her 'special facilities' to 'slough off a sadness and replace it by a hope as easily as a lizard renews a diseased limb': shallowness of feeling or the resilience of youth? Well, her 'proneness to inconstancy' enables her soon to admire the good looks of Lord Luxellian in Hyde Park and to transfer her affection from Smith to Knight. She also transfers to Knight her selfish policy of concealment, her occasional thoughtless cruelty of behaviour, and she convicts herself of the culpable shallowness of which Hardy disapproves in young women. But her faults generally lie not in her action but in her inaction. When she is faced with moral decisions the intelligence that helped her to save Knight's life fails her. She will not confess to Stephen about Jethway until forced to do so, nor will she confess to Knight about Jethway and Stephen: 'Her resolution, sustained during the last fifteen hours, had been to tell the whole truth, and now the moment had come. ... The moment had been too much for her ... [nothing] could string Elfride up to the venture.' Seized with indecision about whether to keep her marriage appointment with Stephen, she abdicates responsibility to Pansy, the horse, and having done so tries to pretend that 'today's rash action was not her own', but she cannot escape responsibility for her feckless irresolution. And later she is unable to decide to send the letter to Stephen about the money that he has sent, 'although never ceasing to feel strenuously that the deed must be done'.

Eventually the force of her inaction leads to her tragedy. The fear which prevents her revelations to Knight – that 'what he might consider as bad as the fact, was her previous concealment of it by strategy' – proves to be justified, and Knight's pompous indignation and contempt throws the reader's full sympathy upon Elfride. She has been betrayed by her chronic inaction and moral cowardice. Because it involves a living sufferer, the picture of her seen by Knight when he leaves is perhaps even more pathetic than her death:

> He saw the stubble-field, and a slight girlish figure in the midst of it – up against the sky. Elfride, docile as ever, had hardly moved a step, for he had said, Remain. He looked and saw her again – he saw her for weeks and months.

This is the impression of Elfride that remains, her shallowness stripped away to reveal a docile, naïve and unsophisticated girl whose efforts to meet her brave new world, so full of promise, have simply failed. She lives and dies by the most venial of mortal sins, and is despatched with a final irony, in a coffin which a railway porter describes as 'Light as vanity; full o' nothing', to Endelstow on the eve of St Valentine's.

The other compulsively interesting character, Henry Knight, is as responsible as anyone for Elfride's decline and death. A 30-year-old bachelor when he first appears, Knight is an intriguing compound of honesty, intelligence, logic, naïvety, sexual peculiarity and pomposity. His very name, resonant with medievalism, is appropriate to his quest for perfection. But the peculiar nature of the perfection he seeks is born of his unusual lack of experience with women: he 'could pack them into sentences like a workman, but practically was nowhere'. Even in the context of Victorian inhibition it is odd that he should attain the age of 32 without kissing any woman other than his mother, and this implies a reservoir of repressed sexuality within him. Even as an observer, and he claims to be an acute one, he is especially naïve to harbour such 'an invincible objection to be any but the first comer in a woman's heart'. But it is this unreason, allied with his straightforward integrity, that destroys him. Knight is the first hopeless idealist in the novels, the first of all those who have an unreal conception of the world and its favours, before discovering at last that it is inimical to their purposes. These people, Hardy suggests with profound sympathy for them, are unfitted for the world.

Knight's tragedy is deeply felt and he is defined with psychological consistency. His notebook analysis of Elfride's intentions and behaviour is acute but underestimates her capacity for deception and the potency of her seductiveness. When he kisses her for the first time, the act releases 'all the ardour which was the accumulation of long years behind a natural reserve': he shares with Miss Aldclyffe years of repressed sexuality, unreasoning possessiveness and jealousy, and a neurotic preoccupation with the sanctity of the kiss. Repression is a condition that fascinates Hardy and it is returned to often in the novels. But Knight also suffers the agonies of self-recognition, eventually admitting his 'great remissness' in not having 'trod out my measure like lighter-hearted men', and he is abandoned to misery and absolute pain on discovery of his folly and his 'peculiar weaknesses'. It is hinted that Knight is a bachelor by nature:

> Perhaps Knight was not shaped by Nature for a marrying man. Perhaps his lifelong constraint towards women, which he had attributed to accident, was not chance after all, but the natural result of instinctive acts so minute as to be indiscernible even by himself.

The germ of his failure, however, is in the obsessiveness that derives from his condition. His case against Elfride is after all slight enough, and his intransigence in refusing forgiveness places him among those too-idealistic men who will 'morally hang [their sweethearts or wives] upon evidence they would be ashamed to admit in judging a dog'. This 'wrongheadedness' of the 'scrupulously honest' diverts him from the path of Christian charity. Knight is powerfully conceived, unusual and even frightening. His intellectual-emotional imbalance, the result of the disconcerting impact of normal emotional activity upon a man who lives by the intellect, is unique in Hardy's fiction.

Stephen Smith is sketched too lightly to engage our interest to the same extent. Part of the problem is his age: he is 'a youth in appearance, and not yet a man in years', with a concomitant lack of pyschological complexity. Like Springrove, the previous architect-hero, Stephen is insipid, and his dramatic presence is diminished since his part is so much confined to the earlier and generally weaker section of the book; he is then despatched to India for so long, while more interesting things happen at home, that his return does not provoke the suspense that might be hoped for. Yet in Stephen we have an interesting portrait of a clumsy and self-educated young man, a more successful Jude,[21] who has learned his chess and his Latin by correspondence. His whole characteristic is passive ('his brain had extraordinary receptive powers, and no great creativeness'), and it is ironic that he and Knight are drawn together: he is 'not quite the man Knight would have deliberately chosen as a friend ... Circumstance, as usual, did it all.' He yields readily to circumstance and falls from Elfie's affections by passively assenting to her return from London to Endelstow after their abortive expedition. 'The emotional side of his constitution', the narrator tells us, 'was built rather after a feminine than a male model.' So Elfride has to make an odd choice between Stephen, with his pretty face and feminine constitution, and Knight, who is not shaped by nature for a marrying man.

Four other characters show Hardy's newly refined ability to inter-relate different planes of characterisation. Swancourt is both a comic parson and a disagreeable, snobbish and ambitious old man. In his former role, with his tales which are 'too bad – too bad to tell', he could have been a mere humour. But it is a rude shock to discover that he will marry Mrs Troyton for her £3,500, and that he can utter such un-Christian sentiments as this: 'Uniform pleasantness is rather a defect than a faculty. It shows that a man hasn't sense enough to know whom to despise.' By no means the last parson to be satirised by Hardy for his worldly failings, Swancourt is brought alive by the antilogies in his make-up. William Worm, on the other hand, the 'dazed factotum' (as he is designated in the list of Persons), a 'poor wambling man' with fish frying constantly in his head, is a one-dimensional figure who is consistently good fun. Mrs Jethway is no more real. Her inexorable presence at crucial moments is contrived: she is present at the railway station, in the church-yard, in the woods, and on the sea passage; her dark form seems to emerge incongruously, a Gothic *voyeuse*, from behind every tombstone and every tree, ominously gloomy. But her ubiquity helps to define her function as a poetic symbol. Lord Luxellian is yet more unreal. Hardy settles for a suggestive name (presumably intended to convey a notion of luxury and wealth) and a definitive analogy: the peer, with his musical laugh and lack of any talent, is like 'a good-natured commercial traveller of the superior class'.

In all these particulars *A Pair of Blue Eyes* anticipates Hardy's later fiction more distinctly than the previous novels, but it owes much to *Desperate Remedies* and may even be read as a matured version of it. Three main characters are derivative (Miss Aldclyffe/Knight, Cytherea/Elfride, Springrove/Smith) and there is some suggestion in the approximation of details that in writing *A Pair of Blue Eyes* under pressure Hardy had some recourse to the earlier novel.[22] These details of self-plagiarism hint that Hardy's development as a novelist is a more organic process than the divarications between the first four (published and unpublished) novels imply. They also suggest in little what further study of Hardy's fiction reveals, that his work bears out

Proust's claim that all great artists have one book in them and write it over and over again. A case could be made for reading all Hardy's novels as constituent parts of one symbolic poem. The recurrence of themes and ideas, the repetition of incidents and types of incidents and reflective observations, and the establishment of various typologies (characters, plots, modes), can be advanced in support of this larger view.

It is no surprise, then, to find affinities between *A Pair of Blue Eyes* and *Tess of the d'Urbervilles*. In the 1912 postscript to the Preface, Hardy says that 'in its action [*A Pair of Blue Eyes*] exhibits the romantic stage of an idea which was further developed in a later book', and this has generally been understood to mean *Tess*. Arthur MacDowall, in briefly comparing the two novels, makes the unconventional observation that *A Pair of Blue Eyes* 'has really more intrinsic interest of character'.[23] But the later novel is one of Hardy's finished works, his execution is equal to his idea and the result furnishes a telling comparison with the earlier work. The novels' themes are analogous: a social gulf separates the lovers and it is the woman's concealment of a past that is the agent of her destruction. Knight is an early version of Angel Clare, and both are bookish, sexually repressed and hopeless idealists who expect perfection in their women. When the 'crimes' of their respective sweethearts are revealed, both Knight and Angel misjudge the quality of the faults and exhibit reactions out of all proportion to their cause. Elfride and Tess find themselves in an identical psychical predicament, wilfully concealing past actions from their lovers through fear and vacillation rather than calculated stealth. Each girl is 'a pure woman' without being wholly innocent, and upon the disintegration of their hopes they each submit themselves to a masochistic, almost ritual, self-sacrifice. The President of the Immortals finishes his sport with Tess in a setting of imposing grandeur, and it is a measure of the difference in tone and scope of the two novels that the pathos of Elfride's end is confused by some preceding scenes of gloomy farce. But what really distinguishes *Tess*, as Ian Gregor writes of that novel, is 'the kind of life which each individual reveals'.[24] By now, 'just as the responsiveness, the life, is now done from within, so the processes that warp and twist are done in a similar manner ... in the close, instinctive response of one person to another.'

A Pair of Blue Eyes is the first stage of this internalising process.

In *Desperate Remedies* believable and even engaging characters co-exist, but their responses are to external events and situations rather than to each other as people. In *Under the Greenwood Tree* less complex and more ordinary characters live normal, uncomplicated lives in which the emotional centre is very near the surface. But here, in a story where much of the tension is psychical, already a new kind of life emerges in the characters. In the modest setting of domestic drama there are already powerful psychic clashes between Elfride and Knight; it is in simple incidents (a game of chess, the discovery of a lost earring), and without any of the paraphernalia of tragedy invoked in later novels, that the larger conflicts of the fictional world are implied. In *A Pair of Blue Eyes* is Hardy's first success in the creation of atmosphere (here an atmosphere of romance and dream, duly undercut by the ironies of reality) to which the characters properly relate as well as to each other. The result is a novel of great charm. But it is still exploratory work, in which inconstancy of mood vitiates the ultimate tragic effect, extraneous erudition betrays still a Stephen-Smith-like desire to impress, and an imbalance of overall structure diminishes the first half of the book. Yet Elfride's story is genuinely touching, and a world is defined where necessity and human delusion, aggravated by a complex operation of irony, is the rule. While writing this novel Hardy took leave of the architectural profession for ever and became, professionally, a writer. Properly so since in this novel, written 'from within outwards', Hardy's individuality is revealed: he has found a method.

4 'The end of the happy endings': *The Hand of Ethelberta* (1876)

The Hand of Ethelberta is an ingenious comedy of manners, and it is more than that, but it has been harshly received by critics unwilling to accept that a novelist's works may, like their creator, be 'so various in their pith and plan' ('So Various'). From its very first appearance in the *Cornhill* in 1875–6[1] it was a disappointment to both readers and critics, because in *Ethelberta* Hardy abruptly rejected the mode of his previous novel, *Far from the Madding Crowd*, which had been received with high praise. Despite the deliberacy of Hardy's striking off on to new ground, it has subsequently tended to be regarded as an unhappy aberration between that novel and *The Return of the Native*. On its own terms it is 'A Comedy in Chapters' (as described in the sub-title). Its pursuit of some of Hardy's deep concerns in an unusual mode is often fascinating and it bears throughout the idiosyncratic stamp of its author. Edmund Gosse saw this clearly in 1890 when he wrote that 'the worst chapter in *The Hand of Ethelberta* is recognizable, in a moment, as written by the author of the best chapter in *The Return of the Native*.'[2]

This applies equally to *Ethelberta* and its predecessor, *Far from the Madding Crowd*, though superficially the novels have little in common. One is a pastoral tale confined to Weatherbury in Wessex, the other is an urban comedy of manners in which the main action takes place in London, Rouen and Paris (as well as Wessex). *Far from the Madding Crowd* is the first novel in which Hardy introduces the term 'Wessex' to promote the historical and geographical consciousness which increases the stature of events and personalities. For all the characters, principals and rustics alike, 'the indispensable conditions of existence are attachment to the soil of one particular spot by generation after generation' (Preface), and we learn that in comparison with cities 'Weatherbury was immutable' (Chapter 22). The characters in *Ethelberta* enjoy no such stability. They are moderns in their restlessness, and in this an important new psychic dimension is introduced into Hardy's fiction. The earlier novel tells a story of tragic stamp (if not tragic issue) in which emotional tension is the organising principle. The elemental passions of the Weatherbury inhabitants are often apparently subject to the caprice of fate or chance, a subjugation already regularly explored in Hardy's fiction – but one which, unusually for Hardy, has no place in *The Hand of Ethelberta*. Here, instead, the potentialities of the individual will are explored, and the outcome is only superficially happy.

It is indeed an unusual novel, unduly disparaged by those who fail to see that Hardy did not intend it to be taken as seriously as the great tragic novels, or to appreciate it as a purposive and positive 'plunge in a new and untried direction' (*L*, 102). Its provenance explains why Hardy chose such an experiment. On 2 December 1874 Leslie Stephen asked for another serial for the *Cornhill*. Three months earlier Hardy had married Emma Gifford and his increased financial responsibilities – 'as he would quote, "to keep base life afoot"' – generated a need for him to consider popularity: 'he would, he deemed, have to look for materials in manners – in ordinary social and fashionable life as other novelists did.' It was not to his taste, of course, and he was uneasy about 'having to carry on his life not as an emotion, but as a scientific game' since he was by now 'committed by circumstances to novel-writing as a regular trade' (*L*, 104). Hardy was in search of security and reputation, so he wrote a novel after the manner of the style of fiction that he took to be the most popular at the time, though he simultaneously satirised it.

But another consideration influenced him too. He fiercely resented (more than ever after *Far from the Madding Crowd*) the disproportionate critical emphasis on the pastoral qualities of his work, the implication that his principal virtue was the pictorial celebration of rural life, which seemed to trivialise other concerns which to him were more important. All this generated his well-known acid comment that 'he had not the slightest intention of writing for ever about sheepfarming, as the reading public was apparently expecting him to do, and as, in fact, they presently resented his not doing.' (*L*, 102) He wanted to be seen as something other than a writer of pastoral novels, just as

Joseph Conrad hated to be thought only a writer of sea-stories.

In all this there is a curious mixture of capitulation and defiance. Hardy was temperamentally unable to take Leslie Stephen's advice to close his ears to the opinions of critics, and he was ready to modify individual novels or the direction of his career in order to win acceptance from readers or critics. Even when *Far from the Madding Crowd* was riding high in 1874, Hardy wrote to Stephen:

> The truth is that I am willing, and indeed anxious, to give up any points which may be desirable in a story when read as a whole, for the sake of others which shall please those who read it in numbers. Perhaps I may have higher aims some day, and be a great stickler for the proper artistic balance of the completed work, but for the present circumstances lead me to wish merely to be considered a good hand at a serial. (*L*, 100)

This last sentence is usually wrenched out of context. Hardy was lamenting the sacrifice of a career as a poet to the necessity of writing novels, and understandably his forthcoming marriage was more important to him at this time than his artistic aims. There is no reason to suppose that he was as indifferent about his novels as critics have inferred, through overlooking the 'circumstances' which Hardy mentions as well as his statement that these are his aims only 'for the present'. But the letter is characteristic in so far as it shows his readiness to capitulate on issues in order to win acceptance. He was also exceptionally willing in early years to respond to advice that he received. He made several unsuccessful attempts to write a novel acceptable to Macmillan, and we have seen the result of his ready response to George Meredith's advice to write a story with a plot in *Desperate Remedies*, and the way in which praise of the rural scenes in that novel (by Macmillan's reader, John Morley, and several reviewers) encouraged him to write *Under the Greenwood Tree*. Now, however, in defiant reaction against the excessive praise of these same pastoral qualities in *A Pair of Blue Eyes* and *Far from the Madding Crowd*, and in search of wider public approval, Hardy turned his attention to the novel of manners.

The decision to attempt something new was courageous: Hardy was well aware of the value of a reputation for a speciality and of the risks involved in departing from it. But he did not believe that the taste for the pastoral would last, not even if he chopped his work into shape to suit the *Cornhill* and its readers. They liked novels about society, and Hardy had to use his talents to entertain society. (He did not greatly care for the literary evaluations of the social set, a sly dig at whom might be suspected in the description of them in *The Hand of Ethelberta* as 'an easeful section of society which is especially characterized by the mental condition of knowing nothing about any author a week after they have read him'.) He would have liked to tell a story which was largely autobiographical, as he was still to do, but at this stage it might have put an end to his income. Instead he becomes closely involved with Ethelberta herself: just as she marries Lord Mountclere to provide an income for others, Hardy accepts his fate as a novelist in order to establish himself as a married man. These circumstances of composition help us to understand the direction of Hardy's satire. *The Hand of Ethelberta* is written in the ironic mode, and in it Hardy offers the public something very close to what it wants, but at the same time satirises the form and satisfies himself.

2

In 1877, the year after *The Hand of Ethelberta* was published as a novel, George Meredith published his essay on 'The Idea of Comedy and the Uses of the Comic Spirit', in which he writes that 'the test of true comedy is that it shall awaken thoughtful laughter.' *The Hand of Ethelberta* passes this test well, since it is not only a spirited comedy but also a satire. The sub-title, 'A Comedy in Chapters', sets the tone and immediately relates the novel to the drama, and especially the comedy of manners of the Restoration and 18th century. Although *The Hand of Ethelberta* contains more powerful, polemical satire than most of these plays, theirs is the convention in which it is written. In its allegorical nomenclature, episodic structure, farcical convolution of plot, unexpected confrontations, fatuous social dialogue in metropolitan settings, and its treatment of love and courtship and marriage as a form of sport, it is very much a latter-day Restoration comedy.

Hardy classifies it among the 'Novels of Ingenuity', partly perhaps in defence against the charge that its plot is incredible and contrived. But all Hardy's novels are full of extremely unlikely turns and twists, and indeed this conforms to one of his primary rules:

> A story must be exceptional enough to justify its telling. We tale-tellers are all Ancient Mariners, and none of us is warranted in stopping Wedding-Guests (in other words, the hurrying public) unless he has something more unusual to relate than the ordinary experience of every average man and woman. (23 February 1893; *L*, 252)

The 1895 Preface prepares us for it:

> A high degree of probability was not attempted in the arrangement of the incidents, and there was expected of the reader a certain lightness of mood, which should inform him with a good-natured willingness to accept the production in the spirit in which it was offered.

The spirit in which it is offered is that of ironic comedy with interludes of farce, and in farce improbability is crucial. Farce is the point at which wild fantasy and daily reality meet, and this conjunction embodies the farcical dialectic. Farce traditionally involves a challenge to innocence by some form of malevolence, and the reader's reaction depends on how the challenge is resolved. In comedy as well as tragedy this involves a process of catharsis. When innocence seems about to triumph the action is farcical and the reader feels secure, but when the enemy unexpectedly reappears the effect is melodramatic and the reader may experience a *frisson* of fear. Here the evil humour is the splendidly vigorous old rogue, Lord Mountclere, and when Hardy unexpectedly reveals him as Ethelberta's companion in the coach in Chapter 47 he is giving the farcical situation a wholly legitimate melodramatic twist.

At the same time Hardy is satirising the expected forms of fiction of the time and light-heartedly playing with the kind of improbability that might feature in them. In an ordinary ironic comedy something closer to life would be expected. *The Hand of Ethelberta* remains open to the charge that it demands flexibility from the reader, who is only sure where he is if he accepts that he must keep awake to changes of emphasis. But the combination of modes reveals a wide scatter of affinities with Fielding, Defoe,

Dickens, Meredith, French comedy and Swift's satire, and extends *The Hand of Ethelberta* beyond the scope of its principal historical model, the Restoration comedy. Departures from vraisemblance are generically necessary: many of the situations are stylised and some of the characters are humours. The members of what Hardy calls 'the upper ten thousand' are plum targets for his satire on account of their urban contrivances: as Ben Jonson ridicules the bourgeois humours, Hardy and Meredith ridicule the humours of *arriviste* society.

Failure to accept the novel 'in the spirit in which it was offered', as an ironic comedy of manners, has generated some unduly harsh judgements about the characters. We should not expect characters on the scale of those in the Novels of Character and Environment. That the characters here exist on various planes is made clear through the use of allegorical names for some of them. Those such as Mrs Menlove, Neigh (the horse-knacker) and Ladywell (the ladies' man) are active humours, and in the context of comedy it would have been inappropriate to make them more round and credible than they are. If Hardy had freed them from their dominant traits and compounded their comical absurdity with emotional stature he would have come dangerously close to involving them in potentially tragic situations. Elsewhere in his fiction Neigh and Ladywell might have been portrayed as two wronged men who had suffered cruelly at the hands of a capricious and ambitious woman, or perhaps as a forlorn Smith and Knight or an unlucky Troy and Boldwood. But here they are the traditional 'blocking characters' of comedy, standing up in order to be knocked down. As real human beings their fate might have inspired pity; as humours they rate only a token sympathy. Anything more serious might disturb the emotional equilibrium of the comedy. So in Neigh and Ladywell, as in many features of the novel, the potentially tragic becomes comic. They are excellent comic foils: Neigh is one of 'the general phalanx of cool men and celebrated club yawners', who could have been a burlesque version of Henleigh Grandcourt in George Eliot's *Daniel Deronda*, which appeared in the same year, while Ladywell is an archetypal fop straight off the Restoration stage.

All the characters on this plane are just as economical and are often defined by their moral functions in the story. The steady and reliable butler, Mr Chickerel, with his honest humility, is a moral norm against which his daughter Ethelberta is measured. His son Sol, an honest craftsman, is a representative of social conscience. Sol and Dan make comically awkward appearances in the London gallery and in France, two sincere but bumpkin craftsmen out of their element, so that Ethelberta's philosophy is also implicitly measured against their *gauche* honesty. Sol speaks out his feelings, unlike the contrasting figure, the Hon. Edgar Mountclere, who, on discovering that his brother has married the socially unsuitable Ethelberta, first represses his feelings and then, in the privacy of his coach, is 'quite overcome with fatuous rage, his lips frothing like a mug of hot ale'. A representative of his class, Mountclere is told by his companion Sol, in an entertaining morality sequence as they journey together, un-availingly, to prevent the wedding, that he is 'a bit of rubbish'.

The other 'above stairs' characters in London society come off, I believe, better than is usually allowed. Hardy resented implications that he was out of his depth and a telling passage in the original typescript of his *Early Life* was omitted from the published version:

> Had this very clever satire been discovered to come from the hands of a man about town, its author would have been proclaimed as worthy of a place beside Congreve and Sheridan; indeed such had been hinted before its authorship was well known. But rumours that he had passed all his life in a hermitage smote like an east wind upon all appreciation of the tale. That the stories of his seclusion were untrue, that Hardy had been living in London for many years in the best of all situations for observing manners, was of course unknown. (*Personal Notebooks*, p. 221)

Certainly Hardy's inability to create convincing society talk has been exaggerated, and there are two points about this. One is that *The Hand of Ethelberta* is a comic satire: in burlesquing the vacuous conversations of polite London drawing-rooms Hardy no more intends to create a naturalistic record than Congreve does. The second is that at social gatherings of a certain type the conversation *is* notoriously contrived and artificial. Here the pseudo-*literati* are allowed their say, a 'gentleman who was suffering from a bad shirt front' gets in his word (we are obviously not to expect great wisdom from such a figure), and several speak, like Neigh, 'just as an exercise in words'.[3]

The four main characters are rounder and set up a further scheme of moral contrasts. Christopher's selfless love is set against the lascivious opportunism of Lord Mountclere, and Picotee's loyalty and honesty is contrasted with the ambiguous morality and ruthless will-power of her sister Ethelberta. Here too the potentially tragic is always averted. Picotee is a lighter Marty South, the loyal but distanced admirer of the hero, lacking in social graces and rendered inarticulate by circumstances. Her pains of unrequited love are no less intense than Marty's, but even the presentation of her suffering is often comic ('"O – O – O – O!" she replied, in the tone of pouring from a bottle, "What shall I do – o – o – o!"'). And whereas Giles Winterborne only becomes Marty's 'own true love' when he is in his grave, Picotee is at last united with Christopher. Hardy is always drawn to the stoical sufferer from love pains and in the novels such trials are usually resolved in death, or at best in the sort of philosophical compromise found in Marty's morbid consolation. But in a lighter mood, in *The Hand of Ethelberta*, he grants that long-suffering may have its reward. Picotee wins Christopher, and he has the best of the bargain between the sisters. Yet there remains a neat irony in the ending: Picotee's closing remarks reveal her continued dependence on Ethelberta, and this suggests that even now she and Christopher will not be entirely beyond Ethelberta's hand. Hardy, true to his imagination, does not resist putting a characteristic sting in the tail.

Christopher is firmly in the tradition of the worthy, constant, downtrodden lover whose moral stature Hardy commends. Like Giles and Gabriel Oak, he survives the final test of his loyalty: 'he had shown himself capable of a transmutation as valuable as it is rare in men, the change from pestering lover to staunch friend.' His reward is indirect but real. He does not win Ethelberta's gratitude (as Gabriel wins Bathsheba's) but something more worthwhile, her sister's hand. And before this the author has sent him away, like Stephen Smith and Angel Clare, as 'a sojourner in foreign lands', and unlike Stephen and Angel he finds that his feelings *are* assuaged by this excursion. Again the potentially tragic perspective is altered. Christopher Julian's fate is a kinder one than Hardy usually grants to characters whom he most admires – a usual signal of his regard is an unhappy end to a life of honourable struggle – but one of the author's aims here is to see that, in accordance with the conventions of comedy, harm comes to no one. Christopher's return is in the spring, the season which (with all its promise of rebirth) represents the conclusion of the archetypal comedy.

All of this shows us how we can glimpse a more characteristic Hardy novel running like a stream below the surface. This stream wells up in the central moving force of the novel, a rich and ambiguous personality who inhabits a plane of characterisation all her own: in Ethelberta herself a real claim for distinction in the novel resides. She only just misses the stature of some of the better-known heroines, since she is trimmed to fit the mode of the novel. But her will-power is unequalled by any of them, and she possesses a unique kind of savage energy. If she is denied the sympathy which Hardy extends to Bathsheba, Tess and Sue, she is at least excused the weight of moral judgements which I feel that the author would have more overtly insinuated if she had not appeared in a comedy of manners.

The comic mode precludes, too, a final edge to her almost atavistic personality. She is the most worldly, ruthless and ambitious of all Hardy's heroines, certainly more dangerous than the dissipated old aristocrat who is her adversary. There is a striking symbolic image in Chapter 1, often remarked by those who read the novel, in which a hawk is seen pursuing a wild duck. We are prepared to see this as an allegory of Mountclere's pursuit of Ethelberta by a comment of the ostler's a few pages earlier: 'Pouncing upon young flesh like a carrion crow – 'tis a vile thing for an old man.' Mountclere's capture of Ethelberta is similarly defined in bird imagery in Chapter 39 when the narrator exclaims: 'Was ever a thrush so safe in a cherry net before!' But, despite all this suggestion of her pursuit and captivity, Mountclere ironically wins the hand of Ethelberta only to find himself ruled by it; it is a Pyrrhic victory at best. The traditional pattern of comedy requires the evil humour to be reformed. But while such archetypal constraints inform the way Ethelberta is presented, they do not disguise what she is.

Ethelberta's achievement is riven with ambiguity; she attains the social and economic status that she wanted, but it is uncertain whether she has not sacrificed more than she has gained. Her progress is epigrammatically expressed as being 'from soft and playful Romanticism to distorted Benthamism', which begs the question which Hardy asks but does not answer:

'was the moral incline upward or down?' Hardy has to be content to make fun of her, but she is nonetheless a moral study and important in the psychic progress of his fiction. The ascendancy of reason in her life course touches one of the intellectual concerns of the time. Ethelberta is the first of the moderns. What she manages to do is suppress emotion and healthy sexuality in pursuit of a much less wholesome ideal, the acquisition of social rank and status and wealth. Her coldness is instanced in a succession of images, and an early clue is given in a comment made about her by one of the Doncastles' guests: 'That's a sign of her actual coldness; she lets off her feeling in theoretic grooves, and there is sure to be none left for practical ones!' She is both a vamp and a symbol of purposive masculinity (epitomised in the description of her at Corvsgate Castle, 'as a person freed of her hampering and inconvenient sex'), which allows her to be ruthless with Christopher, Neigh and Ladywell.

When she contemplates marriage with Mountclere, where does she look for ethical support? Unsurprisingly to John Stuart Mill's *Utilitarianism*, not a conventional manual for prospective brides (though it is later coolly quoted by Sue Bridehead to Phillotson over the breakfast table in *Jude the Obscure*), knowing well what she will find there. It is, of course, a process of rationalisation. The end she posits is to involve the happiness 'of all concerned' rather than herself, 'the disinterested spectator'. Yet her reasoning is casuistic. She is not disinterested, and the happiness 'of all concerned' will not be brought about through marriage with Mountclere. The socio-economic basis of her assumption is false; unlike Tess's family the Chickerels are not penurious, and they neither need nor wish to be provided for through such a materialistic compromise. And in the end Ethelberta is a victim of her own compromise, alienated from her family and an *arriviste* in her new setting, suffering from nightmare dreams and unable to sleep because she sees 'processions of people, audiences, battalions of lovers obtained under false pretences – all denouncing me with the finger of ridicule'. She is full of contraries that make her real.

All this sets her far apart from the heroine of Hardy's previous novel, Bathsheba, whom she superficially resembles in her determination and practical abilities, and apart from all the other heroines. Ethelberta is the heroine of a comedy, mocked and undermined; she cannot attain tragic stature because of the essential triviality of her plotting and high ambitions; she is allowed to do no harm which would draw serious moral censure on her. But her powerful characterisation makes her simultaneously frightening. To an unusual extent in Hardy's novels Ethelberta is in control of her life. She determines her course and runs it; Chance has no significant part to play and her only impediments are mundane and social. But Ethelberta's freedom contains greater responsibility for her own behaviour, and her ruthlessness suggests the sort of positive action that Hardy's women may be capable of when they are given their head. As D. H. Lawrence puts it, 'she has nipped off the bud of her heart.'[4] This gives her a unique place in the context of the women characters because Hardy never ventured further in his investigation of this capacity. Such a complex character is unexpected in a comedy of manners. What is frightening is not so much her career as it is shown to us but rather the intimations of such a person's potentiality.

Despite his apparent ambivalence as an impassive narrator, perhaps Hardy too was appalled by the possibilities latent in his creation. Certainly Ethelberta's suppression of emotion by reason and will-power is no solution for Hardy, and he turned away from it. But it is an integral stage, as I have said, in the psychic progress of his fiction. D. H. Lawrence, in his syllogistic but often brilliant study of Hardy, is as percipient as ever and in two paragraphs gives the best definition of the novel that I have read:

> *The Hand of Ethelberta* is the one almost cynical comedy. It marks the zenith of a certain feeling in the Wessex novels, the zenith of the feeling that the best thing to do is to kick out the craving for 'Love' and substitute commonsense, leaving sentiment to the minor characters.
>
> The novel is a shrug of the shoulders, and a last taunt to hope, it is the end of the happy endings, except where sanity and a little cynicism again appear in *The Trumpet-Major*, to bless where they despise. It is the hard, resistant, ironical announcement of personal failure, resistant and half-grinning. It gives way to violent, angry passions and real tragedy, real killing of beloved people, self-killing. Till now, only Elfride among the beloved, has been killed; the good men have always come out on top.[5]

What kind of comedy, then, is this novel which is paradoxically 'hard, resistant, ironical ... the end of the happy endings'? This is not what we expect from a jovial, often farcical, comedy of manners. But Hardy is joining Meredith in pursuit of 'thoughtful laughter'. Two passages from Meredith illuminate Hardy's purposes as well as his own. In his 1877 essay on comedy Meredith proclaims the socially therapeutic effect of the mode:

> Now to look about us in the present time, I think it will be acknowledged that, in neglecting the cultivation of the comic idea, we are losing the aid of a powerful auxiliar. You see Folly perpetually sliding into new shapes in a society possessed of wealth and leisure, with many whims, many strange ailments and strange doctors. Plenty of common sense is in the world to thrust her back when she pretends to empire.

And in his Prelude to *The Egoist* (1879) Meredith defends stylisation of character and improbability of incident:

> Credulity is not wooed through the impressionable senses, nor have we recourse to the small circular glow of the watchmaker's eye to raise in bright relief minutest grains of evidence for the routing of incredulity. The Comic Spirit conceives a definite situation for a number of characters and rejects all accessories in the exclusive pursuit of them and their speech. ... he has not a thought of persuading you to believe in him.

These passages are instructive, but Hardy's work implies a further dimension which Meredith's does not. Half a century later, in a letter to J. B. Priestley on 8 August 1927, Hardy says:

> Meredith was, as you recognize, and might have insisted on even more strongly, and I always felt, in the direct succession of Congreve and the artificial comedians of the Restoration, and in getting his brilliancy we must put up with the fact that he would not, or could not – at any rate did not – when aiming to represent the 'Comic Spirit', let himself discover the tragedy that always underlies Comedy if you only scratch it deeply enough. (*L*, 439)

In *The Hand of Ethelberta* we do not have to scratch very deeply to discover the potential tragedy; only the author's perspective preserves the comic mode. This gives us the key to the novel and to Lawrence's grim conclusions. As a moral investigation its conclusion is sombre. In Ethelberta's success there is no genuine triumph but compromise and surrender – 'self-killing', as Lawrence calls it. In her rise is also her fall from grace.

In the search for moral truth implicit in all his fiction Hardy may employ tragic or comic strategies or (often enough) mediate between the two. He is always a conscious entertainer and never a mere polemical novelist, so his courses will differ. But however divergent his modes, he is consistent in vision. Here, like Meredith, he chooses to strip Folly by enlisting comedy as his powerful auxiliar, to throw out (in Lawrence's phrase) 'a last taunt to hope'; in *Jude the Obscure*, when hope has long since been taunted and done with, he attempts to do the same thing through tragedy. The folly is social folly, and the tragedy (if we conclude, as I think we may, that in a real moral sense Ethelberta's success *is* a tragedy) in each of these novels originates in that most consistent of Hardy's preoccupations: class division.

The radicalism which had over-reached itself in Hardy's first and unpublished novel, *The Poor Man and the Lady*, is reasserted more powerfully than before in *The Hand of Ethelberta*, though tempered with humour. It is not a socialist manifesto, but it is a humanitarian and compassionate work, in tone and direction like much of Hardy's poetry, describing a period of social change and making a plea for personal dignity while regretting the ironies of prevailing conditions. It satirises both the aristocracy and London society and those who aspire to join them, and those who (like Sol and Dan at one point) indulge in inverted snobbery. Hardy's own position is defined in his notebook on 24 January 1888:

> I find that my politics are neither Tory nor Radical. I may be called an Intrinsicalist. I am against privilege derived from accident of any kind, and am therefore equally opposed to aristocratic privilege and democratic privilege. ... Opportunity should be available for all, but those who will not avail themselves of it should be cared for merely. (*L*, 204)

This does not mean that Hardy condones Ethelberta's enterprise. She both avails herself of, and creates, opportunities, but
she is made to look foolish and hypocritical in the process. She
'gets on' only in so far as she allies herself with already-existing
wealth and privilege, simultaneously dissociating herself from
the honest endeavour represented by her family.

The depressed classes are shown to be rising to Hardy's ideals,
making honest use of such opportunities as they have. Sol and
Dan have enough pride and satisfaction in their work to delight
William Morris, and the Hon. Edgar Mountclere cuts a sorry
figure beside the artisans. Mr Chickerel is proud of his service as
a member of what Ethelberta calls 'a peculiarly stigmatized and
ridiculed multitude' (before she becomes an employer and finds
it necessary to be 'too severe' with her own servants). But the
Chickerels are ground into an excessive humility, and it is
against this unnatural repression of individual dignity, rather
than their economic condition, that Hardy protests. His line of
perspective is challenging and original: to present a novel
'wherein servants were as important as ... their masters;
wherein the drawing-room was sketched in many cases from the
point of view of the servants' hall'. And the usual perspective is
inverted to show 'the sons and daughters of Mr and Mrs
Chickerel as beings who come within the scope of a congenial
regard' (Preface). This is nicely ironical in view of the predilec-
tion of many contemporary readers for drawing-room fiction
(perhaps in part a reflection of some readers' own pretensions?)
and the dehumanisation of servants in fiction and real life. This
preference was based on what Hardy later identified as the
erroneous theory that 'novels which depict life in the upper
walks of society must, in the nature of things, be better reading
than those which exhibit the life of any lower class.'[6] In its
inversion of this assumption the novel fell between two stools: if
it did not satisfy those who admired the pastoral Hardy, neither
did it please those who wanted their society fiction unadulter-
ated by members of the servant class. We are told that Emma
Hardy did not like the novel, complaining that there was too
much about servants in it.

In fact the unusual perspective works very well, and the
reader enjoys a multiplicity of angles of vision of society from
above and below stairs. This enables the author to compound his

ironies in a new way. The ambivalence of Ethelberta's position allows her to be accepted into Mrs Doncastle's select circle and to dine at her table, yet pay surreptitious visits to her father in the servants' pantry of the same house; to accept Ladywell as a suitor, yet view his carriage passing by Arrowthorne Lodge, wherein she sits as a humble cottager. The premise is unusual but not wholly unreal: members of the aristocracy did occasionally marry servants.[7] The logical culmination of the novel's inverted pattern is the circumstance that distresses Mrs Doncastle: 'The times have taken a strange turn when the angry parent of the comedy, who goes post-haste to prevent the undutiful daughter's rash marriage, is a gentleman from below stairs, and the unworthy lover a peer of the realm.' But it is not surprising in view of Hardy's association of moral judgements with social values, when the socially disabled people below stairs are the exemplars of honourable behaviour. London society is shown as one composed, in large part, of vacuous and pretentious snobs and fools, and (in Sol's words) the aristocracy are 'the useless lumber of our nation that'll be the first to burn if ever there comes a flare'.

Ethelberta's ambitions to join them are contemptible to her family, especially to her father and Sol, who severely upbraids her: 'I never see such a deserter of your own lot as you be! ... instead of sticking to ... principles, you must needs push up!' But Ethelberta nonetheless involves herself in the deracination which is so antagonistic to Hardy's conception of community, yet which is so often found in the Wessex novels. It signals individual isolation and further divisiveness in an already unstable society. And it is not clear that Hardy expects much from the new middle classes either, 'the metamorphic classes of society', who will bring in their train increasing urbanisation and erosion of rural values, and amongst whom Ethelberta settles her family in a new suburban villa in Knollsea. Hardy is concerned with the effect of deracination on the individual. In this novel the contrast between country and town, which is sustained throughout, is made more explicit than anywhere else in the Wessex novels. Ethelberta diminishes in moral stature as she passes from one to the other: the 'free habits and enthusiasms of country life' give way to 'the subtler gratifications of abridged bodices, candlelight, and no feelings in particular, which prevailed in town'. And Hardy is one of the early critics of the need to cover the green land with suburbia, with the concomitant effects of this process on the spirit:

> Slush-ponds may be seen turning into basement-kitchens; a broad causeway of shattered earthenware smothers plots of budding gooseberry-bushes and vegetable trenches, foundations following so closely upon gardens that the householder may be expected to find cadaverous sprouts from overlooked potatoes rising through the chinks of his cellar floor. But the other great process, that of internal transmutation, is not less curious than the encroachment of grey upon green.

How much of the original impulse of *The Poor Man and the Lady* survives in *The Hand of Ethelberta* is conjectural, but the satire is fierce. It is an outcry against unfair privilege and social advantage, urban pretensions and hypocrisy, foolish aspirations and ignoble compromise, and a celebration of the spiritual and moral superiority of country life. It is a study of the physical and personal deracination which later leads to the personal and social tragedies in *Tess* and *Jude*. And it is a vigorous protest against all sorts of repressions in London: the aristocracy and upper classes suppress emotions, sincerity and integrity, and deprive lower classes of rightful dignity. Only social forces are involved, not Fate, and man himself must bear the blame. Though man is capable of adjusting the 'moral incline' for himself, however, there seems little chance that he will do so. It is only when we isolate the serious themes of the satire from its humorous mode that we realise what a seminal novel *The Hand of Ethelberta* may be in the Hardy canon; his deepest concerns are packed in, and nowhere else are his social beliefs set out with such clarity.

That Hardy chose to incorporate such social messages in what he later called a 'somewhat frivolous narrative' (1895 Preface) is perhaps one of the reasons for the novel's comparative failure. The frivolity is not strong enough to generate unrestrained laughter, nor is it sufficiently weak to allow the serious themes to emerge unimpeded. Hardy could write pure farce with mastery (as in episodes of *Under the Greenwood Tree*) and when one crosses his satiric-ironic sense of humour with his tragic imagination it is unsurprising that he should reveal, in this novel and elsewhere, a talent for black comedy. But perhaps because the production of

The Hand of Ethelberta was circumstantial rather than planned, the different modes do not wholly cohere.

Though Hardy's style is not always at its best here, however, we cannot leave *The Hand of Ethelberta* without observing that it contains much strong, idiosyncratic writing. The tastelessness of modish urban aesthetics, for example, is epitomised in the decorated tiles of Ethelberta's chimneypiece in London, as she explains to Christopher Julian the method of design:

> 'The flowers, mice and spiders are done very simply, you know: you only press a real flower, mouse, or spider out flat under a piece of glass, and then copy it, adding a little more emaciation or angularity at pleasure.'
> 'In that "at pleasure" is where all the art lies,' said he.

Elsewhere there is a striking view of the Doncastles' servants, dehumanised by their labours, subsumed into their surroundings and transformed into half-human licensed *voyeurs*, grimly sporting in the shadows. They are made to appear to Picotee almost in the guise of sprites:

> Her nerves were screwed up to the highest pitch of uneasiness by the grotesque habits of these men and maids, who were quite unlike the country servants she had known, and resembled nothing so much as pixies, elves, or gnomes, peeping up upon human beings from their haunts underground, sometimes for good, sometimes for ill – sometimes doing heavy work, sometimes none; teasing and worrying with impish laughter half suppressed, and vanishing directly once mortal eyes were bent on them. Separate and distinct from overt existence under the sun, this life could hardly be without its distinctive pleasures, all of them being more or less pervaded by thrills and titillations from games of hazard, and the perpetual risk of sensational surprises.

The Hand of Ethelberta also contains a brilliant scene describing the visit to Farnfield by Ethelberta and Picotee. As they advance through the thickening fog, the light of the full moon struggling through the mists reveals a surrealistic nightmare vision, as memorable as it is moving and bitter:

In the enclosure ... was an extraordinary group. It consisted of numerous horses in the last stage of decrepitude, the animals being such mere skeletons that at first Ethelberta hardly recognised them to be horses at all; they seemed rather to be specimens of some attenuated heraldic animal, scarcely thick enough through the body to throw a shadow: or enlarged castings of the fire-dog of past times. These poor creatures were endeavouring to make a meal from herbage so trodden and thin that scarcely a wholesome blade remained; the little that there was consisted of the sourer sorts common on such sandy soils, mingled with tufts of heather and sprouting ferns.

'Why have we come here, dear Berta?' said Picotee, shuddering.

'I hardly know,' said Ethelberta.

Adjoining this enclosure was another and smaller one, formed of high boarding, within which appeared to be some sheds and outhouses. Ethelberta looked through the crevices, and saw that in the midst of the yard stood trunks of trees as if they were growing, with branches also extending, but these were sawn off at the points where they began to be flexible, no twig or boughs remaining. Each torso was not unlike a hat-stand, and suspended to the pegs and prongs were lumps of some substance which at first she did not recognise; they proved to be a chronological sequence to the previous scene. Horses' skulls, ribs, quarters, legs, and other joints were hung thereon, the whole forming a huge open-air larder emitting not too sweet a smell.

But what Stygian sound was this? There had arisen at the moment upon the mute and sleepy air a varied howling from a hundred tongues ...

This is powerful Juvenalian satire. The cruelty of this pitiful scene symbolises the reality beneath the veneer of manners in London society, the substratum of inhumane activity that makes the money-mill turn.

The incorporation of such scenes emphasises the difficulty in defining the novel, this 'last taunt to hope ... end of the happy endings'. To isolate individual scenes, themes, characters and characteristics is to recognise the polymorphous quality of Hardy's experiment. It may be argued that the author has not entirely absorbed his materials into the mode in which he has

chosen to write; and Ethelberta is arguably larger than the novel
in which she appears, because we are able to see her in the
impressive company of Hardy's women and may prefer to wish
her into a more serious work. The problem is partly one that the
novel shares with *Desperate Remedies*, the tension between an
established form and the author's reading of life, the need to
meet the requirements of a conventional mode which is basically
inimical to Hardy's tragic imagination. This seems to be
acknowledged in Hardy's later regret that he had hurried into
the new form before learning from *Far from the Madding Crowd*
'what there had been of value ... of true and genuine substance
on which to build a career as a writer with a real literary
message' (*L*, 102).

Since the story is ironic, the ending is in key: Ethelberta has
what she wants, and Mountclere has what he wants, but they do
not get what they expected. The comic is realised but not
without a sense that Hardy is constrained by the mode from
investigating the deeper implications of the conclusion. The
cynicism is there, and Lawrence recognised it, but the nature of
the heroine's 'moral incline' has to remain undefined. The novel
has to be understood on more than one plane, but it must be
read as a comedy of manners. The tensions involved in this
inevitably at last partly dissipate the dramatic stature of the
work.

Analysis of the comedy would surely disserve the novel, or
indeed any novel written in the comic mode. But *The Hand of
Ethelberta* is funnier than its solemn critics have admitted and
reveals, though they are not uniformly successful, a wide range
of humorous effects from epigrammatic wit to farce. It lacks
some of the qualities that inform the Novels of Character and
Environment: their characters and fates grand and tragic, local
intensity and historical consciousness, disturbing passions and
cosmic agencies, the psychic interrelationship of individual
minds, and certain poetic and atmospheric qualities associated
with these features. That may seem a daunting array of minuses.
But the scope of *The Hand of Ethelberta* is more modest and its
tone is different. If it is not as good as *The Return of the Native*,
which followed it, that is partly to say that Hardy is better at
writing a different kind of novel. And if the psychic interest is
here subdued in favour of amusing situations and social polemic,
Hardy's imagination is seized by one powerful and potentially

frightening psyche driven by compulsive forces common to
Eustacia and Tess and Sue.

If *Desperate Remedies* is an exceptional sensation novel, *The
Hand of Ethelberta* is an exceptional ironic comedy of manners
which satirises the accepted forms of fiction of the time as well as
the social conventions which they report. As a comedy it is dark
rather than light, as befits a novel which represents 'the end of
the happy endings'. But in the process Hardy is having a great
deal of ironic fun, and undue critical solemnity should not
obscure either what Hardy calls 'the aim of the performance', or
the degree of its achievement.

5 Historical consciousness and pastoral irony: *The Trumpet-Major* (1880)

1

On 28 November 1878 Hardy made a sombre entry in his notebook: 'Woke before it was light. Felt that I had not enough staying power to hold my own in the world.' (*L*, 124) This characteristic feeling of disquietude followed close on the publication of *The Return of the Native* on 4 November, and the note must have been written soon after Hardy had read the review of the novel in the *Athenaeum*, which provoked his reply on 'Dialect in Novels'.[1] The reviewer thought the novel 'distinctly inferior to anything of his which we have yet read', and although Hardy avoids saying almost anything about the novel in the *Life* what struck him most deeply was that he might not be able to sustain the level he had reached. The confident tone of Hardy's reply hid misgivings which were to be deepened by further criticism. *The Return of the Native* was his greatest literary achievement so far, yet there were charges from W. E. Henley of 'insincerity' and 'affectation'; the *Saturday Review* repeated this and concluded that 'in the attempt to amuse us Mr Hardy, in our opinion, breaks down'; the *Illustrated London News* found the descriptions good, the movement slow, the characters uninteresting, the action poor and the conclusion flat; the critic for *The Times* 'could scarcely get up a satisfactory interest in people whose history and habits are entirely foreign to our own' and regretted that readers were taken farther from the madding crowd than ever.[2]

Though Hardy could not have known it, he was at a mid-point in the first phase of his writing career. He had published six novels in seven years, establishing a reputation as a novelist of much more than rural life, but at the expense of puzzling his readers. Even with *The Return of the Native* they seemed unaware of his capacity for exploring serious and tragic issues, for psychic investigation of individual lives and for moving away from the rural idyll into scenes expressing a personalised loneliness. In view of the reception of *The Return of the Native*, which must have influenced his next novel, Hardy's misgivings were understandable; looking back from the present on his writing over the seven years that followed, they can be seen to have been justified. But it would be wrong to regard this period as a *lacuna* between works of genius; the three novels which follow are more limited in scope and execution but each represents a further development of Hardy's talent. In this and the next two chapters the curious interlude between *The Return of the Native* (1878) and *The Mayor of Casterbridge* (1886) will be examined.

The first novel to appear was *The Trumpet-Major*, a pastoral story set in the Napoleonic era. It is reasonable to assume that the subject was already in Hardy's mind while writing *The Return of the Native* in 1877–8, since that novel contains many references to Napoleon and the threatened invasion, especially in the reiterated recollections of Grandfer Cantle and the invocation of Napoleon as an ironic instrument in defining Eustacia, one of whose 'high Gods' he is. Hardy's '*Trumpet-Major* Notebook'[3] shows that he was busy gathering material about the Napoleonic era in the British Museum from the spring and summer of 1878 onwards: internal dating shows that he was there on 30 and 31 May and 6 and 27 July 1878, and again in the spring and at least once in the autumn of 1879. It is not clear when the large amount of detailed contemporary material that Hardy collected coalesced into a definite intention to write *The Trumpet-Major* as such; the first gathering is merely entitled '1803–5 Geo.III. notes – (I.) B. M. &c.', 'Geo.III.' being later stroked through. But as early as May 1875 Hardy had made his first recorded note of intent to write an extended work, in some form, on the Napoleonic wars: 'Mem: A Ballad of the Hundred Days. Then another of Moscow. Others of earlier campaigns – forming altogether an Iliad of Europe from 1789 to 1815.' (*L*, 106) This was obviously realised in *The Dynasts*, but Hardy's first venture into this period was *The Trumpet-Major*. The novel is of course neither a direct precursor of nor a preliminary sketch for the subsequent epic-drama, except in the most general sense. The works are entirely different in impulse, form and scope, united only by a common interest in the period; but while the Napoleonic wars form the subject of *The Dynasts*, they represent only the background (albeit important) to *The Trumpet-Major*.

Hardy's deliberate course of reading and research at the British Museum shows an admirable respect for historical precision,[4] and he never took such pains over the preparation for any other novel. Its value in helping to create a pervasive historical vraisemblance is self-evident, but Hardy's motive for such careful study may have been personal as well as aesthetic. The Napoleonic wars had long fascinated him because of childhood reading and family associations. At the age of eight he

> found in a closet *A History of the Wars* – a periodical dealing with the war with Napoleon, which his grandfather had subscribed to at the time, having been himself a volunteer. The torn pages of these contemporary numbers with their melodramatic prints of serried ranks, crossed bayonets, huge knapsacks, and dead bodies, were the first to set him on the train of ideas that led to *The Trumpet-Major* and *The Dynasts*. (*L*, 16–17)

He also enjoyed in his youth 'extensive acquaintance' with old soldiers of the time (*L*, 19), and thus impressions of the Napoleonic era were passed down to Hardy by word of mouth. The legends of 'Boney' were still alive to the countrymen of Dorset and the 'Corsican ogre' was still a villain of dumb-shows and puppet-shows, feared as an Antichrist.[5] In the preface to *The Dynasts* Hardy recalls that Wessex, in his own memory, had been 'animated by memories and traditions of the desperate military preparations' for the contingency of an invasion. And a likely emotional attraction for Hardy was the involvement of his collateral ancestor Captain (later Vice-Admiral) Hardy at Trafalgar. But personal links, oral traditions and general historical awareness of the period were not enough for Hardy, and his extensive research bespeaks a deeper involvement and interest.

Composition probably began in early 1879, and certainly the manuscript cannot have been very substantial when Hardy submitted the idea to Leslie Stephen, who replied on 17 February 1879 that he would like to see the story when it was 'further advanced'.[6] Hardy had asked Stephen's advice about whether to present a historical personage in the story, and Stephen advised him against it: 'a historical character in a novel is almost always a nuisance; but I like to have a bit of history in the background, so to speak: to feel that George III is just round the corner though he does not present himself in full front.' Perhaps because he did not really expect the story to appear in the *Cornhill* Hardy ignored this advice, and George III duly appears 'in full front' on the downs, in the theatre and notably in his encounter with Anne Garland in Chapter 34.

Within three months Hardy had made enough progress to submit a manuscript to Macmillan and Co., presumably for publication in *Macmillan's Magazine* and then in book form. But Hardy had no more success with this publishing house than before, and the only extant evidence of the novel's submission is found in a letter from George Macmillan dated 20 May 1879.[7] Presumably a letter of rejection from Alexander Macmillan followed soon afterwards, since on 9 June Hardy wrote to Blackwood's suggesting that he might submit the manuscript to them, pointing out that it was 'nearer to your own standard of taste' than an earlier story which he had offered.[8] Hardy is at pains to stress the innocuous quality of the story: 'I may just add that it is to be above all things a cheerful story, without views or opinions, & is intended to wind up happily – in short I flatter myself that you would not regret reading it.'

John Blackwood replied with some enthusiasm on 27 June, but by this time Hardy had had some communication (now presumably lost) with William Isbister, publisher of *Good Words*, for on 20 June the editor of that journal, Dr Donald Macleod, wrote to Hardy: 'I am particularly glad to learn from Mr Isbister that there is a probability of your contributing a story to Good Words during 1880.'[9] Macleod's letter is largely, in his own expression, a 'homily', frankly and uncompromisingly defining the kind of story that was acceptable to *Good Words*:

> I have no doubt that you fully appreciate the role which we try to assign to Good Words. We are anxious that all our stories should be in harmony with the spirit of the Magazine – free at once from *Goody-goodyism* – and from anything – direct or indirect – which a healthy *Parson* like myself would not care to read to his family or their friends. Let us have as much humour (oh that we had more!) and character – as much manly bracing fresh air – as much honest love-making and stirring incident as you like – avoiding everything likely to

offend the susceptibilities of honestly religious and domestic souls.

Macleod writes with the urgent fervour of a Presbyterian minister and in a vein which cannot have appealed to Hardy, so often harassed by editorial pleas about the susceptibilities of readers. By this time journals like *Good Words* were widely read by the new middle classes, who were even more stuffy than their predecessors. Certain standards had been set much earlier, but as more people aspired to membership of the middle class their very insecurity made them hyper-respectable, and editors were extremely sensitive to opinion and sales. Macleod's well-intentioned puritanism is more uncompromising than most, but it is impossible to know the actual effect of his forceful letter on the eventual tone of *The Trumpet-Major*. It is unlikely that Hardy had wanted to make the story offend convention – he had already been rebuffed by Stephen and Macmillan, and had stressed its innocuous quality to Blackwood – but if any rebellious instinct remained, Macleod's letter must have repressed it. Hardy was living by the pen and was shrewd enough to avoid gratuitous sensationalism.

Macleod wrote again on 22 August: 'Isbister speaks in glowing terms of what he had read and I am all anxiety to be in a position to judge for myself!'[10] But Macleod's judgement proved slightly less glowing, and he pedantically insisted on a number of trivial changes. Hardy submitted placidly, knowing well enough that in book form the story would appear as originally written.[11] He recalled his dealings with Macleod 46 years later:

> I met Dr. Macleod whenever he came to London & discussed small literary points with him, all of which I have forgotten except two: that he asked me to make a lover's meeting [between Bob Loveday and Matilda Johnson in Chapter 16], which I had fixed for a Sunday afternoon, take place on a Saturday, & that swear-words should be avoided – in both which requests I readily acquiesced, as I restored my own readings when the novel came out as a book.[12]

Textual comparison with the serial version published in *Good Words* reveals that the swearing, which had so slightly polluted the 'manly bracing fresh air' that Macleod demanded, is of the

'Damn!' and 'Good God!' variety.

The novel was half written by September 1879 (Purdy, p. 34) and probably completed early in 1880. It appeared serially in *Good Words* (January–December 1880) and in volume form, published by Smith, Elder, on 23 October of the same year.

2

The appearance of *The Trumpet-Major* after *The Return of the Native*, and its modification of Hardy's tone and scope, again demands flexibility from readers. If it does not sustain the distinction of its predecessor this is because it was written as a popular entertainment calculated to satisfy the undemanding standards of the general late-Victorian reader of fiction. (The subscribers to Mudie's Circulating Library, for example, were not notably intellectual.) There is not even a moderate challenge to propriety, the novel exhibits pastoral charm and pathos, and there is some pleasing humour and lively action. But there is also a serious undertone and a great deal more irony than its contemporary readers probably suspected. The pictorial charms of the idealised world can be delusive, and Hardy's classification of the novel among the 'Romances and Fantasies' does not imply romantic escapism. Even when he is celebrating rural charms in a more benevolent mood than usual Hardy does not curb his fundamental impulse to truth. It is not perverse to regard the powerful elegiac note of the story's concluding paragraph as the key to the real meaning of the novel, the climax to a series of ironies upon which the story is structured; to realise that it is not the archetypal wedding celebration that matters, but the passing of the good, defeated by the fickle and the mediocre, into undeserved oblivion. John Loveday goes the way of Clym, Henchard, Giles Winterborne, Tess and Jude. The apparently idyllic world of Overcombe has no better fate to offer. Contemporary readers seem to have found nothing so sombre about the novel, beyond approving the pathos of John's departure, but by means of an equivocal conclusion Hardy may have satisfied both his own veracity of vision and his readers' more ideal expectations.[13]

After the indifferent reception of *The Return of the Native* the new novel was warmly acclaimed. This is a measure of how accurately Hardy could now gauge the ingredients for an innocuous popular success and tells much about the tastes of Victorian reviewers and readers. A typical verdict is that of Julian Hawthorne, in the *Spectator* (18 December 1880), who prefers *The Trumpet-Major* to its predecessor since he believes that Hardy 'is not capable of the loftier and more powerful efforts of tragedy', so that *The Trumpet-Major* 'is calculated to show the author in his happiest light'; a well-meant conclusion but one unlikely to have appealed to Hardy. The most telling comment about the nineteenth-century popularity of the novel is made by W. P. Trent in a survey of Hardy's novels in 1892: 'It is one of the cleanest, most interesting, most wholesome stories that can be recommended to readers old or young.'[14] The Grundyism and concern for the moral welfare of the Young Person implicit in this would have appealed to Dr Macleod and no doubt to the cosseted general reader, but it represents a confusion of social, moral and literary values. The qualities here commended could later inspire Emma Hardy to remark disparagingly of the novel, 'Yes, that's one of the pretty ones!',[15] and it is the prettiness and wholesome cleanliness that have led more recent critics to regard it as trite. Among the laudatory epithets adjectives like 'modest', 'charming' and 'competent' predominate.

The Trumpet-Major is a novel of moderation; no issue is forced, and human nature is subjected to no extremities of behaviour. The elements of suspense upon which the reader's interest is to be maintained are themselves moderate. Will Bob or John marry the heroine? Will Bob be killed at Trafalgar? Will the villain Festus be foiled? There is little doubt about the outcome of any of these dilemmas, and the reader's historical knowledge precludes any anxiety about the threatened invasion. There are some isolated incidents of excitement – such as Anne's escape on the careering horse and Bob's escape from the press-gang – but nothing very stirring, since it soon becomes clear that the story is not to depart from any of the pastoral conventions and that a happy conclusion may be expected. Even John's death, by lending a few moments of agreeable pathos, can be made to conform to this pattern.

The lack of any philosophising is conspicuous, but the absence of formulated ideas does not necessarily imply a lack of serious purpose. It is easy but imprecise to believe that Hardy is only 'serious' in novels of the stature of *The Mayor of Casterbridge* or

Tess; he is just as serious, though in a different way, in *Desperate Remedies*, *A Pair of Blue Eyes*, *The Hand of Ethelberta* and the present novel. In *The Trumpet-Major* overt philosophical reflections are eschewed in favour of a straightforwardly descriptive narrative bearing only the occasional moral aphorism. Again this would satisfy readers who did not wish to be implicitly harangued about the inadequacies of their religious systems and who would shy away from Hardy's alleged pessimism. The Macleods among his audience, those 'honestly religious and domestic souls', wanted nothing which might challenge or change their fixed ideas. Hardy's own disclaimer that the novel was to be 'without views or opinions'[16] should, however, be read with caution: its context reveals it to be a shrewd gambit to win the interest and approval of John Blackwood, and no doubt to distinguish *The Trumpet-Major* from its maligned predecessor. But it is impossible for the most austerely objective author wholly to suppress 'views or opinions', which must invariably emerge in some form, and Hardy is incapable of producing so bland a work of fiction as his disclaimer implies. The absence of authorial philosophising cannot be taken to mean that Hardy's impulse to disturb has been thwarted. Both within and beyond the village of Overcombe there is much that is disturbing, all the more so because it is subtly interwoven into the apparently harmless tale, and the percipient reader will find little to comfort him in the story, which is predominantly ironic and sometimes bitter.

As a love story *The Trumpet-Major* is unexceptional. In Anne's constant vacillation between Bob and John Loveday there is little to quicken the reader's interest, and no sense of the emotional complications that give dramatic effectiveness to the dilemmas of Cytherea, Elfride, Bathsheba, Thomasin and Eustacia, among those who precede her. The heroine, for all her ingenuous charms, seems insufficiently worth the winning. As a conventional comedy, despite the involvement of Festus Derriman, Uncle Benjy and Anthony Cripplestraw, it is no more than averagely amusing, though there are some hearty moments. But it is as an historical novel that *The Trumpet-Major* comes into its own, not in the conventional sense of describing romance and adventure in an historical setting, but in the evocation of time and war and man's inhumanity to man, and in the ironic shades which the Napoleonic background casts over the happenings at

Overcombe and Budmouth. The international tragedy is the informing presence of the story and the fate of John Loveday its emotional correlative within the microcosm of the action, so that it is impossible to accept *The Trumpet-Major* as the innocuous idyll which it is usually taken to be.

Hardy's conscientious research contributes to the historical realism of the narrative and the period atmosphere, but the pervasive historical consciousness is more important than any particularity of detail. 'Hardy's whole art', as Ian Gregor says, 'requires the backward glance, it is memory that primes his imagination.'[17] It is more than a sense of period. The insistence of the past is ever present in the mill at Overcombe, whose passageway is worn down 'by the ebb and flow of feet that had been going on there ever since Tudor times' and whose walls are marked with 'the tawny smudges of bygone shoulders'. Miller Loveday himself is 'the representative of an ancient family of corn-grinders whose history is lost in the mists of antiquity', a living personification of former days, and his presence is a constant factor in a world of change. He stands for the timeworn and innocent serenity of Wessex, now as so often in the novels under threat of invasion and incipient fragmentation; the psychic movement of Hardy's fiction is implied beneath the surface.

It is around the miller and his mill that the action revolves, from the initial discovery there of the quiet homesteads of the miller and the Garlands to the subdued closure of the story in the same place with the poignant departure of John, and the union of Anne and Bob to signify the continuation of the line. The structure of the tale is cyclical: 'Time present and time past/Are both perhaps present in time future,/And time future contained in time past.'[18] The events contained by the cycle, depicted and reported, range from the trivial to the terrible. There is nothing melioristic about Hardy's 'cheerful story': by the end no one (with the possible exceptions of Miller Loveday and Widow Garland) is better off. For all her prim carefulness Anne is to be united with the least worthy brother, the mercurial and unreliable Bob; old Squire Derriman is dead; Festus and Matilda are brought together in a match which promises disaster; the noblest character, John, is dead, along with many others among his soldier friends, all good men and true; and the war is still in progress. The solid, good-natured miller is still at the centre of the community, but Bob will not be an equal successor. Nothing has occurred to enhance the quality of life, and much human endeavour (in both love and war) has been shown as an exercise in futility. The prospects for the future, in the wider implications of the historical cycle, are not promising.

The most sombre influence in the novel is the war itself, and its presentation is the more effective for being suggestive and unforced, while its implications lour. The emphasis each reader accords the war must determine, or be determined by, his interpretation of the novel. Many of its contemporary readers probably enjoyed reading about the colourful soldiers, with their dashing appearance and gallant aspect, on a purely superficial level, and attached no more significance to them than as attractive set-pieces: Edmund Gosse wrote to Hardy, 'I think the first volume of the T. M. ranks with the very cream of your writing – I delight in this deep green landscape starred over with the scarlet & white of the cheerful military.'[19] But this is to overlook, as Hardy does not, the bitter poignancy of their cheerfulness. At the miller's party Sergeant Stanner lightheartedly mocks 'Boney' in song, but

> Poor Stanner! In spite of his satire, he fell at the bloody battle of Albuera a few years after this pleasantly spent summer at the Georgian watering-place, being mortally wounded and trampled down by a French hussar when the brigade was deploying into line under Beresford.

All these genial men in red and white enjoy the party without premonition: 'There is not one among them who would attach any meaning to "Vittoria" or gather from the syllables "Waterloo" the remotest idea of his own glory or death.' The laconic delivery of these observations should not obscure them.

Napoleon and his wars serve to dramatise time itself, and the cycle of events depicted in the span of the novel is shown to be only a fraction of the larger cycle. Much later in the novel, when the downs are described after the King's review, the passing glory is undercut to reveal the realities behind the panoply, and the past and present are united in a sudden ironic intensity:

> They still spread their grassy surface to the sun as on that beautiful morning not, historically speaking, so very long ago;

but the King and his fifteen thousand armed men, the horses, the bands of music, the princesses, the cream-coloured teams – the gorgeous centre-piece, in short, to which the downs were but the mere mount or margin – how entirely have they all passed and gone! – lying scattered about the world as military and other dust, some at Talavera, Albuera, Salamanca, Vittoria, Toulouse, and Waterloo; some in home churchyards; and a few small handfuls in royal vaults.

It is compassion that moves the author, not martial splendour or romantic glory.[20]

Since the Napoleonic wars take place offstage, they are not the subject of the novel, nor are their incidents dramatised as they are in *The Dynasts*. But neither are they merely a convenient peg on which to hang the story. The distant wars play a pervasive metaphorical and ironic role. Napoleon broods over the action like a malignant spirit, a potential Mephistophelian Visitant, the fear of whose invasion threatens the peaceful folk of Wessex and whose war claims several of them elsewhere. He is the Jungian 'shadow', the force of evil which must be reckoned with: in a sentence strikingly appropriate to describe that more recent demagogue, Adolf Hitler, he is called 'the mighty little man who was less than human in feeling, and more than human in will'. For Hardy, here as in *The Dynasts*, he is a fascinating but terrible phenomenon. (In so far as he has a local metaphorical counterpart as a 'shadow' or villain, it is the buffoonish Festus Derriman with his aggrandised ambitions to inherit Oxwell Hall. Festus is a parody of Napoleon in his vicious pretensions: just as Napoleon is the villain of the macrocosm, Festus is the villain of the microcosm, and the reader knows through historical hindsight that Napoleon's ultimate fate is as derisory as Derriman's, each suffering the failure of his overweening ambitions in a state of exile.)

Nothing in the actual story of *The Trumpet-Major* is dramatically comparable with the great events in the background, but the domestic narrative derives its deeper tones from the sombre world picture. The eponymous hero is John Loveday, the trumpet-major, whose experience is one of frustration, failure and tragedy; there is nothing essentially lighthearted about a novel in which the hero is thus subjugated to pain and death, despite its reputation for a convivial atmosphere and bucolic humour. Several critics have compared the pattern of *The Trumpet-Major* with that of *Under the Greenwood Tree*, and it is easy to understand why: the slender narrative of each novel concerns some mild rivalry for the hand of an *ingénue*, the stories each unfold in a pleasant rural backwater, and each concludes in conformity with the conventions of romance and comedy with an archetypal wedding. But there is an important distinction: in *The Trumpet-Major* the hero does not win. The imminent wedding is not entirely satisfactory – a rather foolish girl is to marry an inconsistent and fairly insensitive man – and any premature rejoicing is inhibited by the knowledge of John's coming death. The most vivid image which remains in the reader's mind is the moving elegiac note of the final paragraph:

> The candle held by his father shed its waving light upon John's face and uniform as with a farewell smile he turned on the doorstone, backed by the black night; and in another moment he had plunged into the darkness, the ring of his smart step dying away upon the bridge as he joined his companions-in-arms, and went off to blow his trumpet till silenced for ever upon one of the bloody battle-fields of Spain.

The novel which ends on this tragic note is full of country freshness and romantic shades, though this geniality does not obscure its more fundamental and disturbing forces. But there is always much to enjoy in the evocation of an idealised rural Wessex, regardless of palimpsestic meaning, and there is much that is pleasing in Overcombe, with its enduring downs and domestic charms, its rural quietude and communal hospitality. It is a setting of languorous but perpetual activity, where 'the water, with its flowing leaves and spots of froth, was stealing away, like Time, under the dark arch', and where the unsensational events of the narrative proceed at the same slow but confident pace. The story is as slight in incident as that of *Under the Greenwood Tree*, and the sequence of events is rather loosely structured; *The Trumpet-Major* comprises a series of episodes rather than a developing drama, so the effect can sometimes be tedious. But the central theme, though timeworn, is modestly effective and concerns the choice of a husband for Anne Garland. The formal emphasis of the title-page[21] invites us to see *The Trumpet-Major* as a study too of the emotional vicissitudes of two contrasting personalities, John and Bob. It is the vacillations of two of the central characters that prove destructive to the third, and there is a premonitory image of the changeable natures of Anne and Bob in Chapter 2: 'This revolving piece of statuary could not, however, be relied on as a vane, owing to the neighbouring hill, which formed variable currents in the wind.'[22] If the love story has a moral it is one characteristic of Hardy: that the steady virtues of honour, loyalty and patience go unrewarded while victory crowns the inconstant and less worthy.

In common with most of Hardy's novels *The Trumpet-Major* may be read as a symbolic morality play in which characters of different fictional substance interact without any irritant feeling of disparity in their presentation. The more prominent among them (John, Bob, Miller Loveday, Anne and Mrs Garland) are all psychologically credible; the characters involved in the sub-plot (Festus, Uncle Benjy, Matilda, Cripplestraw), whence proceeds the humour, are not necessarily incredible – indeed all the characters are true to life, in whatever mode they are presented – but they are purposely stagey. All the characters, the credible and the histrionic, fulfil a symbolic function in the story and contribute to the controlled network of ironies which dominates the plot. The Lovedays, with their strong family affections, represent the desirable norm of human relationships, until their loyalties are threatened by internecine rivalries between the brothers. Like 'Fancy Day' and 'Dick Dewy' in *Under the Greenwood Tree*, their name is suggestive of life-giving, life-enhancing qualities – it is, as King George says, 'a good name' – and it is as appropriately pastoral as Garland.

The miller is a traditional figure, approaching 60 with great good humour, a survivor from better times, 'hale all through, as many were in those days'. As the scion of a long line of millers, Mr Loveday's personality is reflected in Overcombe Mill itself: in its genial simplicity and continuing usefulness in supplying flour, 'the blessed staff of life', this 'hard-worked house' images its owner. The miller's best qualities are inherited not by Bob, who will succeed him, but by John, four years Bob's senior and in almost all respects his superior. Each brother has an antecedent in *The Return of the Native*: if John takes on the mantle of Diggory Venn in his loyalty and passive fortitude, Bob takes on that of the fickle Damon Wildeve. John and Bob thus assume familiar roles within the typology of Hardy's characters and enact the author's continuing preoccupation with the contrasting fortunes of the passive and fastidious man on the one hand and the devil-may-care precipitate on the other.

If Hardy's novels contain a series of psychological explorations of character types which fascinated him, or with which he identified, to read *The Trumpet-Major* with this in mind is to lend an added piquancy to the presentation of Bob and John. While Hardy commends the ethical ideal of the self-denying men whose unselfish actions are dictated by what they regard as a higher cause than their own interests, and his own sympathies are with the reticent and true, it is not clear with what pragmatic regret he regards their qualities. Perhaps there is even an implicit criticism that they do not combine with their goodness a normal share of male initiative. Certainly the author is no advocate of wilful asceticism – Jude is as much an extension of Hardy's own personality as Gabriel Oak or John Loveday – which can almost degenerate into moral masochism, as in the painful excesses of Giles Winterborne's self-denying loyalties.

John Loveday is the spiritual successor of Springrove, Stephen Smith, Oak, Julian and Diggory Venn, the latest in a series of quiet and good men who engage Hardy's admiration even as they lack a certain emotional maturity. Hardy is aware of this: the chant of the rude boys when they encounter John walking out with Anne ('Why don't he clipse her to his side, like a man?') poses a pertinent question which might be asked of a number of Hardy's passive heroes. Bob Loveday and his kind, on the other hand, the lively extroverts whose sexual proclivities tend to be overabundant than otherwise, do not engage Hardy's respect. Perhaps they may even, as a side-effect of that curious symbiosis which unites the writer and his creation, excite his envy. Hardy may have unconsciously compensated for the lack of marked aggressiveness in his ill-fated heroes and for his own reticence and late development not only by emphasising the tendency of his more full-blooded creations to become reprobates but also by seeing that they are usually overtaken by due retribution. The moral is important for Hardy. Sergeant Troy is shot dead, Damon Wildeve is drowned, Alec d'Urberville is stabbed: Bob Loveday alone among the sexually aggressive is reprieved. There is of course hope for his redemption – he has shown valour at sea and family affection at home – but he is a known philanderer who is indiscreet, unreliable, selfish and insensitive. It is ominous that Hardy allows him to win the day, and this distinguishes *The Trumpet-Major* from those novels in which his spiritual companions appear.

The unhappy resolution of the brothers' rivalry is convincing because true to life. It is the way of the world that impetuous charm and pre-eminent masculinity appear more romantically attractive than less spectacular but more solid virtue, and Hardy's ironies often derive from this circumstance. Anne's choice of the wrong man is entirely in character for an impressionable *ingénue*, but it is equally true to life in an even more fundamental sense: the heart is ruled by more delicate impulses than objective reason can supply. Even Anne comes to realise the incontrovertible quality of genuine love: 'Gratitude is not love, though I wanted to make it so for the time.' But just as Ethelberta had shown the emotional sterility of allowing reason to dominate over passion, Anne's behaviour shows the result of the opposite excess, the exclusion of reason from her eventual emotional decision.

As the heroine, occupying a central role, Anne Garland presents a problem. The *ingénue* is a difficult character-type to animate, and in her primness of manner and her perpetual vacillation Anne becomes tiresome and exasperating. She lacks the intelligence of Cytherea, Fancy and Elfride, and she is less appealing than Picotee or Thomasin; of all Hardy's heroines who had so far appeared, Anne is the most colourless. But she is a well-realised dull character, and her insipidity is not without point. There are indeed girls like Anne, though one hopes not to be involved with them. Her personality does not develop through experience, and the results of her fluctuating decisions leave no perceptible mark on her. Her detachment extends to the great events of the time, so that she is as incapable of understanding their significance as she is of attaining self-knowledge about her own feelings. The only glimmer of percipience is implied in her parting remarks to John though, ironically, even this simple discovery is long overdue. Anne combines the less pleasing qualities of Emma Woodhouse and Harriet Smith, her fictional contemporaries in 'the days of high-waisted and muslin-gowned women', and Hardy is critical of her genteel pride and inanimate dullness. Even Mrs Garland is 'more girlish and animated than her daughter', and she duly chides Anne for being so 'prim and stiff about everything'.

Anne thus takes her place in the ironic scheme of the story. Her primness does a great deal of harm, albeit unintended, to herself and her friends, and there is nothing to commend in her self-conscious social attitudes,[23] while her emotional immaturity leads her to treat John cruelly (she admits that she can take pleasure in inflicting pain). Anne is deliberately drawn to alienate the reader's affection. The narrator reports her shallow preference for 'a dashing presentment, a naval rank, and telling scars', but he does not condone it: 'Youth is foolish; and does a woman often let her reasoning in favour of the worthier stand in the way of her perverse desire for the less worthy at such times as these?' Her choice may be natural but it is folly for all that, and her more serious flaw is the extent of her perversity, which amounts to callousness. That the apparently harmless heroine contains such latently disruptive qualities adds a new dimension of irony, though an early clue is given in the first chapter: 'beneath all that was charming and simple in this young woman there lurked a real firmness, unperceived at first, as the speck of colour lurks unperceived in the heart of the palest parsley flower.' By the end of the novel there is an ineluctable feeling that Bob and Anne deserve each other. The revelation that they will acquire Oxwell Hall bears implications no more cheerful: the apparently meek shall inherit the earth, whether they deserve it or not.

The remaining characters are all functional and, apart from Captain Hardy, psychologically unrealised. A familiar chorus of Wessex rustics contains some typical Hardyan oddities and grotesques, such as Corporal Tullidge with his gruesomely morticed skull and bone-crunching arm. The sub-plot is entirely constructed and characterised according to stage conventions and takes the form of a dramatic metaphor: Festus is a classic cowardly braggadocio, reminiscent of Captain Bobadill in *Every Man in his Humour*, Uncle Benjy is a comical Jonsonian miser, and Matilda Johnson is an actress whose role-playing is not confined to the stage.[24] The old man is purely a figure of fun. Like Overcombe Mill, Oxwell Hall images its owner. In its state of declension and decay it reflects Uncle Benjy himself, and in its state of siege by Festus it is representative too of England under the threat of Napoleon. The old man is as afraid of his nephew as he is of the Emperor, his worst fear being that his title-deeds and documents 'should be stole away by Boney or Festus'. In the comical tergiversations involving his money and property the cunning old squire is no mean player, enacting the dramatic metaphor in his own life as effectively as Festus and Matilda. The hollowness of his pretences is suggested after his death in one of the novel's few arresting images: 'The unconscious carcass was little more than a light empty husk, dry and fleshless as that of a dead heron found on a moor in January.' Yet this description is not without compassion.

Festus, a *miles gloriosus* figure of traditional comedy, has a stagey presence which emphasises his comic function. A 'bouncing Rufus' of florid complexion and angry disposition, Festus is a buffoonish braggart and coward, and it is in his encounters with his uncle and the teasing factotum Anthony Cripplestraw that most of the novel's humour resides. From his initial dramatic entry at the miller's party, where he arrives in martial splendour only to be told that 'you'd look more natural with a spud in your hand, sir', he is the eternal butt or foil, as doomed to fall on his face in the stream as he is to lose his inheritance. As the local parody of the Emperor Napoleon he cuts a nicely derisory figure. There is no real sense of danger in his pursuit of Anne, and the challenge to goodness which he represents is merely symbolic, despite his evil machinations. In Matilda he meets his match, since they are two of a kind in their persistent role-playing. Matilda is a professional dissembler who adopts the currency of her calling to allure the naïve Festus: 'I hold the world but as the world, Derrimanio – a stage where every man must play a part, and mine a sad one!'

These characters are essentially one-dimensional exercises in the comic mode, thrown into relief by the quietly credible Garlands and Lovedays, but the most 'true' character of all is, oddly enough, also a minor one; this is the captain of the *Victory*, and in the truth of his presentation lies a clue about the novel. Hardy's pride and pleasure in introducing his eminent collateral ancestor invests Captain Hardy with a sturdy and believable presence.[25] It is difficult, and perhaps as dangerous as Leslie Stephen hinted, to portray convincingly an historical personage in a fiction which is not in any conventional sense an historical novel: King George's appearance in Chapter 34, for example, is rather unfortunate. But the success of the short scene in which Captain Hardy takes part surely derives from Hardy's emotional engagement with the character, generating a warm response from the reader. The captain apart, however, there is no pervasive sense of Hardy's emotional engagement with the story, and the curious absence of this quality constitutes one of the novel's weaknesses. *The Trumpet-Major* is not written detachedly, but it does have a less individually distinctive flavour than usual, though it is hard precisely to define the reason for this impression. Hardy at his best is a conspicuously personal writer and his narratives bind reader and author into an unusually close relationship.

The manner in which Hardy's presence is evinced in his fiction is more than a matter of rhetorical idiosyncrasies or recurrent themes, prominent though these are in its articulation, but rather the transmission of a sense of Hardy the man. This is not to admit the validity of Eliot's misleading charge that Hardy wrote almost entirely 'for the sake of self-expression'. But certainly Hardy would have disapproved of the impossible notions of authorial detachment proclaimed by Flaubert and James, whose presence is so discernible in their own work despite their austere theories of the novel as an art form. Since all art is an extension of the artist's personality, no artist can clinically excerpt himself from his work; 'The novelist does not come to his desk devoid of experience and memory,' as Evelyn Waugh has said, 'His raw material is compounded of all he has seen and done.'[26] The personal presence of Hardy, the colour of his feelings and the rhetoric of his voice, enriches his fiction and bestows a fundamental unity upon all his novels.

A logical concomitant of the author's perceptible self-projection into his work is the reader's ability to draw the author's features from his work, not in a narrowly biographical sense (as Hardy properly protested) but in terms of personal vision. But, unlike most of the novels, no clear picture of the author or his vision is projected by *The Trumpet-Major*. Hardy's presence seems to brood over the narrative at a remove, and there is only an indistinct and modified sense of the emotional, social and philosophical preoccupations which usually find such idiosyncratic expression in his fiction. To read *The Trumpet-Major* in isolation would be to misrepresent and underestimate Hardy's unique genius.

This begs the question of the novel's exact status. The indeterminate status usually accorded it is probably just; it is difficult to place. It is easy to see why critics have fallen back on nebulous congratulatory epithets like 'charming', for it is a novel which pleases but does not satisfy. Among the lesser novels it makes less compelling reading than *The Hand of Ethelberta* and *A Pair of Blue Eyes*, or even *Desperate Remedies*, although within the canon of Hardy's work it has achieved a moderate critical acceptance which has eluded these others. *The Trumpet-Major* is devoid of the experimental lapses which mar the reputations of these earlier novels, and as a historical fiction it is imaginative and sympathetic, but its ease of movement does not compensate for its lack of sustained distinction. It does not invariably hold the reader's interest and so fails to satisfy a criterion important to Hardy. It lacks the emotional crises and variety of incident of its immediate predecessor, *The Return of the Native*; it is weakened by the episodic narrative; the contrary and unremitting vacillation of the heroine lends an air of tedium to the proceedings; and its characters are perhaps insufficiently engaging to compensate for the lack of a strong story.

The *Trumpet-Major* represents the first change of direction in Hardy's fiction which does not show any substantial progression. It is as if Hardy were warily marking time, restrained by the reception of *The Return of the Native* and the dogmatic editorial hand of Dr Macleod. But Macleod's possible influence must have come late, since Hardy had already written enough to submit to publishers in manuscript before he heard from the editor of *Good Words*, so it is likely that more fundamental speculations about his potential readership may have affected Hardy's initial conception of the novel. The tone of his letter to Blackwood on 9 June 1879, promising a bland novel 'without views or opinions', gives a clue. Hardy never allowed himself easy assumptions about his readership, and he was always unsure of his audience, so each novel involved a process of discovery, especially when he decided to strike out towards something new. He was too shrewd to ignore the preponderant demands in fiction or the external pressures upon him from those who would publish his work. After deriving fulfilment from writing *The Return of the Native*, as a professional writer keeping 'base life afoot' he could afford to turn his hand to something unchallenging, a popular entertainment which would appeal to late-Victorian susceptibilities. And indeed he was rewarded with a unanimous chorus of critical praise.

Yet between the lines of *The Trumpet-Major* the reader may perceive another novel, similar in incident but different and darker in tone and emphasis, closer to the inward investigation of individual lives towards which Hardy's imagination is increasingly primed, and it is this glimpse of unrealised potential that elevates *The Trumpet-Major* above the more modestly esteemed novels while preventing it from becoming a major one. A fiction may be successfully written on more than one level, but it is likely to be less successful if the meaning at one level works against the meaning at another. There is an unresolved tension (as there is for different reasons in *Desperate Remedies* and *The Hand of Ethelberta*) between the novel that his wider public wanted and the one that Hardy might have been happier to write. Hardy's imagination does not by now allow him, despite his protestations to Blackwood, to write a novel which is 'above all things a cheerful story'. It is not that Hardy fails in writing a conventionally pleasing pastoral but rather that his imagination is better suited to writing more conspicuously serious novels.

The novel is not just, as many Victorians thought, a story of bucolic celebration tempered with some military glamour. Athough it shares with Hardy's earlier pastoral, *Under the Greenwood Tree*, simplicity of form, dependence on external rather than psychic movement, and a superficially untroubled rustic vision not to be found again in the novels, it is in the ironic undercurrent that its serious implications are found. Never content to abandon his talents to a shepherd's song, Hardy satisfies his own veracity of vision by undermining the idyll from within. The real picture which emerges is moving and sad. *The Trumpet-Major* is an ironic tale of human foolishness and individual responsibility. If there is nothing of the psychic inwardness of the later novels, where individual problems are more clearly seen to proceed from within, in a process made prominent, at least the source of individual problems is identified as clearly as in the preceding and succeeding novels. It is not Crass Casualty or a malign Providence that wreaks havoc and leads to pain and suffering, but man's misuse, through disinclination or disability, of his own free will.

6 'A man hit by vicissitudes': *A Laodicean* (1881)

1

'There is mercy in trouble coming in battalions,' wrote Hardy in autumn 1880, 'They neutralize each other. Tell a man that he must suffer the amputation of a limb, and it is a horror to him; but tell him this the minute after he has been reduced to beggary, and his only son has died: it hurts him but feebly.' (*L*, 147) Hardy was seeking comfort in his present accumulation of troubles: the apprehensions in his note of November 1878 (quoted at the beginning of Chapter 5) had by now been realised in a situation which he could not have foreseen. The adversity under which Hardy was now forced to work had taken the unexpected form of a severe and painful illness, from which there was a possibility that he might not recover. Its onset had been sudden. After a week's visit to Cambridge Hardy and Emma returned to London on 23 October 1880, the day on which *The Trumpet-Major* appeared in three volumes, and already Hardy felt unwell. A serious internal haemorrhage was diagnosed, and he was offered the choice of a dangerous operation or a prolonged period of prostration 'on an inclined plane with the lower part of his body higher than his head' (*L*, 145). Hardy chose the latter, remaining in bed from October until the following April.

This ordeal was complicated by his obligation to supply a new serial story to launch the English edition of *Harper's Magazine*, the first issue of which was due to appear within six weeks of the onset of the haemorrhage. In his determination to complete the story under such duress Hardy showed considerable fortitude, and although *A Laodicean* clearly bears marks of weakness consequent upon his illness, it represents in the circumstances a very respectable achievement. Even though critical judgement must stand free of any special pleading, the novel is not the complete failure it is usually taken to be. It is a pity that the promising start is not maintained, but it is a measure of Hardy's stature that even at his weakest he is more than a good hand at a serial.

Hardy felt impelled to continue and complete the story, 'at whatever stress to himself', on both ethical and personal grounds: he wanted 'not to ruin the new venture of the publishers' and to safeguard 'the interests of his wife, for whom as yet he had made but a poor provision in the event of his own decease' (*L*, 145). He was, therefore, more than ever subject to the constricting requirements of Grub Street. He had entered into correspondence with Harper and Brothers, about supplying them with a new serial, by 16 April 1880 (Purdy, p.39), by which time he had presumably just completed *The Trumpet-Major*. It is not clear when the idea of *A Laodicean* was conceived, though an early (if oblique) clue may be contained in the fact that he met Matthew Arnold, 'probably for the first time', during February (*L*, 134). Hardy incorporated some of Arnold's ideas in *A Laodicean*: whether this meeting suggested their applicability to the theme of the projected story, or whether (conversely) ideas deriving from Hardy's consequent further reading of Arnold's essays influenced his conception of the story, is conjectural.[1] But the conjunction of the meeting and the explicit incorporation of some Arnoldian themes in *A Laodicean* may be suggestively coincidental in estimating when Hardy was shaping the novel in his mind.

The negotiations with Harpers were finished by 24 May, when they sent a formal acceptance of the story.[2] Hardy was to be paid £100 an instalment, his highest fee yet, itself a powerful incentive to continue composition when he fell ill. On 11 June Hardy wrote to Harpers about the illustrations by Du Maurier,[3] and those for the first two instalments had been completed by 28 July (Purdy, p.39). But the most valuable evidence of Hardy's progress is found in the surviving proof-sheets of the *Harper's Magazine* serial publication: Purdy's examination of these sheets reveals that the first thirteen chapters were in print when Hardy fell ill in October.[4] By July Hardy must have been satisfied enough with his progress to take a holiday with Emma, and they set out on a European tour on 27 July, returning to England a month later.

When the haemorrhage began the project was too far ad-

vanced for any retreat on Hardy's part to be practicable even if
he had wished it, so, with Emma as his amanuensis, the story
had to be 'strenuously continued by dictation to a predetermined
cheerful ending' (Preface). Hardy was not allowed out of bed
until April, and he completed the draft in pencil on 1 May 1881.
During that month he went outside again for the first time and
celebrated his recovery by repeating to himself, on Wandsworth
Common, some lines from Gray's 'Ode on the Pleasure arising
from Vicissitude':

> See the wretch that long has tost
>   On the thorny bed of pain,
> At length repair his vigour lost,
>   And breathe and walk again.

Meanwhile the serial composed in such unhappy conditions
continued to appear in *Harper's Magazine* until December, and
Hardy received his final payment on 26 November 1881.[5] *A
Laodicean* was published in book form in New York (by Harper
and Brothers) and London (by Sampson Low) in November and
December respectively. Within two months the London edition
had been remaindered to Mudie.

The unusual circumstances of composition obviously account
for many of the novel's irregularities. It has frequently and fairly
been remarked that Hardy lost control of the story in Books Four
and Five, which describe at excessive length the European tour.
Hardy was clearly falling back upon his own tour with Emma
during July and August (see *L*, 138–9), but the transference of
geographical detail is not very successful: the sequence becomes
a travelogue, flat and unenlivened, and the details of the plot
could have taken place anywhere. There is no useful correspondence between the characters and their surroundings. A more
imaginative use was made of the author's recollections of a
garden-party at Mrs Macmillan's, during which a thunderstorm
occurred, in July 1879 (*L*, 128; cf. *A Laodicean*, Book 2, Chapter
1), and of controversies in his youth over Paedobaptism (*L*, 29–
30; cf. *A Laodicean*, Book 1, Chapter 7). The argumentative sons
of the Baptist minister in Dorchester, Mr Perkins, were friends of
Hardy when he was twenty, and from them he learned the
necessity for 'plain living and high-thinking'. He imported some
of the vigour of the family's arguments over Paedobaptism into

the story, and Mr Woodwell is 'a recognisable drawing' of the minister himself.

These latter recollections, however, were presumably exploited by Hardy before he fell ill, and it is in Book Two onwards that his recourse to autobiographical padding can be seen. Some of the recollections may even have been prompted by Emma as she took Hardy's dictation. In later years she would often make exaggerated claims that she had had a hand in the composition and editing of several of her husband's best novels, and it is possible that these delusions may have originated in her help with *A Laodicean*. The tale may have appealed to her, since the basic situation of the poor man and the lady, and of the young architect carrying out renovation work in the near presence of his loved one, was (as in *A Pair of Blue Eyes*) that of Emma and Hardy at St Juliot; and she would be able to recall details of their recent tour and make other useful suggestions. But she may also have been influential, as an amanuensis, in another way. Fiction writing is essentially a private activity, and the introduction of an audience, however small, subtly modifies the author's freedom, especially if the audience is not minutely sympathetic to all the author's most personal impulses and convictions. Hardy must have been affected by Emma's presence, which was likely to inhibit rather than stimulate. Writing by dictation was a new and unfamiliar experience for Hardy, and Emma's intimate involvement, for the first time, at this stage of the creative process may have imposed greater discretion upon him than usual. It is hard to estimate how much of the novel's pallor may derive from this. But certainly the sheer physical effort of continuing the story in this way effected a perceptible change of mood: sensational devices and complications of plot take the place of the subtleties of social comedy, and the narrative becomes externalised as action predominates over ideas.

The story sags most notably as the European tour proceeds but at the end, like its author, recovers well. Yet the implications of Hardy's illness go beyond the journeywork aspect of spinning out a tale, and as a result *A Laodicean* is a personal work in a more fundamental sense. Hardy once told William Lyon Phelps that '*A Laodicean* contained more of the facts of his own life than anything else he had ever written. That was published in 1881; during its completion he was dangerously ill and did not believe he could recover. He thought it was his last illness ... '[6] Hardy's remark is telling and should not be too narrowly interpreted. The autobiographical features of the narrative are self-evident, but the novel as a whole contains questionings that appear to be Hardy's own.

It reflects the subjectivity of a prolonged and incapacitating illness, when Hardy's interest was inevitably turned inward upon himself. This spiritual introspection makes *A Laodicean* much more revealing than *The Trumpet-Major* had been. In a condition of constriction, like Shakespeare's Richard II imprisoned in Pomfret Castle, the imaginative may read their own situation as an analogy of the wider human predicament and attempt to distinguish universal principles through the process of their own attainment of self-knowledge. This impulse inspired a note made by Hardy as he lay in bed in late November 1880 (*L*, 146):

> Discover for how many years, and on how many occasions, the organism, Society, has been standing, lying, etc., in varied positions, as if it were a tree or a man hit by vicissitudes.
> There would be found these periods:
> 1. Upright, normal or healthy periods.
> 2. Oblique or cramped periods.
> 3. Prostrate periods (intellect counterpoised by ignorance or narrowness, producing stagnation).
> 4. Drooping periods.
> 5. Inverted periods.

Hardy's use of his own plight as a curious metaphor for social analysis lends a piquancy to his claim that *A Laodicean* 'contains more of the facts of his own life' than any other novel. It suggests that we might expect to learn something more unguardedly personal than usual about Hardy's diagnosis of the condition of society, and about his own uncertainties.

2

A suggestive pattern emerges in the first half of Hardy's career as a novelist, since after each pastoral novel he turned his attention to contemporary themes. Following the rural idyll of *Under the Greenwood Tree* he found a more ironic method in the contemporaneous *A Pair of Blue Eyes*; after *Far from the Madding Crowd* he wrote a present-day social satire in *The Hand of Ethelberta*; and after the romantically distanced setting and story of *The Trumpet-Major* he set out to analyse the ethics of modernism in *A Laodicean*. Each time there is a sense of a turning to more intimate preoccupations, and it may be no coincidence that each of the contemporary novels contains directly autobiographical features. Hardy cannot have found *The Trumpet-Major* deeply satisfying, and certainly he never again attempted a novel in the same historical mode. Although *A Laodicean* was forced to become Hardy's most unusual novel it exhibits throughout a personal commitment and involvement lacking in its predecessor. The author's voice is more discernible, and *A Laodicean* is a fascinating exposition of his social beliefs and his concern about the aesthetic and cultural implications of social revolution and technical progress.

The sub-title strikes a note of deliberate contemporaneity: *A Laodicean* is 'A Story of To-Day'. That his imagination was most readily stimulated by retrospection does not mean that Hardy was incapable of writing about his own time, though successive generations of readers have cast the novels in which he does so – *Desperate Remedies, A Pair of Blue Eyes, The Hand of Ethelberta, A Laodicean* and *Two on a Tower* – as lesser works. Chronological settings are determined by theme, and some of his novels require a distancing of the action by anything up to 80 years before the date of their publication. Hardy is always alive to the potential of different historical periods. The dramatic structure of *The Mayor of Casterbridge* requires the story to pre-date the railway age, while the presence of buzzing telegraph wires and machines would make nonsense of the internal harmonies of *The Return of the Native*. But certain modern conveniences are required to support the way of life of the sophisticates in *The Woodlanders*, and the cultural conditions of its time are essential to *Jude the Obscure* (in which the time span extends from the mid-fifties to the mid-seventies of the nineteenth century). The carefully distinguished time settings of all Hardy's fictions cover almost the entire century and, while it is unnecessary to identify the presumed time period of each novel as precisely as Carl Weber has done, each novel is set in a precise and subtly exploited context.

Hardy's interests in the possibilities of period are not just antiquarian or nostalgic, so he dispenses with historical distancing when it is irrelevant to his purpose (as in *Desperate Remedies*, a sensation novel which needs no historical identification) or when contemporaneity must inform the theme (as in *The Hand of Ethelberta*). But the present is often less appealing than the past, and his readers preferred something recognisably romantic to home-truths about the present. There is less poetry in the railway cuttings near Stancy Castle than in the Roman amphitheatre near Casterbridge, but each of the novels in which they appear presents a different and appropriately constructed fictional world. The description of a telegraph message in *A Laodicean* has been dismissed by more than one critic as absurd:

> The cheering message from Paula to Somerset sped through the loophole of Stancy Castle tower, over the trees, along the railway, under bridges, across four counties – and finally landed itself on a table in Somerset's chambers in the midst of a cloud of fog.

But there *is* something absurd about even the most sophisticated technological achievements, and here Hardy captures the essence of a new-fangled phenomenon with humour and common sense. The passage is not to be read with great solemnity. The reader should be alive to the wryness of his presentation of a piece of the paraphernalia of modernism.

Hardy's 'stories of today' (as we may call them) have always had a cool reception. Contemporary readers were unwilling to accept him as a social critic; they preferred diversion to social investigation and found his radical notions disturbing. Now these novels are overlooked for different reasons. Their themes are less dramatically expansive: Hardy's is a generously romantic imagination, and when he writes of society of his own time he is constrained to operate on a narrower scale. The stories of character and environment make more compelling reading, partly because they suit the form of fiction. But the 'stories of today' do illustrate the formation of those social and cultural ideals which impel the moral protest that attains its fullest expression in *Tess* and *Jude*. Among those novels *A Laodicean* is unique. Written under the stress of physical incapacity and spiritual introspection, it dramatises some of Hardy's most personal preoccupations: class, heredity, modern practicality and the ambiguous qualities of medievalism. Beneath melodramatic trappings which at times thwart the novel's serious purpose there is an original and often subtle insight into the problems of conflicting ideologies. It is not so much the psychic life of individuals that is the novel's concern but (through the effects of changing external circumstances upon them) the psychic life of the community as a whole.

Hardy again addresses some of the problems explored in a more fiercely satiric vein in *The Hand of Ethelberta* but does so now in the context of a slightly later stage of social evolution. The feudalism and medievalism represented by Lord Mountclere have fallen into further decay, while the rising manufacturing classes have thrown up the generation of Paula's father. In *A Laodicean* Hardy examines the further implications of 'the incongruities that were daily shaping themselves in the world under the great modern fluctuations of classes and creeds', and this state of ideological flux constitutes the novel's theme.[7] The new ideologies are recognised as essential but easier to posit than to implement in personal terms: the new order is uneasily assimilated since 'human nature at bottom is romantic rather than ascetic.' This is a maturer insight into the problems of adjustment to economic, social and aesthetic progress, reflective of Hardy's own experience and a usefully realistic coda to the unqualified radicalism proposed in the earlier novel. At the centre of the dilemma provoked by the onset of modernism, Paula is the touchstone of sensibility and uncertainty.

As Hardy shrewdly distinguishes the ambiguities of the transitional period some of the contraries in his own attitudes are thrown into relief. He may be emotionally identified with each of the main characters in turn, since each dramatises a different aspect of his own process of self-discovery and resolution of the conflicting demands of the medieval and the modern. So the novel may be read as an allegory of an important stage in Hardy's intellectual development. Like Paula, Hardy is (in Somerset's words) a member of 'that other nobility – the nobility of talent and enterprise', an apostle of 'modernism, eclecticism, new aristocracies'; and he too is something of a Laodicean in his religious and social outlook. He shares Paula's humanist scepticism and her distrust of the harsh puritanism of the late Mr Power's Baptist faith.[8] And while Hardy is sensible of the defects and inadequacies of medievalism, he too is romantically attracted to some of its qualities. When Paula admits that she has 'a *prédilection d'artiste* for ancestors of the other sort' she is articulating an instinctive feature of the author's outlook. As

Lawrence has remarked, Hardy shares this *prédilection d'artiste* for
the aristocrat, and it is one of the interesting ambiguities in his
make-up that he accompanies this regard with moral antagon-
ism. The creation of Paula as a spiritual and intellectual
doppelgänger brings her to life, and in his 1912 Preface Hardy
could justly look back on her with real affection. He writes of her
as 'individualised with some clearness, and really lovable,
though she is of that reserved disposition which is the most
difficult of all dispositions to depict'. Her suitor, George
Somerset, is another architect *alter ego* of Hardy, based freely on
the author's own characteristics and precepts and as a result the
most convincing of the passive heroes in the lesser novels.

Both Somerset and Paula are representatives of modernism –
his beauty is 'more of the future human type than of the past' –
and both come from meritocratic backgrounds. Their qualities
are complementary, Somerset having enough common sense to
rescue Paula's mind from the warp of medievalism. But he is not
unimaginative, and Hardy shares his delight in the friendship of
the two girls from 'antipodean families', Paula and Charlotte de
Stancy:

> It was an engaging instance of that human progress on which
> he had expended many charming dreams in the years when
> poetry, theology, and the reorganization of society had seemed
> matters of more importance to him than a profession which
> should help him to a big house and income, a fair Deiopeia,
> and a lovely progeny.

This fusion of idealism and practicality in Somerset mirrors
some of Hardy's own hopes and ambitions. But the relationship
of Paula and Somerset also shows that in one respect the new
aristocracy is as bad as the old: the dilemma of the poor man and
the lady still remains, and Somerset is harshly schooled in the
difficulties arising 'when the woman is rich and the man is poor'.

The personal embodiments of medievalism are the de Stancys,
an 'unfortunate line' in decline. There is something of Hardy in
Captain de Stancy too, since he also thought of himself as
coming at the end of a decayed family line; and, like de Stancy,
he might also be said to have 'adopted Radical notions to
obliterate disappointed hereditary instincts'. But the spirit of
medievalism is now dead and Hardy applauds the pragmatism

of old Sir William: 'Nothing can retain the spirit, and why should we preserve the spirit of the form?'[9] By the end the family is in final and hopeless disarray. Sir William is dead; de Stancy is isolated, humiliated and sick at heart; and the inoffensive Charlotte retreats into an Anglican order, as if in expiation of the sins of her forbears. The once-powerful family is impotent and doomed to extinction. Their home is a 'fossil of feudalism'; Sir William's doctrine, 'accommodate yourself to the times', is sensible but the advice comes too late, since there is no place for feudalism or its remnants in the modern world. Captain de Stancy's attempt to win Paula's hand is the family's last desperate attempt at survival, and even here lingers a suggestion of the brute force upon which the feudal spirit had depended: as Paula observes the de Stancy portraits she experiences a 'feeling that the de Stancys had stretched out a tentacle from their genealogical tree to seize her by the hand and draw her into their mass'. But she does not surrender, since the modern spirit is independent. Paula and de Stancy are symbolically incompatible, and the need for the new is manifest in the corruption of the old. The past is not so much overtaken by the present as defeated by itself; medievalism contains the seeds of its own destruction, and its final extinction is imaged in the ironic climax as Stancy Castle itself, the dominant symbol of feudalism, is destroyed by fire by its last degenerate scion, William Dare.

This dramatic conclusion, as well as resolving the melodramatic plot with a flourish, contains a moral judgement in the architectural imagery which frames the story. The central contrast is also conceived in terms of architectural symbolism. Hardy endorses Ruskin's insistence that art is a direct function of the moral temper of the age and that the cultural and moral condition of society is most truly reflected in its architecture. Somerset is an independent spirit in 'these neo-Pagan days' of the 1870s, 'when a lull has come over the study of English Gothic architecture'. When he sees the newly built Baptist chapel he exclaims with reason: 'Shade of Pugin, what a monstrosity!' The building exactly represents the tenets of the Baptist faith. Built of red brick, blue slate and plate glass, clean and geometrically oppressive, it is a monument to 'the new utilitarianism. . . . The chapel had neither beauty, quaintness, nor congeniality to recommend it.' The minister's home is equally eloquent of its tenant and his puritanical faith: 'a house which typified the drearier tenets of its occupier with great exactness', lacking 'any natural union' with the earth from which it is separated by a 'stiff straight line', and a house wherein 'all was clean and clear and dry'. The architectural metaphor extends to the home of Sir William, accommodating himself to the times in a specimen of 'mushroom modernism' and 'genuine roadside respectability'. Hardy uses architecture as an instrument of social criticism, and these edificial examples of the modern spirit, the immediate results of the fluctuations of classes and creeds, are not encouraging.[10]

The new architecture represents no advance on the old. While medievalism does not meet the needs of the present, neither puritanism nor utilitarianism furnishes a credible alternative, and Hardy's enthusiasm for the new is tempered by the knowledge that change *per se* is no more likely to attain an ideal perfection than reaction. During his dictation of *A Laodicean* Hardy made this note on 17 February 1881:

> Conservatism is not estimable in itself, nor is Change, or Radicalism. To conserve the existing good, to supplant the existing bad by good, is to act on a true political principle, which is neither Conservative nor Radical. (*L*, 148)

This principle contains the honest ambivalence of Hardy's (and Paula's) attitude to medievalism, which finds its best expression in the dominating symbol of Stancy Castle. This medieval building signifies the meeting point of past and present. Hardy intensifies this image of temporal conjunction by means of an ingenious idea, exposing the ambiguities of both the ancient and the modern in the coexistence of Stancy Castle and the incongruous telegraph machine:

> There was a certain unexpectedness in the fact that the hoary memorial of a stolid antagonism to the interchange of ideas, the monument of hard distinctions in blood and race, of deadly mistrust of one's neighbour in spite of the Church's teaching, and of a sublime unconsciousness of any other force than a brute one, should be the goal of a machine which beyond everything may be said to symbolize cosmopolitan views and the intellectual and moral kinship of all mankind. In that light the little buzzing wire had a far finer significance

to the student Somerset than the vast walls which neigh-
boured it. But the modern fever and fret which consumes
people before they grow old was also signified by the wire; and
this aspect of to-day did not contrast well with the fairer side
of feudalism – leisure, light-hearted generosity, intense friend-
ships, hawks, hounds, revels, healthy complexions, freedom
from care, and such a living power in architectural art as the
world may never see again.

It is a picture of contraries, each containing good and evil
attributes. The problem for Hardy and for Paula is not in
identifying the 'true political principle' but in implementing it,
in finding how to conserve the good and supplant the bad; the
answer is elusive and is never found in the novel.

It is made clear, though, that the solution does not lie in
compromise, in putting new wine into old bottles. The problem
is explored in terms of the architectural motif and the restoration
of Stancy Castle. Since architecture is concomitant with its
cultural context, the debate about restoration bears wider social
implications. The ethics of Gothic restoration were exercising
many Victorians with whose ideas Hardy is entirely sympathetic. In 1877 William Morris had founded 'Anti-Scrape', the
Society for the Protection of Ancient Buildings, and he had
written to the *Athenaeum* on 10 March of 'those acts of barbarism
which the modern architect, parson, and squire call "restoration"' and of 'the ruin that has been wrought by their hands'.[11]
Morris shared Ruskin's belief that the basis of medieval
architecture lay in the lives of the craftsmen of the Middle Ages:
since their way of life had long departed, attempts at restoration
were merely forgeries. And for Ruskin the division of labour
meant the division of the man. In an age of specialisation and
toilsome work no one could recreate the spirit and freedom of the
medieval master-craftsman.[12]

The worst barbarism of all was the introduction of eclectic
styles into the process of restoration, and it is this which Paula
proposes in her scheme for the anachronistic introduction of a
Greek court. But just as Paula does not yield to the compromise
offered by medievalism, in the form of marriage with Captain de
Stancy, neither will Stancy Castle submit to modern compromise in the form of her neo-Greek modifications. Rather than
ingloriously submit to the whims of the new order the medieval

spirit proudly turns its last destructive impulse upon itself.[13] When Dare sets the castle alight his ancestors' approval is imaged in their portraits:

> ... the framed gentleman in the lace collar seemed to open his eyes more widely; he with the flowing locks and turn-up mustachios to part his lips; he in the armour, who was so much like Captain de Stancy, to shake the plates of his mail with suppressed laughter; the lady with the three-stringed pearl necklace, and vast expanse of neck, to nod with satisfaction and triumphantly signify to her adjoining husband that this was a meet and glorious end.

This self-willed abdication of medievalism resolves the course of the future and clears the way for the final stage of the architectural metaphor. Paula and Somerset are liberated from the dead hand of the past, and in deciding not to rebuild the castle but to erect 'a mansion of independent construction' nearby they assert their own determination to 'keep straight on' in pursuit of eclecticism and a new society.

The foundation for that society is established in their own meritocratic backgrounds. Instead of aristocratic pedigrees theirs is the genealogy of constructive advance. Paula descends from the apostles of engineering science, 'Archimedes, Newcomen, Watt, Telford, Stephenson', while Somerset's intellectual line of descent is much later traced through 'Pheidias, Ictius and Callicrates, Chersiphron, Vitruvius, Wilars of Cambray, William of Wykeham, and the rest of that long and illustrious roll'. Paula, unable to accept the Hebraistic precepts of the Baptist faith, conceives the new society in terms of Hellenism: she declares her intention of becoming 'a perfect representative of "the modern spirit" ... representing neither the senses and understanding, nor the heart and imagination; but what a finished writer calls "the imaginative reason"'. The 'finished writer' is Arnold, and the reference is to a passage in his essay on 'Pagan and Medieval Religious Sentiment' celebrating 'an epoch in Greek life, – in pagan life, – of the highest possible beauty and value'.[14]

The concept of 'the imaginative reason' appealed to Hardy. In a notebook entry made in January 1881, four months before he completed *A Laodicean*, Hardy adapted Arnold's formulation in a note on style:

> Style – consider the Wordsworthian dictum (the more perfect-
> ly the natural object is reproduced, the more truly poetic the
> picture). This reproduction is achieved by seeing into the *heart
> of a thing* (as rain, wind, for instance), and is realism, in fact,
> though through being pursued by means of the imagination it
> is confounded with invention, which is pursued by the same
> means. It is, in short, reached by what M. Arnold calls 'the
> imaginative reason.'

This implies that he who possesses imaginative reason has the
most realistic insight. But it is not clear that Hardy is endorsing
'the modern spirit' as a realistic panacea. Paula's allegiance to
modernism is sounded in a bold clarion call: 'I'll keep straight
on; and we'll build a new house beside the ruin, and show the
modern spirit for evermore.' But this is followed by a drastic
qualification, suggesting that the ghosts of medievalism will not
be laid so easily: 'I wish my castle wasn't burnt,' she tells
Somerset, 'and I wish you were a de Stancy!' The tone is comic,
and the story ends on a note of suggestive irresolution. In this
typical reversal Hardy is finally refusing to define his position,
and in doing so he challenges the reader. For although Paula has
declared her allegiances, her eventual decision not to trim has
not been quite freely conceived. It is only after the burning of the
castle, and the decision 'to make an opportunity of misfortune',
that Paula articulates her manifesto for the future, and Hardy
says elsewhere that social progress owes at least as much to
circumstance as to personal choice. In October 1884 he noted:

> Query: Is not the present quasi-scientific system of writing
> history mere charlatanism? Events and tendencies are traced
> as if they were rivers of voluntary activity, and courses
> reasoned out from the circumstances in which natures,
> religions, or what-not, have found themselves. But are they
> not in the main the outcome of *passivity* – acted upon by
> unconscious propensity? (*L*, 168)

So Paula remains something of a Laodicean to the end. The
new society will be constructed according to the eclecticism
which Somerset and herself advocate, yet eclecticism by defini-

tion implies an inability to choose. But eclecticism also implies pragmatism and common sense, a recognition that dogmatic allegiances to any extreme aesthetic, social or religious creed are all equally unsatisfactory. Hardy was an eclectic, often as unwilling as Paula to commit himself on broad issues, and there are examples of deliberate equivocation throughout his work. As a sceptic, distrustful of extremes, Hardy now modifies the fierce radicalism of his own younger days.

The shedding of some illusory ideals of his youth is mirrored in Somerset, who had earlier been too young to know that 'in practice, art had at all times been as full of shifts and compromises as every other mundane thing; that ideal perfection was never achieved by Greek, Goth or Hebrew Jew, and never would be.' But by the end of the story Somerset has adopted eclectic ideals and is set to implement them. Hardy regrets but endorses the compelling need for this disillusionment.[15] His social vision here is mature and realistic and a notable advance on the simpler radicalism of *The Hand of Ethelberta*, and if anything it preaches the doctrine of common sense. A nineteenth-century society dominated by medievalism would exemplify, in terms of Hardy's metaphor, one of the 'prostrate periods (intellect counterpoised by ignorance or narrowness, producing stagnation)'; but with the decline of medievalism this stage has passed and society is (for the moment) pronounced 'upright, normal or healthy'. Yet this is not because a solution has been found but because it continues to be sought. However unattainable the ideal may be, 'man's reach', in Browning's famous phrase, 'should exceed his grasp.' What is needed is the continuing state of ideological flux, the constant striving for the new even as man's innate romanticism regrets the passing of the old. Man must strive even at the price of incurring what is called in *Jude the Obscure* 'the modern vice of unrest'. Flexibility and freedom must be sought in place of rigidity of ideas. Paula's final statement, in its refusal to submit to dogma, appears to have Hardy's approval; it is a reassuring affirmation of human nature.

Unfortunately the novel's execution does not entirely meet the demands of its theme. Its main faults are the long sequence of melodramatic intrigue, during which Hardy seems to lose sight of his original purpose, and the mixture of modes in which the story is written, and both derive from the circumstances of composition. Clearly Hardy did not originally intend a conscious reversion to the techniques of *Desperate Remedies*. The novel begins well as an ironic social comedy and promises to be Hardy's most successful exercise in this genre; it is a novel in which ideas are to be as important as the action, but the comic irony gives way to mysteries and convolutions of plot and the action overtakes the ideas. It is with the accelerated incidence of melodramatic intrigue in that portion of the story written after Hardy fell ill that the course is set for *A Laodicean* to become (like *Desperate Remedies* and *The Hand of Ethelberta*) a 'novel of ingenuity'. Hardy had to abandon the subtleties of social comedy in favour of a technique which would have a reductive effect on the novel as a whole but which was easier to execute; and for him, as Arthur MacDowall remarks, melodrama was always 'the line of least resistance'.[16]

The melodramatic ingredients include plot devices involving concealed identities, unreliable messengers and marvellous coincidences; a preternatural satanic figure and a conspiratorial bomb-maker; characters indulging in criminal duplicity, black-mail, eavesdropping, erotic *voyeurism* and arson. And the techni-cal paraphernalia of modernism (the railway, the tower clock, the telegraph) is supplemented by a grotesquely deforming photographic process, revolvers and bombs. The problem is not that Hardy invokes melodrama – an interest in the sensational is fundamental to his imagination and features in all the major novels – but that here the sensational devices are not systemati-cally incorporated. The intrigue has little relationship with what has gone before, and several of the incidents contribute nothing to plot, characters or theme. The melodrama is not altogether bad but it is overdone. To dismiss the novel, as J. I. M. Stewart does and other critics intimate, with the claim that 'it disinte-grates into melodramatic nonsense such as it would be idle to summon before the court of criticism'[17] is altogether too harsh. This verdict fails to acknowledge the extent to which, in the last book, the novel recovers the pace, tone and direction of the opening chapters, or the fact that ideas (which are never entirely suppressed by the melodrama) are usually handled subtly and well.

There are, however, other defects which weaken the central section. There is a serious structural imbalance in the whole episode of de Stancy's troublesome persistence, which exhibits much movement but little progress. The European trip is a piece of journeywork writing into which Hardy was forced by illness but it also reveals his deficiencies in writing about unfamiliar territory. The dead hand of the travelogue lays hold of the tale and rotund phrases like 'a heated phantasmagoria of tainted splendour' are not enough to bring Monte Carlo to life. But other structural devices are used persuasively and well. The exchange of letters and telegrams between Paula and Somerset in Book 4 is a triumph of epistolary narration and a considerable refinement of the technique rather clumsily employed in *Desperate Remedies*. And the 'play within a play' in Book 3, Chapter 8, in which de Stancy takes the role of Ferdinand, King of Navarre, and Paula that of the Princess of France, neatly furnishes a prelusive clue that in real life the leading players will not eventually marry. The analogy between the lives of the players and their roles is clear. The King, like de Stancy, has abjured the company of women, warring against (to borrow the phrase used elsewhere in Shakespeare's text) 'the huge army of the world's desires',[18] but his resolve is weakened by the arrival of the Princess of France. The Princess for her part is as hesitant a figure as Paula. De Stancy's real-life experience realises the implications of the play's title, *Love's Labour's Lost*.

Two episodes in the novel have attracted critical scorn, but each deserves a brief defence. The photographic ploy, in which Somerset's image is made to appear 'in the distorted features and wild attitude of a man advanced in intoxication', may be far-fetched but it is both original and ingenious, a grotesque instance of the perversion of modern technical advance. But the episode most widely mocked comes in Book 2, Chapter 7, as Paula is secretly observed doing her gymnastic exercises. The spectacle of Paula 'bending, wheeling and undulating in the air like a gold-fish in its globe', wearing a pink flannel costume, is an easy target for humour, especially as these are said to be 'the most love-kindling, passion-begetting circumstances that can be thought of'. But it is unfair to take a patronising twentieth-century view of the pink flannel outfit, which was unlikely in 1881 to diminish the sexual fascination of Paula's performance. The scene was erotic enough to upset the reviewer for the *Athenaeum* (31 December 1881), who complained that

the modern version of the story of Gyges will displease many readers. Without being in the least degree a 'fleshly' writer,

Mr Hardy has a way of insisting on the physical attractions of women which, if imitated by weaker writers, may prove offensive.

More recent hilarity presupposes that Hardy was unaware of the comic aspect, but in fact he admits that 'it would have been comical to an outsider'. Hardy is again disclosing the tragedy that underlies comedy, and it is not in the scene itself but in its pathetic undertones that the seriousness resides: 'to one who had known the history and relationship of the two speakers, [the scene] would have worn a sadder significance.' The incident illuminates the predicament of de Stancy, in whom Paula's erotic performance effects an almost Jekyll-and-Hyde transformation. The sudden release of his repressions provides a convincing motivation for his subsequent behaviour and simultaneously furnishes a challenging pre-Freudian insight into the psychology of the *voyeur*, a weakness exploited by Dare.

The twentieth-century derision provoked by this sequence measures the critical reversal from which *A Laodicean* has suffered. The novel was received with general approval, the now maligned intricacies of plot being (oddly) preferred to the characters, with only the occasional carp. In 1883 Havelock Ellis could write that the novel was

> more faultless, and certainly less mannered, than anything that [Hardy] had yet produced. ... He has written no other novel which succeeds so entirely in satisfying the reader's emotional sense. ... it marks distinctly the continuous development and versatility of his genius. (*Westminster Review*, April 1883)

But in 1886 *The Mayor of Casterbridge* appeared, to be followed by *The Woodlanders* in 1887, and by 1889 the modern view was crystallising: J. M. Barrie could remark of *A Laodicean* and Hardy's next novel, *Two on a Tower*, that 'they are both dull books: here and there nasty as well, and the besom of oblivion will soon pass over them.'[19] His prophecy was indeed accurate, but Hardy does not seem to have shared the critical predisposition to consign the novel to oblivion. In later years he never seems to have written slightingly of it, as he did of *Desperate Remedies*, and even his usual semi-depreciatory comments in the preface seem to betray a quiet pride rather than disfavour. Over the years he sent out presentation copies to various friends, including Florence Henniker, and even as late as 24 April 1922, when Hardy sent five of his own books to the library of Dorchester Grammar School, *A Laodicean* was among them.[20] Since the novel contains an intimate account of some of the author's own intellectual conflicts it is not surprising that Hardy should have retained an affection for it. A large measure of his regard is obviously centred in his feeling for Paula, but all characters in a novel may represent different aspects of an author's psyche. This is especially true of *A Laodicean* and helps to explain why every character (with the possible exception of Abner Power) has enough imaginative appeal to survive the inequalities of the novel and transcend its technical deficiencies.

Captain de Stancy brings to his symbolic role as the exemplar of the old aristocracy a credible presence. His complex personality yields to no easy definition, probably because (like Paula and Somerset) he embodies in his character some of the contraries of Hardy's own. De Stancy is a 'gambler seasoned in ill-luck, who adopts pessimistic surmises as a safe background to his most sanguine hopes'. This was Hardy's own practice, formulated over twenty years later in a notebook entry (*L*, 311):

> January 1 (1902). A Pessimist's apology. Pessimism (or rather what is called such) is, in brief, playing the sure game. You cannot lose at it; you may gain. It is the only view of life in which you can never be disappointed. Having reckoned what to do in the worst possible circumstances, when better arise, as they may, life becomes child's play.[21]

Hardy's sympathies for the 'easy, melancholy, unaspiring officer' are warm. While de Stancy's endeavours to be 'purified from the dross of his former life' are tinged with absurdity, and he is subjected to a comic transformation into an impassioned but hopeless lover, the sadness of his lot is kept in view.

In de Stancy the figurative impotence of Hardy's passive men is invested with a new subtlety since his ascetic self-repression (perhaps like Hardy's) contradicts his instincts. Far from lacking normal male aggressiveness, as some of the other passive figures appear to do, de Stancy has nobly (if unhealthily) suppressed his emotions in remorse over a youthful indiscretion: 'a chamber of his nature had been preserved intact during many ... years, like the solitary sealed-up cell occasionally retained by bees in a lobe of drained honey-comb', but 'the love-force that he had kept immured alive was still a reproducible thing.' As with Miss Aldclyffe, its sudden release induces an uncontrolled emotional reaction. De Stancy's dull roots are cruelly stirred with spring rain, and his subsequent career is not only a comical survey of a passionate but ill-fated courtship but a poignant study of retributive suffering. In de Stancy, with his preoccupation with honour and fairness as well as self-interest, there is the germ of a tragic hero. Like Henchard, with whom he shares some telling similarities, his suffering far exceeds his original offence.

De Stancy's spiritual isolation extends to the rest of his decayed family. Old Sir William preaches self-sufficiency and self-containment ('each man's happiness depends upon himself') which is at least the practical wisdom of maturity even as it implies the failure of other relationships. But the unluckiest victim of the family characteristic is the innocent and emotionally immature Charlotte, of whom Somerset's estimate is accurate: 'She was genuine, if anybody ever was; and simple as she was true.' Charlotte is the real bridge between the medieval and the modern, both in her friendship with Paula and in her timely prevention of the wedding, even against the interests of her own family. But her good deed requires self-immolation and the emotional repressiveness which she shares with her brother: in the matter of her love for Somerset we learn that Charlotte 'had schooled her emotions on that side cruelly well'. There is even something ambiguous about her relationship with Paula, to whom she is devoted with almost undue passion. When she speaks of Paula to Somerset at the beginning, 'a blush slowly rose to her cheek, as if the person spoken of had been a lover rather than a friend.' This suggestion of moral ambivalence is maintained and is another sign of the emotional inadequacy of the old family. Charlotte's deepest affection seems to be reserved for Paula, and although she loves Somerset she is afraid of the implications: '"I don't like you to put it like that – that I love him – it frightens me," murmured the girl, visibly agitated.' Eventually she practises the ultimate withdrawal and joins an Anglican order, abandoning the real world for purely cerebral fulfilment.

The emotional repression of the de Stancys reaches its climax in their last representative, William Dare. More symbolic than human, Dare is a cosmopolite with Mephistophelian attributes,[22] but eventually his origins (after several prelusive clues) are revealed as being more local. His diabolic behaviour may be assigned to genetic causes ('As for my conduct, cat will after kind, you know'), and Dare is the instrument of the worst medieval impulses of his family. He too is impotent and isolated, as much of a *voyeur* as de Stancy. His fate is ambiguous, since it is not clear whether or not he perishes in the fire which he starts. Dare is a figure of romance, and although his presence is vivid he is not as credible as some of the other 'Mephistophelian Visitants', such as Diggory Venn or Donald Farfrae. Yet the novel's oddest character is Abner Power. He too is a mysterious interloper 'from afar' who has cosmopolitan features: 'the manner of a Dutchman, the face of a smelter, and the clothes of an inhabitant of Guiana'. Abner is a grotesque, Gothic in conception and diabolic in conduct:

> His visage, which was of the colour of light porphyry, had little of its original surface left; it was a face which had been the plaything of strange fires or pestilences, that had moulded to whatever shape they chose his originally supple skin, and left it pitted, puckered, and seamed like a dried water-course.

He is totally unreal and does not begin to come alive, moving stiffly through the story until, after a comic confrontation with Dare in the vestry, he is once more despatched overseas. He is less acceptable than Dare, since he has no organic relationship to the story. His physiognomic presence ('the appearance, as from the tomb, of this wintry man') lends him a preternatural suggestiveness, and as the erstwhile manufacturer of 'combustible inventions' used for murderous purposes by revolutionaries he is the symbolic exemplar of the dangerous extremes of radicalism. But his introduction seems to be an afterthought designed to generate further mystery and suspense, and his presence is at odds with the tone of the early chapters.

Abner Power seems especially incongruous beside the main protagonists, Somerset and Paula, each of whom has a credible inner life. Somerset shares the passivity of his fictive forbears; an early deficiency of initiative – he misses opportunities with Paula by not pursuing courses that 'any other man would have had wit enough to do!' – is succeeded later by the adoption of a stoical philosophy which enables him to practise 'the sad science of renunciation'. Significantly it is Paula's comical and unconventional pursuit of him through Europe, and her virtual proposal of marriage, that eventually effects their engagement. But Somerset is intellectually dominant throughout, independent in taste and proficient in the exercise of his profession. Although Paula is 'more woman than Somerset was man', her own sexuality is unconventional and she too undergoes a maturing process. She is interesting and 'lovable', since there is no fixity in her personality; her emotions as well as her intellect are in a state of flux. Superficially she is the symbolic and actual representative of scientific progress and the new aristocracy of monetary wealth: 'Miss Steam-Power', as de Stancy calls her. The ramifications of her Laodiceanism on her religious, social and cultural beliefs have been noticed; it induces no less tantalising ambiguities in her emotional life. Her unwillingness to undergo the immersion ceremony is Freudian in its implications; she is unwilling to make a sexual commitment. Hers is 'emphatically a modern type of maidenhood' and in many ways she remarkably anticipates Sue Bridehead. Her Hellenic alignment – like Sue she is 'a Dissenter, and a Radical, and a New-light, and a Neo-Greek' – is accompanied by a similar emotional reticence and sexual timidity. Accidentally alone with Somerset for the first time, she has to withdraw on account of 'a curious coyness' and she is very much 'the fair Puritan' when she adopts delaying tactics: 'To everything there is a season, and the season for this is not just now.' Like the earlier modern thinker, Henry Knight, Paula has never been kissed.

Though she does not practise the epicene cruelty of Sue, Paula's letters from the Continent occasion some pain to Somerset, especially when she preaches a stoical philosophy: 'Remember M. Aurelius: "This is the chief thing: Be not perturbed; for all things are of the nature of the Universal." '[23] But there is no falsity in this as Paula herself is a Stoic. Like Sue, her desire to attract and captivate is instinctive, while her tendency to evade the implications of her sexuality derives from her Hellenism and her innate Laodiceanism. She is, as she describes herself, 'one of that body to whom lukewarmth is not an accident but a provisional necessity, till they see a little more clearly'. The burden of the novel is in the discovery whether Paula is to declare herself 'cold or hot' (Revelation, Chapter 3, verse 15), and her declaration is eventually implied in her firm commitment to Somerset. Paula's pursuit of him across Europe, with a modern disregard for convention, signals her liberation from her inhibitions and constitutional Laodiceanism.

A Laodicean ought to have been a much better novel than *The Trumpet-Major*, as the opening chapters promised, and even in the modified form of the original conception which survived Hardy's illness it is still a more interesting work. It enjoys the emotional and intellectual engagement of its author. *A Laodicean* is an extension of the study of modernism initiated in social and satirical terms in *The Hand of Ethelberta* and in cultural terms in *The Return of the Native*. In his espousal of Heine and the need for the modern spirit Hardy is aware of the attendant problems of implementation. In Paula, and later in Sue Bridehead, he endorses a Hellenistic, secular ideal, but each case has a different issue. For Hardy the secular ideal is a doctrine of freedom, and it is in the difficulty (and sometimes impossibility) of attaining this freedom that the seeds of tragedy may lie. *A Laodicean*, Hardy tells us in the Preface, attains a 'predetermined cheerful ending', yet in Hardy's fiction endings are never entirely cheerful; unmodified optimism, he always makes clear, is not true to life and certainly not true to the kind of life he discerns and depicts. Paula attains her freedom from outdated creeds and the past at the expense of subduing some of her innate instincts; Somerset attains his freedom to implement eclecticism unfettered by tradition at the price of his 'soaring' youthful idealism having suffered a 'reduction to common measure'. Yet progress will be made as the Somersets 'keep straight on' in their pursuit of a new society. It may be an elusive pursuit, and the victory of common sense and reason is not an unmixed blessing, but it is the most hopeful prospect that there is; the novel realistically appraises what the future must bring. The price of progress is uncertainty and unrest and the evils of alienation and isolation which are drawn in their train.

Hardy does not unreservedly endorse Hellenism as a practical ideal, and indeed in other novels it is seen to be responsible for varying degrees of misfortune. Eustacia Vye is a Hellenic anachronism on Egdon Heath, and later Angel Clare's Hellenic paganism is inadequate. But for Sue Bridehead, Paula's spiritual successor and the definitive embodiment of Hellenism and the modern spirit, it is shown as nothing less than tragic that she is forced back to conventional Christianity and superstition. Paula is far from these straits but the incipient socio-cultural problems in *A Laodicean* furnish a prelusive view of the tragedy of the later novels. In *Tess* and *Jude* Hardy gives full expression to his fears about the implications of living out the philosophy of the modern spirit, defining them in terms of individual psychic predicaments; the characters suffer what he calls, in a poignant phrase in *Tess* (Chapter 19), 'the ache of modernism'. It is here that Tess can express her fears of 'numbers of tomorrows just all in a line' which 'all seem very fierce and cruel and as if they said "I'm coming! Beware of me! Beware of me!"'; and it is in *Jude* (Part 6, Chapter 2) that we see 'the outcome of new views of life', in which children 'seem to see all its terrors before they are old enough to have staying power to resist them. ... it is the beginning of the coming universal wish not to live.'[24] In *A Laodicean* 'the ache of modernism' is already anticipated in the emotional dilemmas of Paula and Somerset and the repression and wilful self-extermination of the de Stancys. The deracination of society is aided by the railways upon which the new aristocrats' wealth is based and reflected in the uprooting of the de Stancys, the aimless wandering of Dare and Abner Power, even in the tourism of Paula and Somerset. The 'modern vice of unrest' which convulses into tragedy in *Jude* has already been set in train. Only Paula and Somerset survive to face the future, and although they do so blithely the painful exigencies of the modern spirit are within them.

The movements in *A Laodicean* enhance our understanding of the later novels. The progress of society and of the individual mind is dramatised in terms of Paula Power's inability to make up her mind about fundamental issues that confront her. Her constant vacillations – between nonconformist faith and humanist scepticism, between incorporating or abjuring neo-Greek modifications in Stancy Castle, between Somerset and de Stancy, between emotional reticence and commitment, between past and present – make her attractively ambiguous. *A Laodicean* is a story of the age of the railway and the telegraph, curiously titillated by sensationalism but capturing 'that form of romanticism which is the mood of the age' (*L*, 147), to use a prescription for imaginative literature noted by Hardy during his illness and the writing of the novel. It is a romanticism subdued by scientific reason and so fortified to meet the future, but which continues instinctively to flourish. And the novel plays out Hardy's own introspection in a time of personal vicissitude, and in it the author achieves as clear a resolution as possible of his Laodiceanism in intellectual preparation for the new age. The problems of reconciling reason and emotion are enormous and modern tendencies only exacerbate them; eventually, as we see in *Tess* and *Jude*, it is the emotions that will suffer. This is the culminating tragedy towards which the Wessex novels move: 'the ache of modernism' is at last no longer a function of external circumstance but psychically resident in the individual mind.

Although the subject of *A Laodicean* comes close to Hardy's inner experience it is not a totally satisfying fiction because of the compromise forced on him by sickness. But it is also because his whole cast of mind is strongest in considering things affectively; it is strong, but not as strong, in its exploration of ideas through the genre of fiction. At times he can bring the two abilities together and this is the sign of the major novel, but the peculiar circumstances of composition preclude this here. Yet despite its defects *A Laodicean* offers a distinct line of thought, and the irony of the ending (which as so often seems to portend melioristic possibilities) lies in the fact that even now there is no achieved resolution, since man is emotionally ill-equipped to adapt to the exigencies of a defective if progressive society. An added piquancy is given to the conclusion by Hardy's own notebook reflections on 9 May 1881, immediately relevant to the theme of his novel, made one week after completing *A Laodicean* (*L*, 148–9):

> May 9. After infinite trying to reconcile a scientific view of life with the emotional and spiritual, so that they may not be inter-destructive I come to the following:
> General Principles. Law has produced in man a child who cannot but constantly reproach its parent for doing much and yet not all, and constantly say to such parent that it would have been better never to have begun doing than to have *over*done so indecisively; that is, than to have created so far beyond all apparent first intention (on the emotional side), without mending matters by a second intent and execution, to eliminate the evils of the blunder of overdoing. The emotions have no place in a world of defect, and it is a cruel injustice that they should have developed in it.
>
> If Law itself had consciousness, how the aspect of its creatures would terrify it, fill it with remorse!

7 Life-loyalties: *Two on a Tower* (1882)

1

For Hardy 1881 was a year of physical recuperation, travel, and a final move from London to Dorset. The poem 'A Wasted Illness', though not explicitly autobiographical, almost certainly alludes to the author's debilitating illness of 1880–1 and his recovery:

> I roam anew
> Scarce conscious of my late distress ... And yet
> Those backward steps to strength I cannot view
>   Without regret.

But here Hardy is enjoying a typically ironic view of the process of recovery, a feeling that in surviving he has lost a positive opportunity to attain what he calls in another poem 'numb relief'; death would be 'the deft achievement' whereby he could escape 'the Wrongers all' ('After the Last Breath'). In real life a different attitude is shown in his quotation (aloud on Wandsworth Common) from Gray: 'The common sun, the air, the skies,/To him are opening Paradise.'[1]

His renewed vigour and the ending of the lease of the Hardys' home in Tooting finally decided Hardy to leave London and establish his permanent home in Dorset, since 'both for reasons of health and for mental inspiration ... he found ... that residence in or near a city tended to force mechanical and ordinary productions from his pen, concerning ordinary society-life and habits.' (*L*, 149) *A Laodicean* was presumably classified among these 'mechanical and ordinary productions'. His next novel, *Two on a Tower*, the first and only one to be written at his new home at Wimborne, certainly reflects an impulse towards the experimental. But this was not begun until six months after

the Hardys moved to Wimborne in summer 1881. After a trip to
Scotland in August Hardy corrected the proofs of *A Laodicean* in
September, and his only prose productions during the rest of
1881 were two short stories, 'The Honourable Laura' and 'What
the Shepherd Saw', both written in the autumn.

Meanwhile, Thomas Bailey Aldrich, editor of the *Atlantic
Monthly*, wrote on 28 September asking for a serial from Hardy
(Purdy, p.44). Hardy records that in December he was in
London, where he 'did some business in arranging for the
publication ... of a novel that he was about to begin writing,
called off-hand by the title of *Two on a Tower*' (*L*, 151). The new
novel's theme probably began to germinate as early as 25 June,
the first night Hardy and Emma spent in their new home, when
they 'saw the new comet from the conservatory' (*L*, 149). It must
have been clearly established by 26 November, when Hardy
applied to the Astronomer Royal for permission to view the
Greenwich Observatory,[2] and a letter from W. C. Unwin dated
12 December 1881 (DCM) provides further evidence of Hardy's
researches:

> I have been very unsuccessful as yet in finding the
> information you wanted. I send you a book I found on my
> shelves which contains some account of lens grinding. Also
> Mr. Lancasters catalogue in which at p.30 is some account of
> telescope making.
>
> Was it not the astronomer Horrocks who did some good
> star mapping with rude instruments when a youth.

This shows the particularity of Hardy's inquiries and, though his
astronomical research for *Two on a Tower* must have been much
less extensive than his historical research prior to writing *The
Trumpet-Major*, he obviously went to some pains to ensure
technical accuracy. The originality of the astronomical setting
was praised by a reviewer in the *Athenaeum* (18 November 1882):

> Mr Hardy may fairly claim for [*Two on a Tower*] the credit of
> having added to the novelist's stock of 'properties' and
> 'business.' We have known military novels, sporting and
> dramatic novels, law and police novels, musical novels, but an
> astronomical novel never.

Astronomical precision was especially important for verisimilitude, since Hardy's avowed aim was 'to make science, not
the mere padding of a romance, but the actual vehicle of
romance'.[3] While details of plot sometimes turn on the minutiae
of astronomical technology, the astronomical theme itself carries
the emotional burden of the author's stated aims.

Composition began in January 1882, and Chapters 1 to 9 had
reached Boston by 8 March; the last part arrived there by 19
September (Purdy, p.44). The actual writing was hurried, and
Hardy later regretted not taking the chance to revise the story for
book publication.[4] *Two on a Tower* appeared in the *Atlantic
Monthly* from May to December 1882 and in book form at the end
of October. It was written more rapidly than most of the
previous novels – the exceptions being *Desperate Remedies* (eight
months), *Under the Greenwood Tree* (three months) and *A Pair of
Blue Eyes* (like *Two on a Tower*, nine months). Only one novel was
subsequently written more rapidly and that was *The Well-Beloved*
(six months). There appears, unsurprisingly, to be some correla-
tion between Hardy's speed of composition and the eventual
critical estimation of the novels. Almost all the 'major' works
were over a year in the writing: *The Mayor of Casterbridge* and *The
Return of the Native* (both thirteen months), *Far from the Madding
Crowd* (fourteen months), *The Woodlanders* (fifteen months). And
the final masterpieces – *Tess* (twenty-five months) and *Jude*
(twenty months) – were the longest of all in composition.[5] *Two on
a Tower* was written faster than any novel since *A Pair of Blue Eyes*
a decade earlier; even *A Laodicean* was written over eleven
months. This haste has left its mark on the novel but in omission
rather than commission:[6] whereas the plot manipulations of *A
Laodicean* eventually overwhelm, the main problem in *Two on a
Tower* is that promising themes are insufficiently developed and
opportunities are missed with less excuse than in the previous
novel. It is doubtful whether any revisions which Hardy had
projected would have made much improvement, since the faults
of *Two on a Tower* lie in its direction and development rather than
in detail.

It was written at the mid-point of Hardy's novel-writing
career, twelve years after *Desperate Remedies* and twelve years
before *Jude the Obscure*. It was followed by the longest break yet in
the sequence of novels which Hardy had been assiduously
producing at regular intervals over more than a decade. That

Hardy was not satisfied with *Two on a Tower* seems clear not only from his comments to Gosse in 1883 (see note 4) but also in his prefatory description of it in 1895 as a 'slightly-built romance'. Havelock Ellis, writing in 1883, speculated that Hardy would probably henceforward 'pursue the vein of comedy which began in *The Hand of Ethelberta*' and that 'it is probable that, of stories in this manner, *A Laodicean* and *Two on a Tower* will not be the last.'[7] It may seem odd that Ellis should have isolated the strain in Hardy's novels which subsequently proved critically the least important in his development as a writer, but it shows the extent to which at least one critic (and there were surely more of the same mind) was unsure what to expect next from Hardy, because of the range and variety of his earlier productions. Hardy may have found this partially satisfying, since it meant that his reputation was no longer defined by association with sheepfarming; but perhaps too he felt some dissatisfaction that even now he had not clearly defined a consistent course in his fiction.

After more than a decade of writing to meet the sometimes dissonant demands of the serial-reading public and of his own thoughts and imagination, Hardy now let eighteen months pass before starting his next novel and almost four years pass before publishing it.[8] This may have been a writer's sabbatical, a contemplative time for an author for whom the ability to produce a 'slightly-built romance' was not enough; a time to define for himself the most fitting mode in which to direct his genius. If so, Hardy's delay was not in vain, and he proved Havelock Ellis wrong in his guess about the future track of Hardy's fiction. After the period of continued experimentation in form and subject-matter which issued in succession *The Trumpet-Major*, *A Laodicean* and *Two on a Tower*, and the eighteen-month lacuna that followed it, Hardy began work in spring 1884 on *The Mayor of Casterbridge*, arguably his most artistically successful novel. The 'major' novels written henceforward (*The Mayor* itself, *The Woodlanders*, *Tess* and *Jude*) are more of a piece, progressive refinements of psychic investigation and products of Hardy's comparative freedom to follow, increasingly, his own impulse rather than the demands of the market-place. *Two on a Tower*, in its chronological centrality, is thus of special artistic interest too, since it brings to a close the all-important first and exploratory phase of Hardy's career as a novelist.

2

The astronomical setting of the novel is ingeniously conceived, yet the author's prefatory description of its intention has often drawn charges of extravagance. Hardy says that it was

> the outcome of a wish to set the emotional history of two infinitesimal lives against the stupendous background of the stellar universe, and to impart to readers the sentiment that of these contrasting magnitudes the smaller might be the greater to them as men.[9]

The novel is frequently undervalued because Hardy is supposed not to have satisfied a too grandiose aim, yet there is nothing unusually ambitious about Hardy's project: the enacting of a human emotional drama against a natural background, whether it be the stellar universe or a more locally defined earthly setting, is common to all the Wessex novels. And the astronomical theme is unusual and original, and its incorporation through plot and imagery is more complete, than is generally supposed. But concentration upon the presumed weakness of this prominent feature of the novel has tended to obscure the fact that *Two on a Tower* may cogently be read as an excursion into the philosophy of celestial immensity and as a logical companion piece to *A Laodicean*. It signifies a new departure in setting, but not in direction or purpose.

The intellectual, social and cultural ramifications of man's attempts to reconcile the impulses of reason and emotion had been shrewdly investigated in *A Laodicean*. We saw at the end of the last chapter that Hardy's concern with the question was still manifest after he had finished the novel and that on 9 May 1881 he recorded his 'infinite trying to reconcile a scientific view of life with the emotional and spiritual, so that they may not be interdestructive' (*L*, 148). This 'trying' continues with renewed vigour in *Two on a Tower*, where the difficulties arising from the conflicting demands of head and heart in both a human and a universal environment are explored, so it is not only in external detail that Hardy seeks to make 'science' the vehicle of the romance. Hardy's typical depreciation of *Two on a Tower* as a 'slightly-built romance' cannot hide potentially more important prefatory clues which indicate the 'serious view' and 'high aims' with which he had approached his subject.[10] Hardy had hoped to write 'in a manner not unprofitable to the growth of the social sympathies'; but recognition of this, he implies in the resigned tone of an author who has long felt himself to have been misunderstood, may be limited to 'some few readers'.[11]

The social sympathies which Hardy hopes to excite are those inspired by 'the pathos, misery, long-suffering and divine tenderness' of Lady Viviette Constantine, in the face of the harsh scientific rationalism of the young astronomer, Swithin St Cleeve, to whose priorities Viviette has soon to demur: 'The immensity of the subject you have engaged on has completely crushed my subject out of me! Yours is celestial; mine lamentably human! And the less must give way to the greater.' Yet the melioristic irony of *Two on a Tower* is contained in the inversion of these traditional assumptions of human insignificance in the face of the vastness of the universe. It is the love and self-immolating nobility of Viviette that proves to be of far greater value than the stellar immensities with which Swithin is concerned.

Hardy's presentation of the universe, however, is as a nightmare vision. It is an archetypal example of Northrop Frye's demonic divine world, which personifies 'the vast, menacing, stupid powers of nature ... with the inaccessible sky, and the central idea that crystallizes from it ... the idea of inscrutable fate or external necessity. The machinery of fate is administered by a set of remote invisible gods.'[12] The universe in *Two on a Tower* is peopled with 'horrid monsters' that 'lie up there waiting ... impersonal monsters, namely, Immensities'. It makes a human feel that 'it is not worth while to live' and that 'nothing is made for man.' As Swithin tells Viviette, 'it is better – far better – for men to forget the universe than to bear it clearly in mind.' In *Two on a Tower* Hardy dramatises 'the flashing firmament' and 'ghast heights of sky' described in 'In Vision I Roamed': in the poem, as in the novel, the initial assumption of man's insignificance is undercut by realisation of Earth's bounty, so that the speaker is happily left 'uncaring all that lay/Locked in that Universe taciturn and drear.'[13] The poem 'At a Lunar Eclipse' has a similar burden, questioning the place of 'continents of moil and misery' in the wider context of the sun, moon and stars:

And can immense Mortality but throw
So small a shade, and Heaven's high human scheme
Be hemmed within the coasts yon arc implies?[14]

Yet, as elsewhere in the novels, it is made clear that attribution of demonic or antagonistic qualities to natural phenomena, whether they are cosmic or closer to Earth, is a man-projected delusion. There is no causality in the powers of nature beyond that imagined in the mind of man. Though the hurricane seizes hold of Rings-Hill Speer in Chapter 16 'with the determination of a conscious agent', it is not the wind itself but man's attitude towards it that has altered: 'The disposition of the wind is as vicious as ever [Viviette tells Swithin]. It is your mood of viewing it that has changed. "There is nothing either good or bad, but thinking makes it so."'

Similarly it is man's implacable striving in vain endeavour to comprehend the universe that invests his conception of it with terrible apprehensions about macrocosmic magnitudes:

'There is a size at which dignity begins,' [Swithin] exclaimed; 'further on there is a size at which grandeur begins; further on there is a size at which solemnity begins; further on, a size at which ghastliness begins. ... So am I not right in saying that those minds who exert their imaginative powers to bury themselves in the depths of that universe merely strain their faculties to gain a new horror?'

In this formulation, ingenious in its psychological gradations, Swithin reveals the falsity of his own perspective. The universe is only vast and menacing when he thinks it so. It is a metaphysical problem with which we all live, but it is only a trouble to 'those minds' who busy themselves in seeking solutions to humanly unanswerable questions. The perception that there is such a philosophic concept as infinity is the furthest that human understanding can be stretched, and after acknowledging this and the intellectual limitations which it implies man can proceed with the business of daily life.

Swithin is not entirely seduced by such philosophical imponderables even though, in awe and wonder, he is fearfully aware of them, but he is enthralled by the horror and the glory of the heavens. His scientific pursuit of knowledge is carried on (initially at least) to the exclusion of human emotions, yet there is something primitive in his subjugation of what is humanly normal to his fascination with the skies: 'Not unaptly might it have been said that he was worshipping the sun' (an image compounded many chapters later by his tower being seen as 'the temple of that sublime mystery on whose threshold he stood as priest'). Unlike those mortals in *A Laodicean*, whom Hardy more readily approves, with their diligent quest for a new human society, Swithin's inquiry is directed outwards, away from human sympathies and towards inhuman phenomena. His paradoxical mix of scientific rationalism and primitive obsession is regressive in personal and social terms.

It becomes hard to distinguish who is the master of Swithin, himself or the heavens, and it is only when his initial priorities are undermined by sexual attraction that he is restored to a normal human perspective and the menacing universe recedes to its proper place. The 'growth of the social sympathies' is achieved not only in the exemplary virtues of Viviette but also in the bringing of Swithin St Cleeve, literally, down to earth. Swithin graduates to awareness not only of human passions but also to awareness of what Viviette refers to ironically as 'such ephemeral trivialities as human tragedy'. These human matters, infinitesimal as they may seem in comparison with the cosmos, dwarf all astronomical stupendousness.

Hardy explicitly grants no more credence to the idea of an antagonistic cosmos than he does to that of an anthropomorphic God. In *Two on a Tower* the universe is shown as subservient to man once its enthralling powers have been reduced by the ascendancy of human values; it is of interest to man only in so far as it may be of use to him and exists only as a background to his activity. The heavens are a scientific fact, but in the human environment emotional values prevail. It is unusual to find Hardy championing man's chances against the impersonal universe, but in *Two on a Tower* he sounds an optimistic note that should not go unheeded. Yet the end of the story is not exactly comforting. While the primacy of emotional values is established it is simultaneously made clear that they are vulnerable; and, in so far as a main concern of the novel is Swithin's psychic history, the future is left indeterminate. We are shown Swithin working at the Cape: 'In these experiments with tubes and glasses, important as they were to human intellect, there was little food

for the sympathetic instincts which create the changes in a life.'
His discoveries are 'of the highest importance to him; and yet
from an intersocial point of view they served but the humble
purpose of killing time.' But the story happens to be about
intersocial affiliations (as Hardy might say), because that is
what novels are, and, from one point of view, by the end
Swithin's intersocial life has diminished to vanishing point,
including the death of Viviette. Though Hardy conceals the
outcome, the logic of the story suggests that he will be easily
consoled by Tabitha, who is simply younger, but he may remain
just as interested in the stars as he was before. This possibility is
perhaps as likely as any other from which to draw out our plan of
his life, but Hardy as narrator remains typically uncommitted.

The author's handling of astronomical technicalities is unquestionably competent. He handles confidently much talk of
object lenses, equatorial telescopes and gigantic refractors;
ascensions and declinations and tangent and parallax; sidereal
observations, the mysteries of the solar system, Swithin's new
discovery about the variable stars and his expedition into the
southern hemisphere. There is some exhaustion, perhaps, implicit in the 'Is it not all written in the chronicle of the
Astronomical Society?' with which, in Chapter 40, Hardy
eagerly excuses himself for further particularity. All this makes
the novel technically convincing and gives it a believable aura of
astronomical inquiry; and even in detail the astronomical
imagery permeates the story, usually in connection with Viviette,
whose snowdrop bed is 'like a nether Milky Way'; later the
whiplash cut on her cheek is described as being 'straight as a
meridian', and at the end her hair is touched by 'a faint grey
haze, like the Via Lactea in a midnight sky'. Yet the material
calls for an imaginative transformation that is, in part, lacking.

What comes nearest to vitalising the astronomical theme is the
tower itself, the earthly monitor of the heavens, which is invested
with a curiously poetic quality. The intermediary between Earth
and stars, from the perspective of men below the tower wears an
almost celestial aspect, aggressively reaching out (like its
incumbent Swithin) towards the heavens. But in fact it is
conspicuously terrestrial, and imagery suggests its union with
natural surroundings: 'Pads of moss grew in the joints of the
stone-work, and here and there shade-loving insects had en-
graved on the mortar patterns of no human style or meaning.'

The tower is the meeting-point of the human emotional drama and Swithin's scientific aspirations, and as the pivotal setting it is specially piquant since it is a monument to human vanity and the futility of earthly ambition:

> Here stood this aspiring piece of masonry, erected as the most conspicuous and ineffaceable reminder of a man that could be thought of; and yet the whole aspect of the memorial betokened forgetfulness.

There is a final sense, though, that the author fails to infuse the reader's mind steadily with awareness of the universal environment which frames the story and characters. The astronomical theme, excellent in conception and in its introduction in the early chapters, does not pervade the story as the woods in *The Woodlanders* or as Egdon Heath in *The Return of the Native*. These natural settings, as universal in their implications as the universe itself, are more imaginatively appealing; they are microcosms as opposed to the macrocosm, easier to assimilate since they are created in terms of the familiar. In *Two on a Tower* the sense of the infinite universe is much more elusive, and, lacking in immediate human application, it fails to charge the reader's imagination. Man does not usually live consciously on a cosmic plane, so the heavens, vast and unimaginable as they are, can only be invoked by a deliberate effort as agents in the story; they are, in effect, unnatural. The characters are shown in their universal environment but, except in the most literal sense, this is not where they live and move and have their being. And if the stellar universe does not permeate the story, neither does it consistently impinge upon the main protagonists, Viviette and Swithin, whose career together is for a long time complicated by purely earthly intrigues. Hardy does not forget the astronomical theme, but he does periodically subjugate it to other plot considerations, and the love story is intermittently detached from the astronomical dilemma that forms its basis.

It was not, however, the success or failure of the novel's original setting that attracted contemporary critical attention but its unconventional presentation of a moral lapse and an infatuated bishop. Hardy protested in his 1895 Preface that his 'high aims' had been overlooked in favour of critical insistence 'first, that the novel was an "improper" one in its morals, and, secondly, that it was intended to be a satire on the Established Church of this country'.[15] The novel does bear Hardy's first overt challenge to convention and contemporary moral codes and in this anticipates the problems he was to face more than a decade later over *Tess* and *Jude*, but he was right in saying that too-exclusive attention had been given to these features of *Two on a Tower*. Yet his tone of surprise seems disingenuous. Hardy's reaction to the reviews is worth examining, since it involves, first, a determined rejoinder in print claiming that he had been misunderstood, yet subsequently the introduction of exacerbating details into a later edition of the novel, which strongly suggests that he had not.

The novel's critical reception was almost uniformly antagonistic. Harry Quilter's review in the *Spectator* (3 February 1883) is representative: he finds it 'a story as unpleasant as it is practically possible', notes (like many others) the 'repulsive' elements in Viviette's relationships with Swithin and Bishop Helmsdale, and concludes that 'the book, as a whole, is bad – the worst the author has written', pronouncing it 'melodramatic without strength, extravagant without object, and objectionable without truth'. To castigate the novel so excessively is to strain language, but a more moderate expression of similar views had already drawn a retort from Hardy. An anonymous reviewer in the *St James's Gazette* (16 January 1883) acknowledges the novel's readability but regrets that Hardy has selected his theme 'with a disregard, apparently, of all moral purpose'. He continues:

> There is no reason, of course, why an ecclesiastical dignitary should be *ex officio* less liable than anybody else to have untimely paternity thrust upon him; but Mr Hardy's choice has a suspicion of burlesque about it, and may even be regarded in certain quarters as a studied and gratuitous insult aimed at the Church.

In view of his later revision of certain details of the story Hardy's unusual rejoinder is worth quoting in full, since the episode is revealing. His letter, in the issue of 19 January 1883, is written (perhaps pointedly) from the conventionally respectable Savile Club:

> In your candid review of *Two on a Tower* you express an

opinion that in some quarters the choice of a bishop as a
victim (in a situation which, for unknown reasons, is supposed
to have a ludicrous side) may be regarded as a studied insult
to the Church.

Will you allow me to state that, however the choice may be
regarded, no thought of such an insult was present to my mind
in contriving the situation. Purely artistic conditions necessi-
tated an episcopal position for the character alluded to, as will
be apparent to those readers who are at all experienced in the
story-telling trade. Indeed, that no *arrière-pensée* of the sort
suggested had existence should be sufficiently clear to everybody from the circumstances that one of the most honourable
characters in the book, and the hero's friend, is a clergyman,
and that the heroine's most tender qualities are woven in with
her religious feelings.

There is some ingenuity in Hardy's denial. His invocation of
Parson Torkingham, a minor character who is himself lightly
burlesqued, is unconvincing, and it is difficult to believe that
Hardy's presentation of the bishop is devoid of ironic intention.
The grounds of his defence had slightly altered by 1895: in the
preface of that year, in place of the earlier plea of artistic
necessity he merely says that 'the bishop is every inch a
gentleman.' But there is a sense of wry irony about this too; only
in the next paragraph does Hardy declare his intention to begin
'to take a serious view', and he makes no attempt to exculpate
himself from the charge of satirising the Church.

It is also disingenuous of him to describe, in his letter to the *St
James's Gazette*, the bishop's victimisation as 'a situation which,
for unknown reasons, is supposed to have a ludicrous side': a
letter Hardy had written to Edmund Gosse a month earlier
shows him well satisfied by private assurances from eminent
critics 'that the affair of the Bishop is a triumph of tragi-comedy'
(see note 15). In fact Hardy's values in *Two on a Tower* are those
of a humanist: it is essential to his conception of the story that
the representative of accepted views should be a bishop, and the
cleric is individualised as a most suitable victim for Hardy's
irony. As far as reviewers and public libraries were concerned,
people had not yet quite got used to the so-called 'cynicism' of
Thackeray's attempts to be moderately realistic about human
nature; the private correspondents who wrote to Hardy, on the

other hand, may well have been enjoying Flaubert. Though Hardy could have been bolder and less defensive, the exploitation of the bishop is quite a brave attempt on his part.

Bishop Helmsdale is unprepossessing – self-centred, pompous and even (it is hinted) hypocritical, reminiscent of Browning's bishops. Having intolerantly censured Swithin and having refused to interpret his case charitably – there is little charity in him; he is a social figure – the bishop meets Viviette: 'Who could believe the Bishop to be the same man that he had been a moment before? The darkness left his face as if he had come out of a cave; his look was all sweetness, and shine, and gaiety, as he again greeted Viviette.' The bishop's immoderate obsession with his worldly dignity is indicated after his death by Mr Torkingham: 'To speak candidly, he had his faults, of which arrogance was not the least.' The bishop is deliberately set up as the deserving victim of the deception practised at his expense, and his courtship and marriage, though comically presented, are replete with harsh ironies. His marriage to Viviette is induced not as he thinks by his own 'persuasive force' but because 'a tempter had shown it to her' as a means of delivering herself, Swithin and the child she is carrying from the disgrace that would otherwise ensue.

It is bitterly ironic that a bishop should be thus deluded, through his own pride, by a satanic impulse ('a tempter'), and there is a further Juvenalian irony in showing the bishop, in his ignorance of this, as having 'the air of a man too good for his destiny'. Perhaps the bishop's predicament is not entirely deserved, yet in the fact that he is a bishop there is (as the *St James's Gazette* reviewer concluded) nothing wrong: he is a man like anyone else. That he holds high ecclesiastical office will make some readers uneasy because of the tendency to take the characters of a novel as typical, in spite of what an author may say. Yet he is not just a pompous bishop; Hardy has a certain animosity to him and what he believes. If the bishop has his revenge, in the last sentence of the novel, in this exposure of the bishop Hardy appears to be having *his* revenge, and it is as pointed as some of the remarks in *Tess* or 'A Tragedy of Two Ambitions', the story of the two brothers who are clergymen and who let their father drown. The pages of Chapter 39 rather deftly extract a cruel fun from the bishop's pomposity and complacency. The evidence suggests that Hardy knew very well that

his story contains an ecclesiastical satire but that he was afraid
to say so.

What worsens in conventional eyes the ironic deception
perpetrated on Bishop Helmsdale are the circumstances under
which the child has been conceived.[16] After the announcement
that Sir Blount's death had occurred later than supposed, and
the attendant invalidation of the marriage between Viviette and
Swithin, it becomes clear that Viviette's child will be born a
bastard. Without any further particularity about the date of the
child's conception this may be accepted as, at worst, a brutally
unfortunate legal mischance. If the child has been begotten in
what was 'intended' to be legal matrimony (as Hardy's Preface
implies) then the parents are at least morally innocent, yet
Hardy goes to some lengths in the novel's third edition (1883) to
remove this element of benevolent doubt by introducing a
specific detail of dating, and he clarifies the point still further in
the 1895 edition by adding two new and explicit passages. All
this makes his prefatory claim about 'the scrupulous propriety
observed . . . on the relations of the sexes' astonishing. But Hardy
knows what he is about. When he says that 'there is hardly a
single caress in the book outside legal matrimony, or what was
intended so to be', this is strictly true, if misleading. For the one
'caress' which does occur is a crucial one, and it occurs *after*
Viviette and Swithin discover that their marriage is invalid.

The intriguing text variations through which Hardy makes
this increasingly clear have been discovered by J. C. Maxwell.[17]
The first edition of 1882 includes only the date of the child's
birth, April 10 (Chapter 40); in the third edition (1883) Hardy
specifies the date of the final meeting of Viviette and Swithin as
July 7 (Chapter 36); in 1895, to make it entirely clear that the
child was conceived on this occasion, Hardy introduces in the
same chapter the explicit information that 'Viviette yielded to all
the passion of her first union with him,' and in Chapter 40 he
adds this sentence to Viviette's letter to Swithin: 'I ought not to
have consented to that last interview; all was well till then!' So
ironically enough the original version, for which Hardy was
blamed for his disregard of all moral purpose, is strictly speaking
quite 'proper'; it is up to the reader to assume immorality. Yet
the version in which Hardy returns the critics' fire in his Preface
is also the one in which he makes explicit those elements which
are provocatively 'improper'. No doubt Hardy privately enjoyed

silently administering this snub to censorious critics. The episode suggests his continuing impulse to disturb and the increasing, if still timorous, confidence with which he pursues the doctrine of 'candour in English fiction' in his assault upon the morality of convention-bound readers. (It is made clear that convention provokes Viviette's deception of the bishop: 'Convention was forcing her hand at this game; and to what will not convention compel her weaker victims, in extremes?')

The dominant mode of *Two on a Tower* is unquestionably ironic, and in a novel of which the superficial design is innocuous the degree and the depth of irony is surprising. There are of course many of the innocuous ironies that delight Hardy, such as the thrill of secretly held information from which piquant misunderstandings arise: the entire relationship of Viviette and Swithin turns upon this and contains one of Hardy's favourite formulations of the 'poor man and the lady' theme. Like the relationship between Ethelberta and the Chickerels, this liaison is privileged information shared only by the reader and the characters themselves. There is irony appropriate to social comedy, and there are some more pointed ironies: we learn, for example, of a pre-marital indiscretion between Anthony Green and his wife Gloriana and that 'it was chiefly Lady Constantine's exertions that had made an honest wife of Mrs Green.' Some ironies which emphasise the harshness of necessity are prelusive of the later Hardy rather than inherited from the earlier. They are the kind of ironies which impelled Swinburne to write to Hardy, after reading *Jude*, 'how cruel you are!' (*L*, 270). He could have written 'how cruelly you envisage circumstance!' for the ironies in that novel, as in *Two on a Tower*, operate through mischances which thwart the hopes and ambitions of the protagonists. Swithin makes an original astronomical discovery, but his findings are anticipated by six weeks in an American journal; he receives a handsome inheritance only when he cannot take it up because of Viviette; Sir Blount's death is misreported so that Viviette's and Swithin's marriage is made void; Viviette becomes pregnant but only discovers this immediately after Swithin's departure; Viviette marries a bishop, entering holy matrimony for unholy reasons; the bishop dies, but when Swithin returns Viviette is growing old and it is too late to recreate their former love.

The final and cruellest irony is that Viviette dies of joy:

'Sudden joy after despair had touched an over-strained heart too smartly. Viviette was dead. The Bishop was avenged.' This perfunctory and tragic ending is not of a piece with what has preceded it. Viviette's death is poetical but too unexpected and too unnatural to be genuinely moving, and its effect is not improved by the un-Christian and awkwardly appended notion of vengeance for the bishop. The incident points up the novel's failure in consistency of tone. *Two on a Tower* is a tragi-comedy, a form Hardy seems to find difficult to manage, and the conflicting demands of tragic irony and comic irony impose more strain on the narrative than it can comfortably withstand. *Two on a Tower* is at first a pleasing social comedy in which Hardy exploits unusual material with a confident lightness of touch; the story is admirably controlled in the early chapters, emotionally moving and psychologically true. Hardy humorously poeticises the romance: 'Darker grew the evenings, tearfuller the moonlights, and heavier the dews.' His tone is affectionate yet properly detached. He even permits himself an unusual direct aside to the reader:

> But Swithin St Cleeve did not decease, a fact of which, indeed, the habituated reader will have been well aware ever since the rain came down upon the young man in the ninth chapter, and led to his alarming illness.

But again social comedy gives way to melodrama and plot manipulation, the promising astronomical theme yields place to terrestrial machinations of a more commonplace order, and the ironies become too vicious to be contained within the atmosphere created in the early chapters; yet nothing prepares the reader for the abruptness of the final melodramatic *coup de théâtre*.

In spite of these defects *Two on a Tower* remains a more pleasing, though less challenging, novel than *A Laodicean*. It is infused with a poetic quality that *A Laodicean* lacks, and its love story is less calculating and more appealing. Hardy includes it among the 'Romances and Fantasies' (with *A Pair of Blue Eyes*, *The Trumpet-Major* and *The Well-Beloved*) rather than the 'Novels of Ingenuity', and as a fantastic tale it succeeds well enough. But *Two on a Tower* ultimately disappoints because, in common with others among the lesser novels, it raises ideas which stir uneasily under the narrative surface but which are not fully embodied in the story. Its investigation of the reconciliation of reason and

emotion, and the correspondent development of social sympathies, is an outgrowth of the theme of *A Laodicean*, but there is
a disturbing sense of opportunities missed. The astronomical
imagery, for example, is admirably sustained but nowhere is it
pointedly exploited, as the architectural imagery had been made
to contain social and moral judgements in *A Laodicean*. The
reader is left with an impression of charm or ingenuity (perhaps
sufficient for a fantasy) but not of substance or an essential truth.
Even the insipid alliterative title reinforces this impression and
Hardy later regretted it; it was 'a title he afterwards disliked' (*L*,
151).

What else Hardy liked or disliked about the novel is hard to
discover, apart from his regrets about its too hasty composition
and his description of it as 'slightly-built.' In summer 1920
Hardy responded to Florence Henniker's request for a copy by
sending her one, remarking that 'instead of assisting you to make
up your set of these novels I ought really to be making you read
my later and more serious books. However you must have your
own way, I suppose.'[18] But he adds in a postscript: 'On looking
into it it seems rather clever.' This is the impression with which
many readers must have been left, and it is unsurprising that
what Hardy finds retrospectively to commend is the novel's
cleverness, a quality insufficient to lend it sustained distinction.
But it is in the telling of the story that *Two on a Tower* falls down.
It could have been told simply, directly and dispassionately, but
Hardy is again betrayed by his tendency to verbosity. The
Saturday Review (18 November 1882) was surely right to criticise
the style. Taking a passage from the text, the critic writes:
'"Paraphrase this briefly," one might say to an intelligent
schoolboy.' After reducing eight lines to a two-line paraphrase
the critic continues: 'One might go on to ask the author, "Why
all this bother and affection of profundity to express so very
simple and commonplace a notion?"' The exercise is not unfair:
Two on a Tower could have been 'slightly-built', and it should
have been, but it is stretched to fill three volumes as usual, and
this over-expansion of a good idea is bound to affect the balance
of the work too.

Among the 'Romances and Fantasies' *Two on a Tower* has
much in common with its predecessor of a decade earlier, *A Pair
of Blue Eyes*, since both novels share a peculiar charm not found
elsewhere in the Wessex novels, and a framework of ironic

counterpointing; but they also share indeterminacy of tone, and both end with a cruel and apparently gratuitous fatality. The intervening decade, however, had taught Hardy to have a more reflexive recourse to melodrama when in haste or difficulty. The access of melodrama which leads to Viviette's death is the more irritating for being less easy to isolate than that in *A Laodicean*, where the melodramatic declension becomes so obvious that it can almost be assimilated by the reader. In *Two on a Tower* it is more insidious, so that Viviette's death, when it occurs, is still unprepared for.

Although the original conception of a romance set in the awe-inspiring universal environment is enfeebled by melodramatic opportunism, in the relationship of Viviette and Swithin Hardy captures something of the spirit of an age, and it is here that his presence and conviction must be sought. Though less pervasively so than in *A Laodicean*, *Two on a Tower* marks a further stage in Hardy's investigation of modernism, and here Viviette and Swithin are the touchstones in social, intellectual and moral dilemmas of their age. Contemporaneity is less deliberately exploited than in the previous novel, though it is implicit in the story and in detail. (The Transit of Venus, for the viewing of which Swithin joins his expedition, took place in December 1882, neatly contemporaneous with the novel's publication.) The process of social levelling continues and promises an incipient meritocracy in which Swithin's endeavours will be rewarded. The aristocracy has declined yet further and it is here reduced to its decadent representative, Sir Blount Constantine, whose brute medievalism of temperament leads him to a retributive death by his own hand in Africa, and his wife Viviette. Lady Constantine herself, however, in her love for Swithin effectively erases the false social distinction between the lady and the poor man, and she engages Hardy's respect because she likes 'to dwell less on her permanent position as a county lady than on her passing emotions as a woman', which is getting her priorities right. Swithin's social position is an anomaly: he is the son of a parson who contracted a socially undesirable match with Farmer Martin's daughter. As a result, Amos Fry tells Viviette, 'what with having two stations of life in his blood he's good for nothing.' In fact Swithin achieves the classlessness of the talented scientist. That social distinctions survive is illustrated in the vicar, whose similarly ambivalent standing between the bucolics and the landed gentry is thrown into sartorial relief at Welland House: 'His boots, which had seemed rather elegant in the farm-house, appeared rather clumsy here.'

The social movements are again accompanied by the modern evils of unrest and isolation. Alienated rootlessness is indicated in the intercontinental wanderings of Sir Blount, Louis Glanville and Swithin himself. Viviette and Swithin are both moderns, increasingly alone, Viviette in her great house and Swithin in his tower, itself a symbol of isolation. Even their brief marriage does not qualify their solitude, since the need for seclusion denies them other human society. And each of them, separately, experiences a foreshadowing of the coming universal wish not to live. For Viviette this occurs after Swithin's departure and her discovery of her pregnancy: 'The absence of the dome suggested a way out of her difficulties. A leap in the dark, and all would be over.' Much earlier, when his astronomical discoveries have been forestalled, Swithin experiences 'a wild wish for annihilation'. This anticipates the wishes of the later tragic heroes – Henchard, Giles, Tess (whose 'I'd have my life unbe' in 'Tess's Lament' poignantly conveys the Schopenhauerean will not to will implicit in all these cases), and Jude. The death-wish is not unexpected in a young man who has earlier declared that 'nothing is made for man' and who so far knows nothing of the solaces of human love. But Swithin is not to be a tragic hero, and his case shows that psychologic impulses can operate for the good too: 'The strenuous wish to live and behold the new phenomenon [a comet], supplanting the utter weariness of existence that he had heretofore experienced, gave him a new vitality.' Although the death-wish is overcome by Viviette and Swithin it is implanted within their consciousness, a result of the modern conditions which prevail over them and the spiritual isolation in which they find themselves.

It is in their experience, however, that hope for the future resides. *Two on a Tower*, unreservedly romantic in atmosphere, posits in its proclamation of the holiness of the heart's affections a corrective to the harshly scientific new world foreshadowed in *A Laodicean*. And just as Paula and Somerset survive the deficiencies of that novel, Viviette and Swithin survive those of *Two on a Tower*. These are both books with serious faults but they remain more moving and arresting than many books with fewer faults by other writers because Hardy's sense of character and feeling for his people equips them with protagonists who are assured of our affection and interest. Viviette is an especially rich and fascinating character. In the lesser novels, as I have suggested before, the woman is often the most vital and appealing figure – Miss Aldclyffe, Elfride, Ethelberta and Paula each dominate their respective stories. In *A Laodicean* and *Two on a Tower*, novels generally regarded as having been written at the lowest ebb of his career, Hardy creates two of his most compulsive, endearing and true female characters.

Two on a Tower, like several of Hardy's fictions, is vitalised by the infusion of elements of the author's own history into the principal characters, and this enriches their cognate reality. There is much of Hardy in Swithin, who, as his creator had been, is an aspiring poor man, talented and ambitious yet late in achieving emotional maturity (cf. *L*, 32). Hardy's narrative even suggests (in his uncompromising deployment of mischance in the novel itself, for example) some elements of that inexorably cruel scientific logic that he attributes to the young man. Swithin's grandmother, the octogenarian Mrs Martin, a tidy secondary character, appears to have been based on Mary Head Hardy,[19] Hardy's own 'gentle, kindly grandmother' (*L*, 420), commemorated in the poem 'One We Knew'.[20]

Hardy's choice of the name 'Martin' may be a clue that in conceiving Swithin's relationship with Viviette he may have been inwardly turning back to his own ambivalent relationship with Julia Augusta Martin, the lady of the manor at Kingston Maurward when he was a boy.[21] In his youth he had entertained 'lover-like' (*L*, 20) feelings for her, but the two did not meet again until Hardy was 22 and Julia Martin in her fifties, on which occasion Hardy was shocked to discover how the lady whom he had idealised had aged: 'But the lady of his dreams – alas! To her, too, the meeting must have been no less painful than pleasant.' (*L*, 41) When writing the *Life* Hardy recalled Mrs Martin with a more than ordinary degree of affection: a letter from her in 1875, he says, had revived in him 'throbs of tender feeling' and recalled 'the thrilling "frou-frou" of her four silk flounces' (*L*, 102). But even more revealing is a passage which Hardy heavily crossed through in the original typescript, evidently feeling that he had been much too explicit, and which did not appear in the published version:

Thus though their eyes never met again after his call on her in London, nor their lips from the time when she had held him in her arms, who can say that both occurrences might not have been in the order of things, if he had developed their reacquaintance earlier, now that she was in her widowhood, with nothing to hinder her mind from rolling back upon her past. (*Personal Notebooks*, p.220)

This shows a yet deeper and more lasting affection for the lady whose last recorded letter to Hardy was written on 11 May 1887, when she signed herself, rather pathetically, as 'your old withered-up Friend'.[22] But the influence of this real-life relationship is oblique and, at best, persuasively suggestive.

Hardy is much more playful, ambiguous and uncommitted in his artistic transformation of real experience than biographical exegesis implies. He does not take it raw but distances himself from his experience and weaves it into a myth. Yet we can at least see that the passage deleted from the *Life* is written with the same sensibility that had enabled Hardy 40 years earlier to enter sympathetically into Viviette's anguished plea to Swithin: 'Say you will never despise me, when you get older, for this episode in our lives?' And Swithin's meeting with Viviette, on his return from the expedition, is as pathetically shocking as Hardy's with Mrs Martin in 1862:

Yes, he was shocked at her worn and faded aspect. The image that he had mentally carried out with him to the Cape he had brought home again as that of the woman he was now to rejoin. But another woman sat before him, and not the original Viviette.

By this time Swithin is able to accommodate the emotional demands made upon him by the situation, though his responsibilities are resolved by Viviette's untimely death, since he has attained emotional maturity. Swithin is initially another of Hardy's passive young heroes, intellectually able but sexually retarded. Embodying a peculiar combination of 'youthful ardour and old despair', he is a cool-headed scientific rationalist who can declare that 'nothing is ominous in serene philosophy ... things are either causes, or they are not causes.' Even in his maturity he displays a schoolboy temperament, being oblivious of the effects of a given scheme on others than himself; and, Hardy says, 'there is something in the inexorably simple logic of such men which partakes of the cruelty of the natural laws that are their study.' He shares, in fact, something of that detachment which is a paradoxical feature of Hardy's own compassionate temperament. Superadded to Swithin's scientific outlook is his sexual peculiarity – 'a beloved science is enough wife for me,' he says. He needs to be cured of such abnormal sentiments and weaned from his obsession with equatorial telescopes, and it is in this adjustment of perspective (if it is finally accomplished – Hardy is ultimately evasive) that there is hope for the future.

The transformation of Swithin from disinterested scientist into passionate lover is effected with urbanity and humour, and his maturation is vividly drawn. Like Knight, Miss Aldclyffe and Captain de Stancy, his long-retarded emotions are suddenly released: 'the tardiness of his awakening was the natural result of inexperience combined with devotion to a hobby. But, like a spring bud hard in bursting, the delay was compensated by after speed.' His sexual awakening is achieved through Viviette, who assumes the dominant role because of her 'superiority of experience and ripeness of emotion'. Their relationship to some extent parallels that of Paula and Somerset, in which Paula proved herself 'more woman than Somerset was man' both in her more mature sexuality and in her assiduous pursuit of him across Europe. But Viviette's initiative also derives from her frustrations; she too belongs to Hardy's gallery of emotionally repressed characters. There is a suggestion in her actions of 'the freakishness which is engendered by a sickening monotony', and there is much later a comical account of her temptations to 'be plunging across the ragged boundary which divides the permissible from the forbidden'. But this is an entirely natural response to her predicament, that of a beautiful 29-year-old woman who has been brutally treated by a now-absent husband and who languishes in solitude at Welland House. Her *ennui* resembles that of both Miss Aldclyffe and Mrs Charmond, but what distinguishes Viviette is her unequivocal generosity of spirit, which makes her (in the words Hardy used to describe Paula) 'really lovable'.

With her hair 'black as midnight' and 'Romance blood in her veins', her 'soft dark eyes' and 'slightly voluptuous temperament', she is a passionate heroine in the Hellenic tradition of

Eustacia Vye, of more noble nature (Viviette has more sense and more principle) but equally doomed. Impulsive and spirited, Viviette is a fitting representative of the humane values which the novel sets in opposition to the soulless universe, and her role is sufficiently important for Hardy to make her the most unselfish heroine whom he had yet presented. Her self-immolation in favour of Swithin is admirable: 'To love St Cleeve so far better than herself as this was to surpass the love of women as conventionally understood, and as mostly existing.' In overcoming her natural impulses and in renouncing her claims upon Swithin Viviette demonstrates that circumstance can be overcome by human decisions. That her unselfishness is rewarded with a sudden and unlikely death is a narrative irony which in no way negates the affirmative optimism implicit in Viviette's exemplary loving-kindness.[23] The cruelty is largely to the reader: Viviette dies happily, in the arms of her lover, suddenly and almost painlessly.

Although it may at first seem hard to reconcile Viviette's deception of Bishop Helmsdale with her goodness otherwise, it is made clear that convention and not innate inclination forces her into this desperate dilemma. It is in part effected by the manoeuvring of her devious brother Louis Glanville, an unpleasant relative who returns from afar (like Abner Power in *A Laodicean*) to promote a marriage for his sister which will best benefit himself. But it is of the essence of Viviette's character that her goodness is united to a very forgivable frailty, a certain shallowness shared by most of us. The implication is that she accepts the marriage partly for the sake of the child. And it is an important part of Hardy's design. If we question (as the novel leads us to do) what we feel when faced with the immensities of the heavens, is it not implied that we might well question what we feel when faced with anything else? If, in the terms of Viviette's own quotation from *Hamlet*, nothing is either good or bad but thinking makes it so, can we not apply this to moral questions or matters of belief? Much earlier Viviette has asked: 'Without the Church to cling to, what have we?' and Swithin has provided the answer: 'Each other'. The reply is not just flippant. The story goes on to set off the young astronomer against the older bishop. It is immediately made clear that Viviette is a *dévote* only because of her passions: she seizes only 'the apparatus of religion'. And eventually we have to face the real challenge that our sympathies, unless we have strong principles that prevent them from affecting us, are entirely with this woman who consents to marry a man she does not love and who uses him as a shield against the disgrace of having a bastard son. This is because we have been led to dislike the bishop for good reason and because at heart we entirely sympathise with the two lovers; but most particularly it is a response to Viviette's genuine goodness. We are led just as logically as if we were following the mathematical arguments of an astronomer to reject the conventions not only of society but also those of the Church.

Viviette, in her complexity of temperament and abundance of the life force, is a triumphant creation. It is natural that she should appeal to D. H. Lawrence, who places her in a noble lineage of Hardy's ladies – 'Elfride, Lady Constantine, Marty South, and Tess, all aristocratic, passionate, yet necessarily unfortunate females'.[24] The germ of failure, he says, is within her: 'The physical and spiritual individualist is a fine thing which must fall because of its own isolation, because it is a sport, not in the true line of life: Jude, Tess, Lady Constantine.' This emphasises Viviette's tragic potential: all these isolated individualists are standard-bearers for Hardy's most passionate beliefs. Viviette's 'fall' is poignant not so much in her death as in its prelude. That she should be visited with physical decay (that constant preoccupation of Hardy's) before her unselfishness can reap its earthly reward is genuinely moving, but it is no part of Viviette's philosophy to expect such an earthly benefit. Her individualism is that of 'the purest benevolence ... that charity which "seeketh not her own"', and it is the most hopeful impulse yet revealed in any of the novels.

The novel's ending is ambivalent in so far as it suggests, without making it clear, that Swithin will marry the light-hearted and suggestively named Tabitha Lark, who appears bounding over the fields ('the single bright spot of colour and animation within the wide horizon') even as Viviette dies upon the tower. This union might fulfil the promise implicit in Viviette's charitable renunciation, though Hardy, in a letter to Florence Henniker, suggests an alternative ending:

> History does not record whether Swithin married Tabitha or not. Perhaps when Lady C. was dead he grew passionately attached to her again, as people often do. I suppose the bishop

did find out the secret. Or perhaps he did not.[25]

Hardy is typically wry and teasing and giving nothing away: 'What I discern I will not say.'[26] The ending must remain indeterminately open, like that of *Tess of the d'Urbervilles*. While Tabitha's appearance suggests a conventionally happy ending, Swithin may yet become remorsefully forlorn upon losing Viviette, or he may turn back to telescopes and stars. What is certain is that the love-child of Viviette and Swithin will be well cared for and survive to face the future, and that Viviette's charitable and humane works will not be undone.

Though *Two on a Tower* may have no radically exciting new qualities, it is a novel of poetic charm, unique conception and humane impulses. And like all Hardy's novels it belongs to a consistent and idiosyncratic pattern of exploration of human experience. On 3 June 1882, while writing *Two on a Tower*, Hardy noted:

> As, in looking at a carpet, by following one colour a certain pattern is suggested, by following another colour, another; so in life the seer should watch that pattern among general things which his idiosyncrasy moves him to observe, and describe that alone. This is, quite accurately, a going to Nature; yet the result is no mere photograph, but purely the product of the writer's own mind. (*L*, 153)

Each individual pattern is woven into the whole, and *Two on a Tower* is as surely the product of a writer whose mind is feeling its way towards *The Mayor of Casterbridge* and the novels which followed as any other of the canon.

At the very least the novel, which ran into several editions despite adverse critical notices, met the contemporary demand for romantic fiction and established Hardy in a position of financial security. This in turn enabled him to take his sabbatical writing only shorter works while he contemplated the future course of his fiction. But *Two on a Tower*, for all its faults, has its own sharp and distinctive colour and pattern. The psychic entity of Wessex is shown, briefly, in a celestial perspective and in an individual mode which is not returned to again. Despite Swithin's devotion to stellar grandeur and to science it is (in the phrase Viviette uses in Chapter 4 to describe her 'subject') the 'lamentably human' values that triumph, at least temporarily, as man's will and his charity transcend the forces of darkness and the enthralling powers of the universe. The novel celebrates a turning away from external nature and back to human sympathies. It shares the mood of the poem 'In A Wood', where nature is at last discovered to be indifferent to man and engaged in its own Darwinian animosities. Hardy's own kind, mankind, is at least enlivened by unique qualities and affinities:

> Since, then, no grace I find
>   Taught me of trees,
> Turn I back to my kind,
>   Worthy as these.
> There at least smiles abound,
> There discourse trills around,
> There, now and then, are found
>   Life-loyalties.

It is the 'Life-loyalties' of Viviette that are celebrated and that we appreciate and approve. 'Life-loyalties' furnish the only salvation that can be found; but this implicit optimism is characteristically qualified since its insecurity is made clear. The interior problems of the new scientific age, the rationalism and the psychic isolation, are only with some difficulty being held at arm's length. The emotions will continue to be the casualties in a world of defect.

8 'A fanciful exhibition of the artistic nature': *The Well-Beloved* (1892, 1897)

1

Since *Two on a Tower* marked the end of Hardy's prolonged period of experiment and innovation, and was succeeded by four novels of outstanding cast (*The Mayor of Casterbridge, The Woodlanders, Tess of the d'Urbervilles* and *Jude the Obscure*), the appearance of *The Well-Beloved* (in serial form) in 1892 as his penultimate full-length prose fiction was curious. By any standard *The Well-Beloved* is an oddity. It invites uneasy comparison with the novels of distinction among which it appeared yet in its fabular conception and originality of structure it remains unique in the Hardy canon. But its appearance at this stage of Hardy's career seems less easy to explain than the apparent inequalities of his early years, when the tentativeness of his explorations could account for frequent changes of pace and direction. Taken out of context *The Well-Beloved* might not be recognised for what it is, a late work of a major novelist at the height of his craft.

It was only with the publication of *The Mayor of Casterbridge* (1886) and *The Woodlanders* (1887) that Hardy's stature was firmly established. Though their reviews as usual contain some verdicts which in retrospect seem eccentric, as well as increased charges of pessimism, critics found in these novels a consistency of purpose and concentration of dramatic power that had previously been only intermittently evident. When *The Mayor of Casterbridge* was published Hardy was still regarded as uneven and unpredictable. In October 1886 Gerard Manley Hopkins wrote to his friend Robert Bridges:

> How admirable are Blackmore and Hardy! ... Do you know the bonfire scene in the *Return of the Native* and still better the sword-exercise scene in the *Madding Crowd*, breathing epic? or the wife-sale in the *Mayor of Casterbridge* (read by chance)? But

these writers only rise to their great strokes, they do not write continuously well.[1]

This is true of Hardy, though he was much superior to Blackmore, and this unevenness had not led his readers to expect the masterpieces still to appear. But Hardy had refined his craft through nine novels, varied in mode and content and each with its own distinction, and the maturity of these final novels represents, to borrow Pound's image for the poetry, the harvest of all that had gone before.

These years saw not only the consolidation of Hardy's enduring reputation in prose fiction but also the expansion of his sales. Publishers' figures record commercial success rather than artistic value, but they are revealing about the change in Hardy's status as a popular author between the publication of *The Mayor of Casterbridge* and *Jude the Obscure*. On its publication (10 May 1886) *The Mayor of Casterbridge* sold about 650 copies and 37 were remaindered. *The Woodlanders* (15 March 1887) sold more than 800 copies, with 170 remainders, but a one-volume re-issue later in the year was published in two impressions of 2,000 copies each. *Tess of the d'Urbervilles* sold out all 1,000 copies on initial publication (29 November 1891), with second and third impressions of 500 copies each appearing in February 1892 and a fourth (probably 500 copies again) in March. In a one-volume edition, first published in September, *Tess* sold 17,000 copies in five impressions by the end of the year. *Jude the Obscure* was published on 1 November 1895, and by 15 February following sales had reached their twentieth thousand.

Hostile reviews undoubtedly quickened sales, which may have afforded Hardy some satisfaction in the face of the adverse criticism that he suffered, but the extent of the controversy which surrounded *Tess* and *Jude* is also a measure of Hardy's stature and the seriousness with which his fiction was now received. He was now the leading novelist of his time, but he could surprise as much as he could disturb and in this context of literary eminence *The Well-Beloved* made its unlikely appearance. It is at first hard to understand why Hardy wrote this curious tale at a time in his career when it would seem incongruous, or why five years later, with the masterpieces of *Tess* and *Jude* still fresh in the reading public's mind, Hardy authorised its publication in book form when he had not done so immediately after its serial publication.

Perhaps in the aftermath of *Jude the Obscure* he wanted to demonstrate that that novel did not contain all his essence as a novelist and to show his flexibility again to a readership ever prone to fasten upon one or other characteristic of each of his major works. Perhaps there was some economic consideration, since he was henceforward to devote himself to the less lucrative publication of poetry. But perhaps Hardy was drawn by something more personal, something obliquely autobiographical. Despite the slightness of conception and some weaknesses in execution, *The Well-Beloved* enjoys Hardy's emotional commitment. The fantastic tale, superficially little more than a geometrical exercise in structure riding on the theme of Shelleyan-Platonic idealism, is ingenious in some of its particulars, it bears an unexpected affinity with *Jude the Obscure*, and it is a final palimpsest through which to glimpse the author.

The circumstances of composition and publication offer some explanation for the curious qualities of *The Well-Beloved*. In February 1892 Hardy wrote to Harper's that the story was 'short and slight, and written entirely with a view to serial publication', and insisted that it should not be published in book form until it had been rewritten (Purdy, p.95). Its inception as a serial dates back to an agreement signed by Hardy and Tillotson's newspaper syndicate on 14 February 1890. Five months earlier the agreement to publish *Too Late Beloved* (the original title of *Tess of the d'Urbervilles*) had been cancelled, and now Hardy agreed to provide something more suitable. But he was still busy writing and then bowdlerizing both *Tess* and the stories in *A Group of Noble Dames*, and he did not begin 'The Pursuit of the Well-Beloved' (as the serial was called) until autumn 1891.

Chastened and wearied by the mutilations he had been forced to practise, despite his eminent reputation, Hardy was again labouring to produce something innocuous for the tender serial public. It is exasperating to see that at the height of his career Hardy was still at the mercy of timid editors, and the pains and humiliations he had to endure call on our sympathy. It is hard, therefore, to understand Hardy's willingness to conform with the serial conventions which he so despised as promoting 'not upward advance but lateral advance' and doing so 'under the censorship of prudery'.[2] It could be argued that he was now secure enough to be able to brave the conventions head-on, to omit entirely the serial stage and thus spare himself the increasingly irksome humiliations involved in the compromise required of him. But the equivocation in Hardy's stand was perhaps less a function of his temperament or an ultimate failure of courage than a question of economics, so that to the end his dealings with editors of serial publications, more than any other single factor outside his creative powers, directed the course of his career in prose fiction.

The composition of *The Well-Beloved* again required Hardy to tread softly. Despite his contempt for 'the present lording of nonage over maturity',[3] a prospectus submitted by Hardy to Tillotson's on 17 December 1891 shows him forced to make the familiar obeisance to the interests of the Young Person:

> There is not a word or scene in this tale which can offend the most fastidious taste; and it is equally suited for the reading of young people, and for that of persons of maturer years. (Purdy, p.95)

And on 29 January following Hardy was assuring Clement K. Shorter, editor of the *Illustrated London News*, in which the tale was to be serialised, that there was 'no cutting out required' and that 'every word can be circulated freely in schools and families – ay in nurseries.'[4] The serial appeared in twelve issues of the *Illustrated London News* (1 October–7 December 1892). In a subsequent Preface (August 1912) Hardy refers to it as an 'experimental issue', and he was clearly dissatisfied with its original form. Refusing to publish *The Well-Beloved* as a book until it had been revised, Hardy turned his attention to *Jude the Obscure*, which was begun in 1893.

In autumn 1896, four years after the serialisation of 'The Pursuit of the Well-Beloved', Hardy took up the tale again. Radical alterations were made to the beginning and end of the story, and many shorter passages were added or omitted. These textual variations are of some importance and will be examined. The progress of Hardy's revision may be inferred from his letters to Florence Henniker. At the end of the year he had been 'hard pressed in sending off the copy of *The Well-Beloved* to the printers', but by 24 January 1897 his task was completed: 'I have today finished the correction of the little sketch or story of *The Well-Beloved* (which is to come out I believe next month, and might come out now but for America).'[5] Though publication was scheduled for February an unexpected demand caused publication to be postponed until 16 March; a second edition was issued on 3 April and a third was announced a week later.

No doubt the novel's sales benefited from the notoriety of *Jude the Obscure*, as Hardy had perhaps foreseen. He wrote to Mrs Henniker on 27 April that '*The Well-Beloved* is selling remarkably well for a book written so many years ago (except the three or four last chapters).' But its success was brief, and since then *The Well-Beloved* has not been popular. Hardy himself looked back on it in another letter to Mrs Henniker eight years later: 'It was called, I remember, when it was published, the worst novel of the year, which perhaps it was.' But this is the typical self-deprecation that we have come to expect from Hardy, and he seems pleased to record in the same letter that 'it seems to have come to life again.'

The suggestion of some critics that *The Well-Beloved* is Hardy's deliberate farewell to prose, with its intimation of 'Prospero-like book burning' (as Michael Millgate describes it in *Thomas Hardy: His Career as a Novelist*) in Jocelyn Pierston's final incinerative actions towards his own sculptures, cannot be supported, since Hardy went on to write *Jude the Obscure*. The appearance of *The Well-Beloved* in 1897 seems an issue of circumstance rather than design. But, placed there, the work does have the individual distinction of bringing to a discreet close Hardy's career as a novelist. For with the final revisions of *The Well-Beloved* for book publication

> ended his prose contributions to literature (beyond two or three short sketches to fulfil engagements), his experiences of the few preceding years having killed all his interest in this form of imaginative work. (*L*, 286)

But his decision was already made. Notwithstanding the reviews of *Tess* and *Jude*, the 'experiences' to which Hardy alludes here, their role can be overstressed. The image of Hardy hounded from the platform of prose fiction by indignant critics is misleading. It is more likely that he had nothing more to say in prose that could not be better expressed in poetry, and that Hardy's more positive motive for abandoning the novel form was the urgency of his desire to distil his unique vision into verse, in which, he had long believed, 'was concentrated the essence of all imaginative and emotional literature' (*L*, 48).

2

Hardy had yet to endure some final pains inflicted by a few hostile critics, their minds so keenly trained on the alleged improprieties of *Jude the Obscure* that the newly published novel was bound to suffer from their righteous indignation. Yet it is typical of his career that even on the appearance of so apparently Platonic a story as this Hardy was to find himself in critical trouble over his presentation of sexuality. It is not entirely surprising. Hardy was temperamentally incapable of subduing in his fiction his concern with the sexual impulses which most powerfully motivate men's actions, and his awareness of all that follows in the wake of what he calls (in the Preface to *Jude*) 'the strongest passion known to humanity'. Even when he writes a story more fabular than realistic, treating idealistic philosophy and the psychic migration of one man's love for a succession of women over a period of 40 years, he cannot negate the sexuality implicit in his theme. This being so, it is hard to understand the violence of Hardy's reaction to criticism.

In the month of the novel's publication its author was protesting bitterly about the misrepresentations of reviewers. He retained a letter from Edmund Gosse on 16 March consoling him over one sharp attack in a periodical (DCM). But the review which excited Hardy's most extreme indignation was that which appeared in the *World* (24 March 1897) and which, in the course of a very censorious notice, described the 'Wessex-mania of Mr Thomas Hardy' as one of the 'most unpleasant' forms of 'sex-mania' in his fiction. Hardy said that the article combined 'personal abuse' and 'mendacious malice' and felt that it had been written by a reviewer 'blinded by malignity' (*L*, 286). The day after it appeared he wrote to his friend, Sir George Douglas:

> The one amazing thing about [*The Well-Beloved*] is the review it has received in *The World*. That a fanciful, tragi-comic half allegorical tale of a poor visionary pursuing a vision should be stigmatized as sexual and disgusting is I think a piece of mendacity hard to beat in the annals of the press, & the low cunning with which the charge is insinuated rather than asserted would be shocking if it were not a trifle comic.[6]

Six days later Hardy repeated his charge to Florence Henniker, though in a less petulant and more reflective tone:

... my poor little innocent book *The Well-Beloved* has had a horrid stab delivered it in one quarter, *The World*, which is as unaccountable as it is base. You will imagine how it amazed me when one of my reasons for letting the story be reprinted was that it cld not by any possibility offend Mrs or Mr Grundy, or their Young Persons, even though it cld be called unreal and impossible for a man to have such an artistic craze for the Ideal in woman as the hero has. It is truly the unexpected that happens.[7]

The accusations of 'unmentionable moral atrocities' rankled deeply, and of the *World*'s review Hardy remarked in yet another letter that 'a reviewer *himself* afflicted with "sex mania" might review so – a thing terrible to think of'; but Hardy was surely less than frank when he wrote to Swinburne that 'the writer's meaning is beyond me' (*L*, 287). Declaring his intention not to reply to the vicious review, it was to a journal whose review was moderate and often laudatory that Hardy turned to make his only statement in print. In a letter written to the *Academy* on 29 March (published 3 April) Hardy explains the genesis of the 'ultra-romantic notion of the tale'. He reveals that

it was sketched many years before [i.e. before 1892, the date of serial publication], when I was comparatively a young man, and interested in the Platonic Idea, which, considering its charm and its poetry, one could well wish to be interested in always.

Underlying the fantasy, Hardy says, exists

the truth that all men are pursuing a shadow, the Unattainable, and I venture to hope that this may redeem the tragicomedy from the charge of frivolity, or of being built upon a baseless conceit.

The story which is structured upon the Platonic theory is fantastic enough, and *The Well-Beloved* is well placed among the 'Romances and Fantasies'. The basis of idealistic philosophy is that a man loves not the reality of a woman but the vision or image of her that exists in his own mind. It follows that a man may seek his ideal in a succession of different women. There is nothing unusual about this, but Hardy extends the notion over 40 years of one man's life, adopting this pursuit of the ideal as the structural principle of his tale. The sculptor Jocelyn Pierston suffers through 'the theory of the transmigration of the ideal beloved one, who only exists in the lover, from material woman to material woman' (*L*, 286). He suffers because the phenomenon is subjective, a function of his own mind, and because he can never locate his ideal for long in any one woman.

On 19 February 1889 Hardy had conceived that the idea of 'the story of a face which goes through three generations or more, would make a fine novel or poem on the passage of Time' (*L*, 217). It is the immutable genetically inherited face of the poem 'Heredity' which is invoked in the story:

I am the family face;
Flesh perishes, I live on,
Projecting trait and trace
Through time to times anon,
And leaping from place to place
Over oblivion.
. . .
The eternal thing in man,
That heeds no call to die.

The structural idea of Jocelyn's love for Avice Caro, her daughter and her granddaughter, a successive love for three generations of the 'family face', is unlikely though not impossible. It is a poetic and challenging notion. Taking his epigraph from Shelley – 'One shape of many names'[8] – Hardy presents the distressing spectacle of his hero in pursuit of an elusive quantity. For most of his life Jocelyn's sexuality is merely cerebral. D. H. Lawrence, who believed man to be much stronger in feeling than in thought, was bound to dislike the Platonic restraint of the story: '*The Well-Beloved* is sheer rubbish, fatuity,'[9] he wrote.

Far from being 'sheer rubbish', however, *The Well-Beloved* dramatises a fundamental aspect of Hardy's tragic vision. The theme of pursuit of an impossible ideal permeates his work and most often takes the form of the pursuit of a woman. In his poem, 'The Chosen', the speaker has sought his ideal in five women, without success: though each in turn proves 'a passable maid' he discovers that 'charms outwear'. The novel's companion poem, 'The Well-Beloved', shows the tragedy (which is Jocelyn's in the novel) implicit in loving the idealised vision rather than the real woman. The vision separates itself from the speaker's bride, in whom it has had residence, and tells the groom: 'Thou lovest what thou dreamest her;/I am thy very dream!/... I wed no mortal man!' The idealisation is lifted and the bride is left 'pinched and thin,/As if her soul had shrunk and died.' The moral is one that Hardy had recognised in a note written when he was beginning *The Well-Beloved*:

> October 28 [1891]. It is the incompleteness that is loved, when love is sterling and true. That is what differentiates the real one from the imaginary, the practicable from the impossible, the Love who returns the kiss from the Vision that melts away. A man sees the Diana or Venus in his Beloved, but what he loves is the difference. (*L*, 239)

Time after time Hardy's characters lack this perception and the results are tragic. In the novel which preceded the serialisation of 'The Pursuit of the Well-Beloved' Tess seems to Angel Clare 'merely a soul at large ... a visionary essence of woman ... He called her Artemis, Demeter, and other fanciful names' (*Tess of the d'Urbervilles*, Phase the Third, Chapter 20). But Angel rejects her when his knowledge of Tess's seduction by Alec destroys this fanciful image:

> She knew that he saw her without irradiation – in all her bareness; that Time was chanting his satiric psalm at her then –
> Behold, when thy face is made bare, he that loved thee shall hate. (Phase the Fifth, Chapter 35)

Jude is also in pursuit of the well-beloved, which first finds its unlikely residence in Arabella, of whom Jude has initially a similarly fanciful conception: 'his idea of her was the thing of most consequence, not Arabella herself, he sometimes said laconically' (*Jude the Obscure*, Part First, Chapter 9). But it is not long before 'Arabella herself' is revealed to him, whereupon it is Sue who becomes 'almost an ideality to him' (Part Second, Chapter 4). Yet Jude, the 'dreamer of dreams ... a tragic Don Quixote' (Part Fourth, Chapter 1), has still to suffer further disillusionments in love and the disintegration of his vision.

Hardy's fiction is peopled with tragic Don Quixotes who possess a catastrophic inability to accept that, for love to flourish, reality must sooner or later supplant the imaginary ideal. Jocelyn Pierston, however, enjoys a perception which they lack, and conversely his tragedy lies in the extent of his self-knowledge. It is a capacity for recognition shared only by the cynical Fitzpiers, who tells Giles that 'Human love is a subjective thing ... joy accompanied by an idea that we project against any suitable object in our line of vision' (*The Woodlanders*, Chapter 16).

Jocelyn must search (to quote another verse of the poem from which Hardy takes his epigraph for Part First) 'Till that divine/ Idea take a shrine/Of crystal flesh, through which to shine.'[10] *The Well-Beloved* is distinguished by Jocelyn's ability to understand and isolate the nature of his problem (even if he cannot penetrate its cause), the errant vision of which successive women are only transient conditions: 'Essentially she was perhaps of no tangible substance; a spirit, a dream, a frenzy, a conception, an aroma, an epitomized sex, a light of the eye, a parting of the lips.' He half suspects the vision to be Aphrodite herself, Sappho's 'Weaver of wiles', teasing and tormenting him for translating the beauty of successive embodiments of the vision into sculpture.

The humour of Jocelyn's dilemma is not avoided and the history of his involvements is entertainingly catalogued: 'Four times she masqueraded as a brunette, twice as a pale-haired creature, and two or three times under a complexion neither light nor dark' in one period, and the vision is later said to have appeared in numerous occupational embodiments including 'a dancing-girl at the Royal Moorish Palace of Varieties'. But its tantalising qualities are basically serious and distressing. Jocelyn tells his painter friend Alfred Somers:

> To see the creature who has hitherto been perfect, divine, lose under your very gaze the divinity which has informed her, grow commonplace, turn from flame to ashes, from a radiant vitality to a relic, is anything but a pleasure to any man, and has been nothing less than a racking spectacle to my sight.

But for his perception Jocelyn would be a typical Hardy male, blindly aspiring to realise the unattainable and bound to fail. Even now, though he can define his intellectual problem, he cannot master it. Yet the impossibility of an ideal solution does not diminish his struggles to achieve one, to entrap his vision in one corporeal residence.

In revising the story Hardy toned down a number of remarks about marriage and at the same time took the opportunity to enhance the theme's more philosophic and imaginative qualities, so that the notion of idealistic philosophy and the Platonic Idea more comprehensively informs the tale, distancing its already fabular mode yet further from realism. But this does not make Jocelyn's problem more esoteric. Though it is romanticised, poeticised and presented *in extremis* spanning three generations, his condition is basically that of many (possibly all) men. The practical Somers recognises this when he tells Jocelyn: 'You are like other men, only rather worse. Essentially all men are fickle, like you; but not with such perceptiveness.' This universal application, usually overlooked, makes Hardy's theme much less nonsensical than many commentators have found it and aligns the story with one of his familiar imaginative preoccupations. The idea is carried further in a sensible review in the *Athenaeum* (10 April 1897). Hardy has, the reviewer says,

> imagined a temperament which we believe to be that of the great majority of male human beings ... But conscious as most people must be of possibilities of this kind in themselves, 'it is,' as Mr Hardy's hero says, 'a sort of thing one doesn't like to speak of.'

It is neither instinct nor temperament, the reviewer suggests, but 'hard reason aided in certain cases by the policeman, [that] alone can persuade the normal man to monogamy'. These shrewd and refreshingly straightforward observations, almost unnoticed beside the moral indignation of some other critics, touch upon a latent and challenging substratum in the novel. Hardy's presentation of Jocelyn frankly acknowledges an immutable facet of human nature and male psychology, thus posing an implicit challenge to marital conventions. And it is here that the novel betrays an unexpected affinity with its notorious successor.

The Well-Beloved is basically motivated by the same impulse which afterwards directed *Jude the Obscure*. Though their modes are disparate, and the earlier work has a much less obviously tragic issue, the serial version of *The Well-Beloved*, containing

several subsequently omitted passages which directly prefigure
Jude, makes explicit the thematic unity of the two novels. One
episode survived the serialisation of *The Well-Beloved* to become
common to both novels: Jocelyn's drying of Marcia's clothes
after the storm (Part First, Chapter 5) parallels Jude's drying of
Sue's (*Jude the Obscure*, Part Third, Chapters 3–4). One phrase is
omitted from the episode in the book of *The Well-Beloved*, perhaps
to avert perverse critical charges of lubricity, intimating that
Jocelyn 'kissed each of the articles of apparel'.[11] Other omissions
are more important and turn upon two important alterations to
the story. In the serial Jocelyn marries Marcia: Part First,
Chapter 8, is entirely rewritten for the book, having originally
shown Jocelyn and Marcia returning from a continental honeymoon. The rift between them, initiated as in the book by the
arrival of a letter from Marcia's former suitor, and which in the
later version is effected through correspondence, here continues
'in the home of these hastily wedded ones'.[12] Their problems,
exacerbated by the family feud, engender reflections on the
marital condition that directly anticipate identical sentiments in
Jude:

> In their ill-matched junction on the strength of a two or three
> days' passion they felt the full irksomeness of a formal tie
> which, as so many have discovered, did not become necessary
> till it was a cruelty to them.
>   A legal marriage it was, but not a true marriage. In the
> night they heard sardonic voices and laughter in the wind at
> the ludicrous facility accorded them by events for taking a step
> in two days which they could not retrace in a lifetime, despite
> their mutual desire as the two persons solely concerned.[13]

The Well-Beloved is the poorer for the loss of this image of ironic
mockery, and the omission of these passages undoubtedly
deprives the novel of some of its original point and substance.
Marcia's bitter appeals against legal oppression parallel Sue's:

> 'Was there ever anything more absurd in history,' she said
> bitterly to him one day, 'than that grey-headed legislators
> from time immemorial should have gravely based inflexible
> laws upon the ridiculous dream of young people that a
> transient mutual desire for each other was going to last for

ever!'[14]

And, like Sue, Marcia is a modern, unafraid to be a pioneer. In her last letter to Jocelyn she tells him: 'I fail to see why, in making each our own home, we should not make our own matrimonial laws if we choose. This may seem an advanced view, but I am not afraid of advanced views.'[15]

If Jocelyn is Jude to Marcia's Sue, he is also Phillotson in relation to Avice the third, and he marries her too in the serial. By this time he is comparatively an old man who has suffered 40 years of 'love-tempest' and the future is not appealing to Avice. After the honeymoon, when they are established in their Queen Anne house in London, Jocelyn enters their bedroom late one night, Avice having retired earlier:

> When he moved forward his light awoke her; she started up as if from a troublous dream, and regarded him with something in her open eye that was not unlike dread. It was so unmistakeable that Pearston felt half paralysed ... All of a sudden he felt that he had no moral right to go further.[16]

The similarity between this and the almost identical incident involving Phillotson and Sue need not be laboured. Phillotson also inherits the magnanimity originally attributed to Jocelyn. Aware of his repulsiveness to Avice, Jocelyn decides that by an 'act of charity he will break the laws and ordinances'.[17] Discovering that Avice's former suitor is nearby and dangerously ill, and learning from Avice that she has met him but commanded him to see her no more, Jocelyn is affected to tears by his wife's misery and determines by some scheme to release her from the marital bond. Just as Phillotson confides in his friend Gillingham, Jocelyn disburdens himself to his old friend Alfred Somers:

> 'Now,' proceeded Pearston, 'some husbands, I suppose, would have sent the young man about his business, and put the young woman under lock-and-key till she came to her senses. This was what I could not do. At first I felt it to be a state of things for which there was no remedy. But I considered that to allow everything to remain *in statu quo* was inanimate, inhuman conduct, worthy only of a vegetable ...

Don't attack me for casuistry, artifice, for contumelious treatment of the laws of my country. A law which, in a particular instance, results in physical cruelty to the innocent deserves to be evaded in that instance if it can be done without injury to anyone.'[18]

These instances indicate the extent of Hardy's quarrying in *The Well-Beloved* for material for his next novel. Unfortunately the excision of these passages leaves the narrative rather limp in parts and relieves the story of some of its dramatic tension as well as its most challenging social and moral protests. Yet Jocelyn's marriages to Marcia and Avice the third are profitably discarded, simultaneously tightening the structure and shaping a neater conclusion that accords better with the story's sub-title, 'A Sketch of a Temperament'.[19] The Platonic Idea is now shown in defeat as cold realism breaks through in the form of the aged Marcia and in Jocelyn's effectual abandonment of his artistic ideals. *The Well-Beloved* foreshadows *Jude* not only in theme and tendency but also in certain particulars. The serial version discloses Jocelyn as a prototype for aspects of Jude and Phillotson and shows that Marcia and Avice the third anticipate characteristics of Sue Bridehead. Yet it is possible to make too much of this for in other ways the books are very different, and to suggest that *The Well-Beloved* was a preliminary sketch for *Jude the Obscure* would be wrong. But it does show that Hardy was already formulating and testing ideas, and his subsequent plundering of the earlier text is surely one explanation of Hardy's long delay in authorising the book version.

The degree of the novel's affinity with *Jude* raises the recurrent question of Hardy's identification with his central character, and of how far Jocelyn's experience may represent an oblique commentary on Hardy's own career as an artist. Though biographical inferences are treacherous and require caution, the internal evidence here is persuasive. *The Well-Beloved* is structured upon the theory of idealistic philosophy, but the Platonic Idea is the vehicle, not the subject, of the story. In common with most of Hardy's novels one of its subjects is the author himself. Hardy and Jocelyn have much in common, though the omission of some further passages in the revised version makes the comparison slightly more elusive. That Hardy shared with Jocelyn a lifelong attraction to young ladies is well known. Even as an octogenarian he was very charming and chivalrous with pretty young women, whose beauty he had always celebrated in his poetry just as Jocelyn immortalises them in sculpture. Hardy's definition of Pierston's dilemma may conceal a wryly ironic reference to his own condition: 'His record moved on with the years, his sentiment stood still,' so that like those 'buffers and fogeys', his contemporaries, he had not 'got past the distracting currents of passionateness' and into 'the calm waters of middle-aged philosophy'.

The suggestiveness of the comparison is enhanced by Pierston's later lament: 'When was it to end – this curse of his heart not ageing while his frame moved naturally onward?' It is a threnody common to the narrator's in 'I Look into my Glass':

> I look into my glass,
> And view my wasting skin,
> And say, 'Would God it came to pass
> My heart had shrunk as thin!'

That *this* narrator also represents Hardy is virtually confirmed in the author's note of 18 October 1892 (simultaneous with the novel's serial publication):

> I look into the glass. Am conscious of the humiliating sorriness of my earthly tabernacle ... Why should a man's mind have been thrown into such close, sad, sensational, inexplicable relations with such a precarious object as his own body! (*L*, 251)

Hardy's own 'throbbings of noontide' shaking his 'fragile frame at eve' ('I Look into my Glass', Stanza 3) are perceptively observed in a poem by May O'Rourke, his secretary between 1923 and 1928, describing him as an octogenarian 'with April in his eyes,/And winter on his face.'[20]

The division between Hardy and Emma, the disaffection of 'hearts grown cold' in the poem already quoted, also seems obliquely present in the novel. Jocelyn's fear of 'being chained in fatal fidelity to an object that his intellect despised' shows a caution taught by the author's own experience. Yet more local similarities emerge in the serial. Of the ill-matched marriage of Jocelyn and Marcia, Hardy here observes that

that gradual substitution of friendship, which is indispensable and, perhaps, usual in marriage, was not possible with natures so jarring as these. ... The Well-Beloved had quite vanished away. What had become of her Pearston knew not, but not a line of her was any longer discoverable in Marcia's contours, not a sound of her in Marcia's accents.[21]

Marcia wears the un-idealised form of the later Emma, she who 'had changed from the one who was all'[22] to Hardy. Even the courtship of Jocelyn and Marcia suffers similar social inhibitions, and the sculptor, like Hardy, is a social and geographical *déraciné* now rising to eminence:

In birth the pair were about equal, but Marcia's family had gained a start in the accumulation of wealth and in the initiation of social distinction, which lent a colour to the feeling that the advantages of the match had been mainly on one side. Nevertheless, Pearston was a sculptor rising to fame by fairly rapid strides; and potentially the marriage was not a bad one for a woman who ... had no exceptional opportunities.[23]

But it is not only the vicissitudes of Hardy's marriage to Emma that seem to be reflected in the novel. Jocelyn's later speculations about the possible condition of Marcia 'in the sere' recall Hardy's own 'Thoughts of Phena', written in March of the previous year.

In view of this the original opening chapter, omitted entirely from the book, is especially suggestive. In the poem the speaker (evidently Hardy) laments: 'Not a line of her writing have I,/ Not a thread of her hair.' In the discarded opening chapter, entitled 'Relics', Jocelyn is discovered discreetly burning old love letters and a lock of hair:

He cut the string, loosened the letters, and kindled another match. The flames illumined the handwriting, which sufficiently recalled to his knowledge her from whom that batch had come, and enabled him to read tender words and fragments of sentences written to him in his teens by the writer. Many of the sentiments, he was ashamed to think, he

had availed himself of in some attempts at lyric verse, as
having in them that living fire which no lucubration can
reach. ...

Suddenly there arose a little fizzle in the dull flicker:
something other than paper was burning. It was hair – *her*
hair.

'Good heavens!' said the budding sculptor to himself, 'How
can I be such a brute? I am burning *her* – part of her form.'[24]

A similar real-life conflagration some time before could account
for the speaker's predicament in 'Thoughts of Phena'. And, in
common with Jocelyn, Hardy's own 'attempts at lyric verse' (the
first volume of which was not published until 1898, the year after
the book version of *The Well-Beloved*, from which this potential
biographical clue is perhaps significantly omitted) abound with
autobiographical recollections of the real and imagined loves of a
lifetime. The 'ghosts of Isabella, Florence, Winifred, Lucy, Jane
and Evangeline' which arise from Jocelyn's second batch of
burnt letters imaginatively correspond to the many young
women celebrated in Hardy's poems, to Tryphena herself or
Louisa Harding, or perhaps to the village beauties who caught
the young Hardy's eye, Elizabeth B —- ['sweet Lizbie Browne'],
Emily D —-, Rachel H —- and Alice P —-, all recalled in a note
by the author a few years earlier.[25] Perhaps Jocelyn's disposal of
his amorous relics may imply the nature of at least some of the
materials submitted to bonfires, both before and by direction
after his death, by Hardy. The sculptor's deliberate impulse to
concealment is reiterated in another abandoned passage in the
third chapter of the serial: 'Determined to run no further risk, he
set about destroying [more] letters there and then. He went into
the garden, threw them down, made a loose heap of a portion,
and put a match to the windy side.'[26] Like his creator, Jocelyn is
quietly intent on covering his tracks. When asked by Avice what
he is burning, his offhand reply is as casually vague as Hardy's
could be: 'O, only some papers ...'[27]

In view of the obvious affinity between Hardy and his hero the
novel's exposition of the creative artist bears added (and often
bitter) point. In so far as the story is conceived as 'A Sketch of a
Temperament', or (as the author described it to Swinburne) 'a
fanciful exhibition of the artistic nature',[28] there can be little
doubt that it is as much about Hardy's artistic temperament as

Jocelyn's. (The personal analogies have been identified by Helmut Gerber.[29]) Like *A Pair of Blue Eyes* nearly two decades earlier, *The Well-Beloved* reveals the practising artist's preoccupation with critics, compromise, reputation and commercial success, and it shares with *The Hand of Ethelberta* a real, though moderated, contempt for drawing-room society and its tasteless and superficial attitude to art. Jocelyn Pierston is an idealist, a true artist who 'would have gone on working with his chisel with just as much zest if his creations had been doomed to meet no mortal eye but his own'. In contrast, his painter friend Alfred Somers is shrewd, practical and as willing to compromise in his art as he will opportunistically marry Nichola Pine-Avon. He finds a happiness that eludes the more fastidious Jocelyn, who suffers pains over sacrificing the integrity of his art to the capricious whims of critics and the public.

Eventually Jocelyn's disillusionment leads him to despise his work, apostrophising his creations in the words of the prophet Isaiah: 'Instead of sweet smell there shall be stink, and there shall be burning instead of beauty' (Isaiah, Chapter 3, verse 24). He is no longer in pursuit of the well-beloved. Since the artist's pursuit of the unattainable furnishes his main inspiration, he must renounce art once this goal is achieved or no longer desired. At the end Jocelyn's role is no longer that of the visionary artist. Gerber and other commentators interpret Jocelyn's creative decline as Hardy's deliberate farewell to novel-writing, an embittered leave-taking of prose fiction:

> At present he is sometimes mentioned as 'the late Mr Pierston' by gourd-like young art-critics and journalists; and his productions are alluded to as those of a man not without genius, whose powers were insufficiently recognized in his own lifetime.

Since this concluding paragraph was newly written for the book, and these are Hardy's feelings about his own critical treatment, a valedictory undertone is entirely plausible. But while Hardy's life experience inevitably contributes intimately to the creation of Jocelyn, in his world-weariness, frustrated idealism, integrity and disillusionments over the artist's lot, a complete identification of the artistic temperaments of author and character is too determinedly biocritical. It is doubtful that there is any such conscious direction in the larger conception of the novel, and inferences about Hardy's valedictory intention are only speculative. *The Well-Beloved* could hardly have been planned as his final novel, since *Jude the Obscure* had been conceived in essence, and the absurdity of regarding Jocelyn as a literal portrait of Hardy is emphasised by the sculptor's eventual fate. He becomes utterly insensitive in a manner abhorrent to Hardy: 'finding his sense of beauty in art and nature absolutely extinct', Jocelyn is transformed into an uncontemplative modern, a practical man engaged in the most mundane acts of aesthetic vandalism.

The philosophy of these 'improvements' is all the more repugnant to Hardy in view of his reverence for traditional cultural values. In sharp contrast to Jocelyn's works is Hardy's prefatory celebration of the island, with its ancient customs and buildings, 'the home of a curious and well-nigh distinct people'. The sense of place in *The Well-Beloved* is of the essence. Here the Isle of Slingers (Portland) takes the place of the more familiar Wessex landscapes as the objective correlative of Hardy's historical consciousness. Bearing the stamp of 'centuries immemorial', almost literally insular, and poetic in its comparative isolation, the Isle appeals directly to Hardy's sensibilities, and he invests the 'peninsula carved by Time out of a single stone' (Preface) with a powerful dramatic presence, allowing it to brood over its inhabitants, a fit and timeless setting against which the rigidly schematic chronological pattern of the story can be thrown into relief.

The immutability of the geographical locations, exactly identified and which recur with all their historical and personal associations, provides a counterpoint to the vicissitudes of the sculptor's emotional life. The place exercises a magnetic effect on its inhabitants, who are inevitably, like Hardy to Dorset, drawn back from wherever their wanderings have taken them. Jocelyn is a true scion of his original environment, a 'native of natives' whose peculiar talents have, again like Hardy, been nurtured in this romantic setting. It is a genealogy that he shares with all three Avices. Their common descent among the 'old island breed', and the racial consciousness which permeates the Isle, are features given new prominence in the revised version, and numerous additional sentences and paragraphs enhance the pervasive sense of history.[30] Heard on the wind are 'the stones of the slingers whizzing past, and the voices of the invaders who annihilated them', the battle sounds of the subsequently inter-married progenitors of the common stock to which all local inhabitants belong. The 'ground-quality' which distinguishes Avice from all the other Well-Beloveds is newly stressed: Jocelyn could never love long a 'kimberlin' (a woman not of the island race). His fate is interlaced with ancient superstition which antedates Christianity itself.

In all particulars the preservation of the island's traditional integrity *in statu quo* is the ideal promoted by Hardy. Despite early fears of Avice Caro the first's submission to 'the tendency of the age', the modern vice of unrest and its concomitant neuroses have scarcely penetrated the unsophisticated but vital community. Yet the tendencies of the future are even here finally inescapable, and there is a relished irony in Jocelyn's becoming the instrument of destruction in his demolition of fine Elizabethan cottages 'because they were damp' in favour of 'new ones with hollow walls, and full of ventilators'. Once again architecture is invoked as a social and ethical touchstone as the insidious process of modernisation, heralded by Ethelberta and Paula and Somerset, by Farfrae and by Fitzpiers, by the endeavours of a more restless generation, is shown in continua-tion. But here there is a curious and poignant sense of betrayal in that it is one of the Isle's most sensitive and visionary sons who eventually becomes the agent of unimaginative modernism: now the canker is being generated from within.

Apart from this almost weary acceptance of the intractability of cultural decay there is elsewhere in the novel no dominant sense of social prophecy. There is nothing fierce about the London society satire, which briefly returns after being aban-doned since *The Hand of Ethelberta,* where the contrast with homely rurality is similarly invoked. Though Hardy is contemp-tuous of the gathering's 'one great utterance of the opinions of the hour' he accuses the Countess of Channelcliffe's assembly of nothing more serious than a 'paucity of original ideas'. Perhaps his own increasing attendance at such crushes, at least as frequent as Jocelyn's is implied to be, had led Hardy to tolerate and even approve of them. The extent of Hardy's social life is made clear in the *Life* and even clearer in the social passages which were omitted from the published version, and his notes do not disguise his enjoyment.

Hardy appears to have drawn on personal experiences

immediately preceding the novel for the society scenes, and his own records contain no criticism of these gatherings. In December 1890 Hardy 'chanced to find himself in political circles for a time'; soon afterwards, at another house, he 'chanced to converse with the Dowager Duchess of Marlborough' and cheerfully records the latest political gossip (a practice vaguely disapproved in the novel): 'She deplores that young men like —— should stand in the fore-front of the Tory party.' (*L*, 230) At another dinner, in July 1891, 'the talk was entirely political – of when the next election would be – of the probable Prime Minister – of ins and outs – of Lord This and the Duke of That – everything except the people for whose existence alone these politicians exist.' (*L*, 238) Something of this Trollopian conclave is imported into the novel, though any implicit criticism is very mild: 'No principles of wise government had place in any mind, a blunt and jolly personalism as to the Ins and Outs animating them all.' The younger Hardy's abrasive radicalism has been moderated by his discovery of the more congenial elements in drawing-room society. Perhaps he had now decided that these society junketings, though mannered and superficial and often extravagant, were basically innocuous as well as enjoyable, and accordingly directed his undiminished humanitarian concern (as in *Tess* and *Jude*, both more fundamentally radical than any of his social satires) to more serious and abiding social injustices.

The tragedy in *The Well-Beloved* is in any case personal and aesthetic rather than social. The subdued social satire is of limited importance, though comedy animates much of the narrative and the incongruities of the fantastic plot and the predicaments of Jocelyn sometimes touch grim farce. Hardy is well aware of the comic perspective in which Jocelyn's late courtship must be cast and he freely exploits it, as in Avice the third's appalled and ingenuous reaction to the sculptor's confession that he has previously been not only her mother's but also her grandmother's young man: ' "And were you my great-grandmother's too?" she asked, with an expectant interest in his case as a drama that overcame her personal consideration for a moment.' Yet Jocelyn is saved from being ludicrous by Hardy's determination that his 'inability to ossify', though wearing the aspect of comedy, is of the nature of tragedy. *The Well-Beloved* is a poetic tragi-comedy and, despite the 'frankly imaginative' (Preface) mode of this 'half allegorical'[31] tale, the conclusion is

more incisive than the story's fabular conception would suggest.
Reality defeats the Platonic Idea, with tragic personal effect,
the romantic vision proving unable to survive physical deterioration. Marcia presents herself no longer in the idealised guise of
the Well-Beloved but now as 'the image and superscription of
Age.' Jocelyn's 'curse' is lifted but at the dreadful cost of
incurring an almost callous insensitivity and emotional sterility.
It is a bleak arrangement indeed, induced only by the pragmat-
ism that henceforward directs his life, that he enters into with
Marcia: '"I have no love to give, you know, Marcia," he said,
"But such friendship as I am capable of is yours till the end."'
Even this grim prospect does not approach the bitterness of the
original conclusion. After an unsuccessful attempt at drowning
himself in a small skiff headed into the dangerous currents of
Race, Jocelyn awakens to find himself in bed at his lodgings in
East Wake and is amazed to discover that the aged Marcia, now
'a wrinkled crone', has returned after 40 years. He sees on the
mantelpiece his enlarged photograph of Avice the third, whom
he had recently married:

> The contrast of the ancient Marcia's aspect, both with this
> portrait and with her own fine former self, brought into his
> brain a sudden sense of the grotesqueness of things. His wife
> was – not Avice, but that parchment-covered skull moving
> about his room. An irresistible fit of laughter, so violent as to
> be an agony, seized upon him, and started in him with such
> momentum that he could not stop it. He laughed and laughed,
> till he was almost too weak to draw breath.
> Marcia hobbled up, frightened. 'What's the matter?' she
> asked; and, turning to a second nurse, 'He is weak-hysterical.'
> 'O – no – no! I – I – it is too, too droll – this ending to my
> would-be romantic history!' Ho-ho-ho![32]

This is a startling, abrupt, dramatically arresting conclusion.
Devoid of the subtlety, muted sadness and resignation of the
revised ending, in its almost cruel farce and invocation of an
unmasking reminiscent of Barbara's literal disillusionment in
'Barbara of the House of Grebe', it exposes with added
sharpness the nature of Jocelyn's tragedy. Perhaps even odder
than the unexpected ending is the way in which Jocelyn's ghastly
and ironic laughter is succeeded by a commentary 'Ho-ho-ho!' of

the narrator's own. Though both endings make explicit Hardy's pessimism over the issue of events, this naked bitterness combines something of the mocking relish of the Spirit Sinister with the sly humour of the Spirit Ironic.

In both versions Jocelyn wins our sympathy. As a truly time-torn man his suffering is ultimately no less intense than that of many of Hardy's more obvious heroes, no more easily endurable for being subtle rather than spectacular, and perhaps harder since it can win no sympathetic recognition from those around him.[33] He shares with the other heroes the pursuit of an unattainable ideal and the bitterness of failure to achieve it. Easily overlooked because he appears in an unusual and often neglected novel, Jocelyn is an honourable descendant of all the dreamers and anti-realists and doomed idealists who people Hardy's psychic world, those who pursue one Idea or other in the face of reality. He is a poetical extreme case of a predominant type whose personations Hardy always champions along their ineluctable course to unfulfilment and defeat. Though the idea of an implacably passionate sculptor in pursuit of the ideal woman is light in conception, the implications of his life course are serious and he becomes a tragic figure. 'Time was against him and love, and time would probably win.' Time inevitably does.

Since Jocelyn's amatory career is superficially so implausible, and since the author (as he says in the Preface) deliberately abjures verisimilitude, Hardy's achievement in making him convincing is the more impressive. A man of Jocelyn's extraordi-nary history might have proved impossible to animate yet he emerges from the schematic contrivances of the plot as a credible, engaging and pitiable character. After the initial sketch of him as a compulsive Don Juan, the persistence of his dream gradually turns his enthralment by the Well-Beloved into a nightmare, with a refinement of tone confidently managed by Hardy. Jocelyn is a gentle, generous and honourable man, realistically flawed, with a problem that is recognisable and (in moderated form) possibly universal, and he is guilty of nothing more serious than being over-fastidious and indecisive. It would be perverse to call his behaviour immoral, though perhaps Hardy was naïve in his expectation that Victorian readers would accept Jocelyn as obviously moral and in his protests that the story was fit for circulation in the nursery; or perhaps he was being provocative and tongue-in-cheek.

Yet his claims that Jocelyn remains 'an innocent and moral man throughout'[34] are literally true. The sculptor's idealism is genuinely Platonic and never physical: 'It was not the flesh; he had never knelt low to that. Not a woman in the world had been wrecked by him, though he had been impassioned by so many.' But this may also suggest that, in common with many of Hardy's men, natural and aggressive male sexuality eludes him. If Jocelyn's Platonism is entirely distinct from physical desires he is psychologically abnormal; if not, his failure to satisfy such desires intensifies his predicament. His dilemma is physical as well as metaphysical. But Jocelyn is emotionally immature; he can never progress, despite his advance in years, beyond the role of passive observer. When at the age of 38 he complains to his friend Somers about the constant migration of his ideal beloved, the painter replies with conventional wisdom appropriate to anyone but Pierston: 'Wait till you are older.' But age effects no such maturity for the sculptor, whose frustrations cause him to exist perpetually in a 'highly charged electric condition', like Miss Aldclyffe and Henry Knight and Captain de Stancy before him. This tantalising state of purely cerebral sexuality is alleviated only at the cost of Jocelyn's eventual complete impotence, the reaffirmation of which commentators have identified in a Freudian image at the end of the novel: 'the closing of the old natural fountains in the Street of Wells.'

Jocelyn's sexuality is thus catastrophically introverted. His love is entirely subjective, and his elusive Well-Beloved never progresses beyond being a projection of his own imagination, his own needs. Hardy reverted to this in a late notebook entry (*L*, 432):

> July 1926. Note – It appears that the theory exhibited in *The Well-Beloved* in 1892 has been since developed by Proust still further:
>
> 'Peu de personnes comprennent le caractère purement subjectif du phénomène qu'est l'amour, et la sorte de création que c'est d'une personne supplémentaire, distincte de celle qui porte le même nom dans le mond, et dont la plupart des éléments sont tirés de nous-mêmes.' (*Ombre*, 1.40.)
>
> [*À l'ombre des jeunes filles en fleurs* in *À la recherche du temps perdu*.]

But unlike most people Jocelyn can never decide that he has found his proper complement. He will not commit himself. When he faces reality his fear drives love away: 'a ten-minutes' conversation in the wings with the substance would send the elusive haunter scurrying fearfully away into some other even less accessible mask-figure.' It is part of Hardy's thinking too, celebrating those who attract him in the safely distanced medium of verse and noting on 8 July 1899 that 'love lives on propinquity, dies of contact' (*L*, 220). And it is an idea that is never far below the surface throughout his fiction. It is present as early as the first chapter of his first published novel: 'With all, the beautiful things of the earth become more dear as they elude pursuit; but with some natures utter elusion is the one special event which will make a passing love permanent for ever.' (*Desperate Remedies*, Chapter 1, Part 2)

Love's only true residence for Jocelyn is Avice Caro. Unlike his feelings for the others his love for her is not illusory but real yet, because the departure of the ideal spirit from her has not left her a mere cipher and Jocelyn can say that 'I retain so great a respect for her still,' he decides almost perversely that she cannot have been a true embodiment of the Well-Beloved. It is only when she is distanced by death that Jocelyn becomes obsessed with 'the lily-white corpse of an obscure country girl', poring over his melancholy mass of relics, loving her 'dead and inaccessible as he had never loved her in life', just as Hardy was to celebrate Emma after her death twenty years later. Pierston possesses the time-honoured Hardyan quality of loyalty but it is loyalty to the image of Avice the first that animates his subsequent infatuation with Avice the second and Avice the third. He only loves Avice the second in so far as she is 'the living representative of the dead', 'the resuscitated Avice', 'a perfect copy'. Later her daughter becomes 'the renewed Avice', vital to Jocelyn not for her own sake or as her mother's daughter but again simply as 'a glorification of the first'.

Pierston's error lies in his worshipping only external appearance. Because of their physical likeness he expects Avice the second and Avice the third to be precise psychic replicas of Avice the first, whom alone he loves (and that only posthumously). The sculptor expects nothing less than metempsychosis and fails to realise that each successive Avice possesses her own distinct personality. Further refinement in their characterisation might

have made this clearer to the reader and exerted a more
powerfully ironic sense of Pierston's delusion. Avice the second,
a washerwoman, has none of the imagination and ingenuous
charm of her mother: leading an intensely circumscribed life, she
is 'clearly more matter-of-fact, unreflecting, less cultivated.' But
she is distinguished by sharing Jocelyn's pursuit of the impossible ideal and in being as fickle as he. Avice the third, although
more sophisticated, is hardly defined as an individual, though
her role is larger in the serial, where her growing aversion for her
elderly husband preludes Sue's aversion for Phillotson. Her
definition is otherwise perfunctory. The Caros (whose symbolic
name derives from the Italian for 'dear'[35] though the translation
from the Latin *caro*, meaning 'flesh' or 'body', is equally
suggestive) and Avice the third do not live so much as fulfil
functions in the stylised plot, and no conviction of their being
real people is generated. The force of one character is dissipated
by division into three, and the novel suffers in having only one
dominant and psychologically complete character.

Apart from Jocelyn only Marcia Bencomb has an impressive
presence, and this is confined to the early and late stages of the
book. 'Dignified, arresting ... a very Juno', in her role as
Jocelyn's 'queenly darling' there is a suggestion of the impetuous
Eustacia, and in her modernism she anticipates Sue. Marcia,
like both of them, is vital and vulnerable. Her spirited presence
so enlivens the serial that it is regrettable that her function is
diminished in the book. She shares the pathos of physical
deterioration with Viviette Constantine, though Hardy in a
more mellow mood allows Marcia at least a token union with the
man whom her independence has rejected four decades earlier.
But there is a hint of Hardy's disdain for his provision in the
book of a more innocuous and superficially undisturbing ending:
'That's how people are,' Jocelyn is made to say, 'wanting to
round off other people's histories in the best machine-made
conventional manner.'

Hardy's own history as a novelist resists such easy definition.
The Well-Beloved, by chance rather than design, is an unusual but
not an unworthy vehicle for his leave-taking as a writer of prose
fiction. Its experimental nature is consistent with Hardy's ability
to surprise throughout his career. Perhaps such a romantic
notion could not entirely come to life and too slender characterisation combines with a too rigidly schematic structure to vitiate

any claim to greatness. But *The Well-Beloved* is ingenious and contains challenging and important ideas uniquely tested. Hardy's fiction is always devoid of complacency, and the impulse to disturb operates to the end; temperamentally incapable of satisfying a public eager for neat and optimistic conclusions, Hardy can never resist (even in so mild a pastoral as *Under the Greenwood Tree*) putting a sting in the tail. The novels should be read individually and collectively as symbolic poems – the narratives are 'as near to poetry in their subject' (*L*, 291) as conditions allow – and even in lighter mood Hardy cannot disguise his sombre view. The tragic irony of *The Well-Beloved* is acerbic: for Jocelyn the 'fantast', in his impossible quest for that Protean essence the Well-Beloved, life ends as 'a ghost story', a waste land where the search for happiness in love is always thwarted. For Hardy there is always at least one worm in the bud; the empty relations of Jocelyn and Marcia scarcely even aspire to this dignity. There is no doubt that Hardy feels Jocelyn's tragedy deeply.

After the appearance of *The Well-Beloved* the reviewer in the *Athenaeum* (10 April 1897) optimistically speculated about its author: 'One can only hope that the fact of his now bringing it out in book form indicates a desire to renew those pleasant relations with his readers that should never have been interrupted.' But Hardy had no such desire because 'pleasant relations' had to be bought at too great a price. He turned to the more instinctive craft of poetry with evident relief, remarking at the time that the novel was 'gradually losing artistic form, with a beginning, middle, and end, and becoming a spasmodic inventory of items, which has nothing to do with art' (*L*, 291). These are scarcely failings of which Hardy could be accused. His last published novel, while possessing an unquestionable and indeed unusual formality of structure, flings a final aesthetic taunt at such inventorial naturalism.

9 Conclusion

Hardy's lesser novels are sound and substantial works of fiction. It has been necessary to seek to identify those deficiencies that make them lesser achievements than *The Mayor of Casterbridge* or *Tess* or *Jude*, but there is no ambivalence about this study's final estimation of their worth. They are imperfect, of course, but they are also fascinating and rewarding. And Hardy's genius was never dependent upon artistic perfection. Even his major works are flawed, not least in their style, and it is not sophistic to claim that this is one of his special idiosyncrasies. The Hardy who emerges from this reading is not inferior or second-rate but the same man seen from different angles through the prism of his art. It is often opined that *Desperate Remedies* fails because it is a pot-boiler, yet all Hardy's novels are to some extent pot-boilers, written under economic duress as a distraction from poetry; sometimes one becomes a masterpiece while others retain the too obvious marks of pot-boiling by a poet of genius. What is remarkable is that by conventional standards even some of the major novels may appear so bad in parts (and all Hardy's readers will know what is meant by that) and yet retain their distinction.

Hardy's genius offers something different from the qualities that make the novels of Henry James or George Eliot so highly valued. Those writers were professionals in the sense that they believed in the novel with an almost religious commitment and regarded it as a vocation or mission. Yet it is not a lack of seriousness on his part, or his unwillingness to theorise, that distinguishes Hardy. It is something more fundamental: though he was a professional writer too, in so far as he lived by fiction writing, he remained a poet by vocation and belief. He does not disregard the rules of fiction but, as a poet, often makes a decision of conspicuous daring; sometimes his gamble comes off, sometimes it does not. Some melodramatic episodes, for example, in the lesser novels are objectively no more unacceptable than the death of Little Father Time in *Jude the Obscure*. At the same time, as Virginia Woolf said, 'his own word, "moments of vision", exactly describes those passages of astonishing beauty and force which are to be found in every book that he wrote.'[1] She also said that the novels are 'full of inequalities', and so they are. To put it another way, they are full of surprises. An occasional misjudgement or a piece of clumsy writing may unexpectedly vitiate the dramatic effectiveness of a scene in one of the masterpieces, yet the lesser novels contain some passages that are among his best and some characters who, in their psychic definition and consistency, rival the acknowledged major figures. But Hardy's distinctive presence does not enliven every narrative equally and reasons for this, beyond the inevitable inequalities of all artistic endeavour in an imperfect world, must be sought.

The circumstances in which each novel was written and published undoubtedly affected the nature and quality of each work. I have described the historical reasons for Hardy's excursion into writing an urban comedy of manners in *The Hand of Ethelberta* after critics had assigned his talents almost exclusively to pastoral fiction, and for his decision to present in *The Trumpet-Major* a relatively unchallenging entertainment after his serious intentions in *The Return of the Native* had met with critical disapproval. In each case Hardy had been diverted from subjects and methods more congenial to his imagination; in one case into an ambitious experiment and in the other into a constrainedly moderate ironic tale, neither of which permitted him to rise to grand strokes. But it is in the demands of serial publication, and in particular Hardy's dealings with editors, that a number of limitations of these novels can be seen to have been imposed upon him. It was not only in the famous instances (like *Tess*) that he had to battle to write as he wished, but up to and including his last published novel, *The Well-Beloved*, he never had the freedom he wanted. Like all his immediate contemporaries Hardy was a victim of his time; if he had been writing novels 50 years earlier or 50 years later he would have enjoyed far more freedom.

Lawrence writes of Hardy's characters' wanting to burst out of Wessex and do extraordinary things; their creator too was hampered by conventions. It is not that he wanted to escape the geographical or psychic limits of his fictive world, there being 'quite enough human nature in Wessex for one man's literary purpose',[2] but the analogy is that he too was held back, in his art, by subjection to the *mores* of timid editors. He was galled by what he called 'the irritating necessity of conforming to rules which in themselves have no virtue' (*L*, 111). His early career was dominated by his continuing ambition to write a novel suitable for publication by Alexander Macmillan, and later he was driven to compromise with his editors, who in turn felt driven to please their readers. He was at various times lectured by Macmillan, John Morley, William Tinsley, John Blackwood, Leslie Stephen, Donald Macleod, Clement Shorter and others. As a result a tension is often encountered in the lesser novels between the work Hardy wanted to write and the one he had to write to please his publishers; the one can sometimes be tantalisingly glimpsed through the other.

Hardy did not want to be explicit in description, though he must have found the suppression of such harmless expletives as 'Good God!' and 'Damn!' (in *The Trumpet-Major*) tiresome and trivial, for his candour is mainly shown by implication and suggestion. (He was capable of meeting convention head-on on rare occasions, as in his curious and deliberate exacerbation of 'offensive' circumstances in *Two on a Tower*.) It is in a more fundamental sense that these novels were affected. For Hardy, again in the words of Virginia Woolf, 'a novel is not a toy, nor an argument; it is a means of giving truthful if harsh and violent impressions of the lives of men and women.'[3] The impulse to disturb which informs his fiction was not always what conventional drawing-room readers wanted, and in the lesser novels Hardy is often seen accommodating their preferences and eschewing the harshness and violence which is integral to his truthful illumination of individual lives. And the insidious way in which publishing arrangements may have affected the eventual form, and consequently stature, of each of these novels has been considered in the foregoing chapters.

One of the reasons why the successful novels are more imposing may be that in them Hardy has not so readily deferred to his editors. In writing *Far from the Madding Crowd* he accepted the guidance of Leslie Stephen, but *The Return of the Native* was rejected by both Stephen and John Blackwood before it was eventually serialised in *Belgravia*. (Hardy had to discard his original ending in deference to serial tastes, however, as he makes clear in the well-known footnote to Book Sixth, Chapter 3.) *The Mayor of Casterbridge*, a less provocative text, was published by Smith, Elder, whose misgivings were restricted to the lack of gentry in the story. In *The Woodlanders* Hardy needed to make no significant concession to the sensibilities of his readers, and his extensive difficulties with *Tess* and *Jude* are well known.

By the time he wrote *Tess* Hardy was more determined to write what he felt, even if for serial publication he had to compromise by making cuts which could later be restored, and he accepted as inevitable that many readers would be offended by this novel and by *Jude*, since in extending his psychic investigation of Wessex to its limits he had to touch the raw nerves of his characters and through them those of his readers. But the major novels also suffered less from circumstantial pressures because their stronger stories and situations made the more provocative aspects less exceptionable, and in novels like *The Mayor of Casterbridge* and *The Woodlanders* Hardy found congenial themes which he could deal with both as he wanted and as his public wanted. Although, always sensitive to editors' and critics' opinions, Hardy found the course of his career deflected at various stages, and the nature of some of the lesser novels can be attributed to such accidents of circumstance, his sensitivity was in a way the artist's necessary defect; for 'sensitiveness was one of Hardy's chief characteristics, and without it his poems would never have been written, nor, indeed, the greatest of his novels.' (*L*, 415)

It is not always easy to isolate the artistic reasons why the lesser novels fail to attain the stature of the others. One explanation can be sought in the reasons behind Hardy's own classification, in 1912, of his novels into three categories. The 'Novels of Character and Environment' include all the seven novels upon which Hardy's reputation as a novelist rests.[4] Among the 'Romances and Fantasies' one (*The Trumpet-Major*) has attained a moderate critical acceptance while the others (*A Pair of Blue Eyes, Two on a Tower, The Well-Beloved*) tend to be regarded at best as interesting curiosities. The phrase describing the final group as 'Novels of Ingenuity' (*Desperate Remedies, The Hand of Ethelberta, A Laodicean*) is often regarded unsympathetically as an excuse for three inferior and otherwise indescribable works. But the categories themselves, which suggest a deeper understanding of the exact nature of his own fiction than is often attributed to Hardy, go some way to explaining why certain of these novels elicit less response than others. It is exactly the psychic interplay of 'character' and 'environment' that sustains the reader's deeper interest in the major novels, and while this is not absent from the others, the effect is muted by other factors. Sensationalism dominates *Desperate Remedies* as fantasy of conception dominates *The Well-Beloved*, though both novels could, without substantial adjustments to plot, have been written on the more familiar plan.

The 'Romances and Fantasies' have distinctly suffered from changes in sensibility. They are written with a moderation of tone and a romantic awareness that appeal less to our susceptibilities than the Victorians'. There is a softness in Hardy here to which he does not give way in *Tess* or *Jude*. But there are ironies too, sometimes on the surface but sometimes submerged. There is both a strength and a weakness in such half-concealed ironies, which may have disrupted the leisurely expectations of serial readers percipient enough to have seen them and which often sustain the true implications of the work; yet this ambiguity dissipates their dramatic effectiveness. It is a device which offers Hardy a way of keeping his integrity when he is not equal to an outright challenge, and it is surely not too fanciful to suggest that, while he had to submit to 'rules which in themselves have no virtue', he may have derived private satisfaction or even solace from the irony of knowing that his true meaning had been misunderstood by comfortable drawing-room readers. If the ironic dimension of the 'Romances and Fantasies' had been conveyed more unambiguously to the reader, they might have been more readily seen as congeneric with the major novels.

There is a circumstantial explanation for each of the 'Novels of Ingenuity'. *Desperate Remedies* is an unusually powerful first novel which belongs to, but extends beyond, the sensation genre. It suffers from defects of inexperience yet reveals at once its author's idiosyncrasies. *The Hand of Ethelberta* also derives from another genre, this time of the stage, but like *Desperate Remedies* goes beyond the limitations of its kind. Written to disprove inferences of Hardy's bucolic isolation (and concomitant restriction of range) drawn by critics after *Far from the Madding Crowd*, this ironic comedy of manners reveals an unexpected flexibility, and the experiment is more successful than has generally been acknowledged. But both of these novels (along with *A Pair of Blue Eyes*) are relatively early works and all have a polymorphous quality: they contain an impressive range of concerns and strategies, but are ultimately not focused sharply enough. In Hardy's own phrase he had not yet discovered his 'real literary message', and as a result his shot is scattered too wide. The major works are distinguished by greater concentration and unity of purpose and technique. The third 'novel of ingenuity', *A Laodicean*, deserves to be rescued as much as any, if only because it is usually so uncompromisingly written off as Hardy's worst novel. In fact it is by no means the least interesting, and it is a mistake to assume that, because for a long period it is laden with melodramatic devices, it is not a serious work. Its defects derive from the accident of its having been largely written under the stress of serious illness, and only this vitiated its early promise of being Hardy's most successful social comedy.

A Laodicean, in common with several others among the lesser novels, is (according to its sub-title) 'A Story of To-Day'. This contemporaneity, deliberately adopted since Hardy wanted to address some of the social and intellectual problems of his day, has proved unacceptable to many readers. His sense of the past has such a powerful dramatic presence in most of his novels that when it is absent there is a feeling of something lost. The concept of 'A Story of To-Day', predictably enough, makes a less direct appeal to the imagination than, for example, 'A Story of a Man of Character' or that of 'A Pure Woman/Faithfully Presented'. But the austerity of the sub-title of *A Laodicean*, which could apply equally to *The Hand of Ethelberta* and *Two on a Tower*,[5] should not disguise the nature of Hardy's concern: the place of the emotions in a world increasingly ordered by science and reason. Social movements are in progress in all these novels. They dramatise some of Hardy's most intimate preoccupations and inaugurate his investigation of what he later calls 'the ache of modernism', which finds its conclusion in *Tess* and *Jude*. Our reading of those masterpieces in the total context of Hardy's fiction is incomplete if we ignore the incipient psychic fragmentation in the lives and experiences of the protagonists in *The Hand of Ethelberta*, *A Laodicean* and *Two on a Tower*.

The intellectual movement from *Ethelberta* to *Jude* is a consistent and organic process. And to some extent the character typologies of the lesser novels relate to those in the greater: it is not extravagant to align Viviette Constantine (and Elfride Swancourt) with Tess, or Paula Power with Sue Bridehead. In the chapter studies of individual novels I have tried to substantiate these claims in an attempt to show that in the lesser novels Hardy's intellectual view of his fictional world coheres. It is not seen as a deliberate process, which Hardy always insisted that it was not; his preoccupations take shape not in the form of a philosophy but as responses to experience. In this impressionistic series of individual histories, in major and lesser novels, he maps out the limits of his intellectual concern.

What distinguishes the later novels in this respect is that in them these fundamental 'questionings' (to use another of Hardy's evocative terms) are seen to better dramatic effect. The social comedy of *The Hand of Ethelberta*, *A Laodicean* and *Two on a Tower* is not the best form for these serious themes, which are inevitably constrained by the mode. It is often easier, too, in the lesser novels to isolate their 'subject'; the mature complexities of *Tess* and *Jude* disallow such definition. But a further distinction is that in the 'stories of today' Hardy often moves into society outside Wessex. Whatever the limitations of the countryside, man as Hardy best knows and instinctively understands him belongs in it. However hostile it may be, there is a relationship. Communities in the country, too, are interrelated: they join in choirs, inns, jobs, even in turning against others. And though it may satisfy Hardy to turn to the society outside the scenes with which he is most familiar and which he has brought alive so convincingly, and express his dissatisfaction and restlessness, it is almost bound to seem less satisfactory to many readers. Perhaps Hardy need not have doubted what he later acknowledged, the psychic completeness of Wessex and his conviction that 'the domestic emotions have throbbed in Wessex nooks with as much intensity as in the palaces of Europe.' (General Preface, 1912)

These novels which in their stories escape from Wessex may satisfy intellectually yet seem less satisfying as novels about human relations. But the question arises whether it is not, in part at least, our expectations which diminish these relationships, our unwillingness to let Hardy out of Wessex. Local circumscription is not the equivalent of intellectual circumscription and, as Hardy properly claimed in the General Preface, a circumscribed setting does not imply any diminution of elemental passions; he writes of 'beings in whose hearts and minds that which is apparently local [is] really universal'. And at the same time the view that Hardy suddenly becomes incompetent when his dramas move outside the narrow geographical limits of Wessex needs to be challenged. These lesser novels with contemporary settings and cosmopolitan features have other defects: if their interest is partly to lie in the questions they raise, for example, we need to feel that Hardy is addressing these problems more openly and less obliquely. And these novels are to some extent weakened by internal tensions and individual structural deficiencies. But Hardy's incompetence in describing social situations in urban settings, and the belief that his alleged inability is attributable to ignorance, is simply a popular myth.

The objections may arise partly because the strong personal presence of Hardy in his work encourages the impression that there must be a closer than usual correspondence between the details of his plots and his own experiences, and the (incorrect) assumption that he had moved only in the circles that he normally describes in his fiction. It is naïve to suppose that any of the novels is 'about' the facts of Hardy's life in a direct sense; they are much more diffused translations of his experience. But there is evidence to suggest that he did draw directly upon situations and incidents of his own life, especially in some of the lesser novels. Biographical speculation of the kind which seeks to sensationalise Hardy's relationship with Tryphena Sparks (on the basis of spurious evidence) is irrelevant to serious consideration of his art, and I have deliberately abjured it. What we need to know is how Hardy transmutes his experience, and only biographical influences which may contribute to this understanding have been offered in this survey. Some such references are unavoidable, since in the lesser novels there seems to be an unusually direct relationship, and possibly the extent to which Hardy sometimes has recourse here to circumstantial details of his own life sets another limitation on his art. The similarities between the basic situations of both *A Pair of Blue Eyes* and *A Laodicean* and Hardy's courtship of Emma Gifford at St Juliot need not be laboured. The predominance of a series of passive young men with often remarkable historical and emotional similarities to Hardy himself (Springrove, Smith, Julian, Somer-

set, St Cleeve), three of them architects, establishes a groove of
characterisation from which he escapes in the major novels;
these apparent *doppelgängers* are all distinguished by a relative
lack of animation and contribute little, in terms of personality, to
the novels in which they individually appear.

Elsewhere Hardy's immediate experience enriches his subject:
both *A Pair of Blue Eyes* and *The Hand of Ethelberta* contain
unusually direct comments on fiction and criticism, reflections
on the nature of Hardy's developing craft. And in several of these
novels Hardy's background and immediate experience help us to
understand the direction of his social criticism and satire. *A
Laodicean* is a unique case, since we have Hardy's own word that
it contains 'more of the facts of his own life' than any other novel,
and the weakness of those sections in which, because of illness,
he falls back on such facts is instructive about the extent to
which facts have to be distilled and transformed to be artistically
convincing; yet the comparative bareness of the narrative throws
into prominence Hardy's own fears about the contingencies of
the modern spirit. None of these biographical correspondences
or influences makes any difference to the value we set upon the
novels as fiction, but they are suggestive constituents of the final
texture of the work. Hardy's emotional commitment always
vitalises the narrative, and it is only when he translates
biographical reality, as he does more often in the lesser novels,
that a limitation is imposed on his creative imagination.

It is not only the men who are coloured by Hardy's personal
engagement: one of the most positive features of the lesser novels
is a series of remarkable women, compulsive and psychically
complete. Miss Aldclyffe is powerful and individual; Elfride,
Paula and (especially) Viviette, in their combination of pur-
posiveness, docility and human weakness, are sympathetic and
endearing. Though none of them is unequivocally rewarded,
they are creatures of Hardy's reverence for humane values.
Ethelberta is unique: the most ambitious and wordly of all
Hardy's heroines, the first of the moderns and metaphysically
divided against herself, she is a moral study, and the implications of her psyche are frightening.

Hardy is always at least as interested in examining a life as in
telling a story, and his best fictions are individual histories. His
first novel, *Desperate Remedies*, is dominated by plot, but even here
Manston is no stock villain and Miss Aldclyffe no stock virago.

Hardy's fiction increasingly moves towards a situation where the individual history becomes the organising principle of the story, the proper mode for 'a true exhibition of man'.[6] If in the lesser novels the characterisation is more diffuse, a quality which they share with *The Return of the Native* and *The Woodlanders* in particular among the major novels, the internal tensions which give life to characters are not absent. As early as *A Pair of Blue Eyes* the principal protagonists have moved beyond stereotypes, and in *The Hand of Ethelberta* the possibilities of the individual history are tentatively explored and the potential stature of the central figure is constrained only by the mode in which the novel is written.

At last no single explanation can be assigned for their being lesser works, and their variety resists any generic definition. They each have individual strengths and weaknesses, but all have suffered too from superficial prejudices. Their titles, for example, are often unappealing. *A Pair of Blue Eyes* is weak, *The Hand of Ethelberta* is unprepossessing, *Two on a Tower* is simplistically alliterative (Hardy afterwards disliked it), and *A Laodicean* is for many readers uncertain in origin, spelling, meaning and pronunciation. Hardy's best titles are straightforward (*The Mayor of Casterbridge, The Woodlanders, Tess of the d'Urbervilles, Jude the Obscure*), spatially or personally definitive, and suggestive of the concentration of subject in the novels which they describe.

Each of the lesser novels contains surprises, whether it is the extraordinary definition of Ethelberta's character or the discovery that a clearer account of Hardy's social views can be derived from *The Hand of Ethelberta* and *A Laodicean* than from any of the more conventional sources. The more closely they are read the clearer it becomes that they are a series of essential pivots on which Hardy's entire career as a novelist turns. Created at vital moments in his development, they (the earlier ones especially) usually portend something new which is later subsumed into the texture of the major works. Several of them are experimental, often boldly so, and reveal a flexibility which traditional accounts of Hardy's range deny. A theory of his fiction cannot be evolved from these novels alone, but no such theory is complete if it does not take them into account. I think that anyone who can discover or rediscover these neglected novels with an open mind will find them interesting and often provocative works that surely deserve to be on the bookshelf rather than in the attic.

Bibliography

Until 1975 the lesser novels were not published in paperback but since that date they have been available, in paperback or hardback and with introductions and notes, in the Macmillan New Wessex edition.

The following editions of Hardy's own writings have been specially useful:

L.A. Björk (ed.), *The Literary Notes of Thomas Hardy*, I (1974).
James Gibson (ed.), *The Complete Poems of Thomas Hardy* (1976).
Evelyn Hardy and F.B. Pinion (eds), *One Rare Fair Woman: Thomas Hardy's Letters to Florence Henniker 1893-1922* (1972).
F.E. Hardy, *The Life of Thomas Hardy* (1962).
Harold Orel (ed.), *Thomas Hardy's Personal Writings* (1966).
Richard H. Taylor (ed.), *The Personal Notebooks of Thomas Hardy* (1979).

I have researched in original manuscript materials and in the novels' serial versions, and I have consulted a wide range of contemporary reviews; some of the latter are reprinted in R.G. Cox (ed.), *Thomas Hardy: The Critical Heritage* (1970).

The following books and articles have been generally useful:

J.O. Bailey, *The Poetry of Thomas Hardy* (1970).
Edmund Blunden, *Thomas Hardy* (1942).
Douglas Brown, *Thomas Hardy* (1954).
David Cecil, *Hardy the Novelist* (1943).
J.S. Cox (ed.), *Thomas Hardy: Materials for a Study of his Life, Times and Works* (I, 1968; II, 1971).
David J. DeLaura, '"The Ache of Modernism" in Hardy's Later Novels', *Journal of English Literary History*, XXIV (1967) 380-99.
Ruth Firor, *Folkways in Thomas Hardy* (1931).
Helmut E. Gerber, 'Hardy's *The Well-Beloved* as a comment on

the Well-Despised', *English Language Notes*, I (1963) 48-53.

Ian Gregor, *The Great Web: The Form of Hardy's Major Fiction* (1974).

Ian Gregor, 'What Kind of Fiction Did Hardy Write?', *Essays in Criticism*, XVI (1966) 290-308.

Albert J. Guerard, *Thomas Hardy* (1949; rev.edn.1964).

Albert J. Guerard (ed.), *Hardy: A Collection of Critical Essays* (1963).

Evelyn Hardy, *Thomas Hardy: A Critical Biography* (1954).

Evelyn Hardy and Robert Gittings (eds.), *Emma Hardy's 'Some Recollections'* [1911] (1961).

Desmond Hawkins, *Hardy the Novelist* (1950).

Irving Howe, *Thomas Hardy* (1967).

Trevor Johnson, *Thomas Hardy* (1968).

Lawrence O. Jones, '*Desperate Remedies* and the Victorian Sensation Novel', *Nineteenth-Century Fiction*, XX (1965), 35-50.

Edward D. McDonald (ed.), *Phoenix: The Posthumous Papers of D.H. Lawrence* (1936).

Arthur S. MacDowall, *Thomas Hardy: A Critical Study* (1931).

J.C. Maxwell, 'Mrs Grundy and *Two on a Tower*', *Thomas Hardy Year Book*, no.2 (1971), 45-6.

J. Hillis Miller, *Thomas Hardy: Distance and Desire* (1970).

Michael Millgate, *Thomas Hardy: His Career as a Novelist* (1971).

Charles Morgan, *The House of Macmillan* (1943).

Roy Morrell, *Thomas Hardy: The Will and the Way* (1965).

Simon Nowell-Smith (ed.), *Letters to Macmillan* (1967).

F.B. Pinion, *A Hardy Companion* (1968).

Richard L. Purdy, *Thomas Hardy: A Bibliographical Study* (1954).

William R. Rutland, *Thomas Hardy* (1938).

Clarice Short, 'In Defence of *Ethelberta*', *Nineteenth-Century Fiction*, XIII (June 1958), 48-57.

J.I.M. Stewart, *Thomas Hardy: A Critical Biography* (1971).

Carl J. Weber, *Hardy of Wessex* (1940; rev.edn.1965).

Carl J. Weber (ed.), *'Dearest Emmie': Thomas Hardy's Letters to his First Wife* (1963).

Harvey Curtis Webster, *On a Darkling Plain: The Art and Thought of Thomas Hardy* (1947).

George Wing, *Thomas Hardy* (1963).

Notes

Chapter 1: Introduction

1. 'Thomas Hardy', *Speaker*, II (13 Sep 1890) 295.
2. Preface to *Poems of the Past and the Present* (1920): 'Unadjusted impressions have their value, and the road to a true philosophy of life seems to lie in humbly recording diverse readings of its phenomena as they are forced upon us by chance and change' (Aug 1901).
3. A.H. Hyatt (ed.), *The Pocket Thomas Hardy* (London, 1906).
4. 'The Profitable Reading of Fiction' (1888), in *Personal Writings*, p.112.

Chapter 2: Desperate Remedies (1871)

Chapter title ('Well, that's a rum story'): Mr Dickson to Aeneas Manston, *Desperate Remedies*, Chapter 14, Part 3.
1. See Lawrence O. Jones, '*Desperate Remedies* and the Victorian Sensation Novel', *Nineteenth-Century Fiction*, xx (1965), 35-50.
2. In Simon Nowell-Smith (ed.), *Letters to Macmillan* (London, 1967) p.129, and in *Collected Letters*, I, p.7.
3. Letter of 10 Aug 1968 in Charles Morgan, *The House of Macmillan* (London, 1943) pp.88-91; Morley's comments, ibid., pp.87-8.
4. Letter, DCM.
5. *The House of Macmillan*, op.cit., pp.93-4.
6. Preface to Edward D. McDonald, *A Bibliography of D.H. Lawrence* (1925), in *Phoenix: The Posthumous Papers of D.H. Lawrence* (London, 1936) p.233.
7. For a full account of Hardy's dealing with Tinsley see J.A. Sutherland, *Victorian Novelists and Publishers* (London, 1976) pp.217-25.
8. '*Pendennis* and *Copperfield*: Thackeray and Dickens', *North British Review*, xv (May 1851) 57-89.
9. Anthony Trollope, *An Autobiography* (London, 1883; 1953 edn.) pp.295, 313.
10. The review also contains the famous charge that the author had adopted '"desperate remedies" for an emaciated purse'. Hardy recalls how he sat on a stile reading this review: 'The bitterness of that moment was never forgotten; at the time he wished that he were dead' (*L*, 84).
11. The original form is restored here. In 1912, perhaps now aware of the scene's further implications, Hardy substituted the phrase 'to care for and be cared for by'.
12. Ronald Pearsall, in *The Worm in the Bud: The World of Victorian Sexuality* (London, 1969;1971 edn.), discusses Lesbianism in Victorian England,

pp.576-93. Pearsall remarks that 'George Meredith, of whom no one could say that he was imperceptive, could write of a Lesbian attachment in *Diana of the Crossways* [1885] without realizing exactly what he was doing.' But the question arises therefore whether the attachment can be said to be Lesbian. Pearsall's quotation from Dr A. Forel (author of *Die Sexuelle Frage*, 1905) may have some bearing on the bed scene in *Desperate Remedies*: 'Kisses, embraces, and caresses in bed seem far less peculiar among girls than among boys, and the normal woman submits to such tenderness with far less nausea.' Perhaps the most that can fairly be said is that Miss Aldclyffe's behaviour is psychically consistent with her history.
13. Letter of 17 Aug 1871 to Malcolm Macmillan (Alexander's son); *The House of Macmillan*, op.cit., p.96.
14. 'Study of Thomas Hardy', *Phoenix*, op.cit., p.435.
15. 'He has joined the great majority': *Cena Trimalchionis*, 42.5, in *Petronii Arbitri Satyricon*, the satirical prose romance of Gaius Petronius (? – *c*. 65), who himself committed suicide to avoid being put to death by Nero.
16. J.O. Bailey, 'Hardy's "Mephistophelian Visitants"', *PMLA*, lxi (Dec 1946) 1146-84.
17. Crickett is the predecessor of many humorous rustics, including the Mellstock Quire; then, Lickpan and Cannister; Clark, Coggan, Moon, Tall; Grandfer and Christian Cantle; Fairway, Coney, Cuxsom, Jopp, Longways; Creedle and Tangs; Izz, Marian and Retty. Joseph Chinney is the first simple-minded innocent, and his genealogical successors include Leaf, Worm, Poorgrass and Whittle, all affectionately drawn and shown to be socially accepted. Springrove is the first of several insipid young heroes, several of whom are architects. Springrove and Owen Graye are the first of these architects, and even Manston is one, though there had been a yet earlier one (Will Strong) in *The Poor Man and the Lady*. Later ones include Stephen Smith and George Somerset.
18. *Phoenix*, op.cit., pp.218-19. Lawrence was writing in 1919 about the state of modern poetry, but the notion has a wider application.
19. See J. Hillis Miller, *Thomas Hardy: Distance and Desire* (Cambridge, Mass., 1970) pp.217-22. Miller notes the earnest pleas of some of Hardy's later characters: Henchard desires in his will that 'no man remember me'; Jude quotes Job as he lies dying, 'Let the day perish wherein I was born.'
20. Cf. Hardy's 1870 notebook entry: 'Oct.15. It is, in a worldly sense, a matter for regret that a child who has to win a living should be born of a noble nature. Social greatness requires littleness to inflate & float it, & a high soul may bring a man to the workhouse.' (*Personal Notebooks*, p.6.).
21. One of Hardy's early commonplace book notes reads: '*Subordination*. – "The grand scheme of subordination" [class to class] Boswell' (*Literary Notes*, p.6).
22. *Phoenix*, op.cit., p.435.

Chapter 3: A Pair of Blue Eyes (1873)

1. 10 Sep 1868; *The House of Macmillan*, op.cit., p.91.
2. Ibid., p.91.
3. Ibid., p.95.
4. Ibid., p.99.

5. 20 Oct 1871; Purdy, pp.11-12.

6. The novel was the last to be published by Tinsley, who called it 'by far the weakest of the three books I published of his' (Purdy, p.12).

7. The *Saturday Review* (2 Aug 1873) calls it 'a thoroughly matured work of its kind'; the *Pall Mall Gazette* (25 Oct 1873) finds 'a greater power of mental analysis and working of human nature' than in *Under the Greenwood Tree*; the *Graphic* (12 July 1873) says that it is 'free from the trace of sensationalism which somewhat disfigured *Desperate Remedies*, and has more "body" in it than ... *Under the Greenwood Tree*.' Both the latter reviews find the title vapid ('weak and sentimental', 'silly and unmeaning'). All the reviews commend the novel's humour but its tragic power inspired divided opinions, the *Athenaeum* (28 June 1873) finding something 'very farcical' about Elfride's tragic adventures.

8. 'The Profitable Reading of Fiction', in *Personal Writings*, p.114.

9. Ibid., p.117.

10. David Cecil, *Hardy the Novelist* (London, 1943, 1954 edn.) pp.127-8.

11. *A Pair of Blue Eyes* has to be read twice if proleptic clues are to be spotted. For example, even before Elfride admits to Knight her innocent deception about her age, the clues have been laid. In Chapter 18 she tells Knight she is 'nearly twenty' but in Chapter 12 a conversation between Elfride and Stephen has revealed her to be a month older than him, and in Chapter 3 Stephen has told Mr Swancourt that he is 'just over twenty'. Some considerable time has passed before Elfride claims to be 'nearly twenty'.

12. Hardy admits his contrivances to the reader in telling phrases: e.g., that Knight and Smith discover, after not meeting for many years, that they are both staying at the Grosvenor Hotel, Pimlico, is 'convenient, not to say odd'.

13. Evelyn Hardy and Robert Gittings (eds.), *Emma Hardy's 'Some Recollections'* (London, 1961) p.7.

14. Quoted by Carl J. Weber in *Hardy of Wessex* (New York, 1940; rev.edn.1965) p.86.

15. Moule, like Knight feeling that he had 'missed his mark', committed suicide on 24 Sept 1873, four months after this novel (which he warmly praised in the *Saturday Review*) was published. In Hardy's poem 'Standing by the Mantelpiece', a dramatic monologue which identifies the speaker as Moule, the speaker addresses a woman who has rejected him ('since you have spoken, and finality/Closes around') before he commits suicide.

16. *Literary Notes*, p.109.

17. 'General Preface to the Novels and Poems' (Wessex Edition, 1912).

18. 'Quand on voit le style naturel, on est tout étonné et ravi, car on s'attendait de voir un auteur, et on trouve un homme': Blaise Pascal, *Pensées sur la Religion et sur quelques autres sujets* [1670] (Paris, 1952) p.96; Avant-Propos, para.3.

19. Quoted in *Hardy of Wessex*, op.cit., p.86.

20. *Phoenix*, op.cit., p.412.

21. Impulses of the theme of *A Pair of Blue Eyes* are carried through to *Jude the Obscure*. In each novel the affections of the heroine are sought by a young and an older man. Each young man is self-educated, though Stephen has succeeded where Jude has failed; each of the older men is intelligent but inexperienced in love, and although Knight has made more of a success

than Phillotson he has similarly 'missed his mark'. Each heroine suffers moral weakness and vacillation, and the fate of each is a masochistic self-sacrifice when they fail to realise their hopes.

22. E.g. Knight's aquarium recalls Manston's rainwater-butt in its discernment of a microcosmic community; both Cytherea and Elfride are compromised by letters they have written; in each novel there is an intricately contrived episode in which observers are observed watching an event: in *Desperate Remedies* as Manston buries his wife's body (Chapter 19, Part 6), in *A Pair of Blue Eyes* as Stephen observes Knight and Elfride in the summer house and Mrs Jethway observes Stephen watching them (Chapter 25). And there are scenes in both novels in which the pair of lovers, seated below trees and beside a stream, observe themselves and each other reflected in the water: *Desperate Remedies*, Chapter 13, Part 4, and *A Pair of Blue Eyes*, Chapter 28.

23. Arthur S. MacDowall, *Thomas Hardy: A Critical Study* (London, 1931) p.97.

24. Ian Gregor, 'What Kind of Fiction did Hardy Write?' *Essays in Criticism*, XVI (1966) 290-308.

Chapter 4: The Hand of Ethelberta (1876)

1. *The Hand of Ethelberta* appeared in the *Cornhill Magazine* (July 1875–May 1876) and was published in book form on 3 Apr 1876.

2. 'Thomas Hardy', *Speaker*, II (13 Sep 1890) 295.

3. In another passage ultimately omitted from the *Life* Hardy delights in assuring us that 'Lady Portsmouth ... a woman of large social experience ... told Hardy that Ethelberta in his novel, who had been pronounced an impossible person by the reviewers, and the social manners unreal, had attracted her immensely because of her reality and naturalness, acting precisely as such women did or would act in such circumstances; and that the society scenes were just as society was, which was not the case with other novels' (*Personal Notebooks*, p.224).

4. 'Study of Thomas Hardy', *Phoenix*, op.cit., p.413.

5. Ibid., p.413.

6. 'The Profitable Reading of Fiction', in *Personal Writings*, pp.123-4. Hardy writes that 'considerations as to the rank or station in life from which characters are drawn can have but little value in regulating the choice of novels for literary reasons.' He repudiates the theory that society novels make better reading because 'it proceeds from the assumption that the novel is the thing, and not a view of the thing. It forgets that the characters, however they may differ, express mainly the author, his largeness of heart or otherwise, his culture, his insight, and very little of any other living person.'

7. In Derek Hudson's *Munby: Man of Two Worlds* (London, 1972) the Victorian barrister A.J. Munby (who himself married his maid) is shown to have noted sympathetically the case of Lord Robert Montagu (1825-1902) of Kimbolton Castle, who in 1862 married the housemaid Catherine Wade. Munby's diary records that he had 'heard from ladies of the shocking degradation of poor Lord Robert, & of his hopeless exclusion from family & friends by reason of this inexplicable depravity' (p.145). Some of the servants thought that Catherine had taken wise advantage of

her opportunity and saw her 'as a champion of her class'; yet there were dissensions from this view below stairs too.

Chapter 5: The Trumpet-Major (1880)

1. Review in the *Athenaeum* (23 Nov 1878). There may be a connection between Hardy's waking thought and his letter to the *Athenaeum* (30 Nov 1878; *Personal Writings*, p.91), which he must have just sent off.
2. W.E. Henley, *Academy* (30 Nov 1878); anon., *Saturday Review* (4 Jan 1879), anon., *Illustrated London News* (14 Dec 1878); anon., *Times* (5 Dec 1878).
3. The notebook is reproduced in full, with Hardy's sketches, in *Personal Notebooks*, pp.115-86.
4. See introduction to the '*Trumpet-Major* Notebook' in *Personal Notebooks*, pp.xxii-xxiv.
5. See Ruth Firor, *Folkways in Thomas Hardy* (Philadelphia, 1931) pp.299-301.
6. Letter in DCM. The letter's tone is not encouraging: 'my space is probably taken up for some time to come ... Please do not go out of your way at all with a view to me; but let me know at any time that you wish for a hearing & I can at any rate tell you what my prospects are.' The previous year Stephen had refused *The Return of the Native* since he feared that the relations between Eustacia, Wildeve and Thomasin might develop into 'something dangerous'.
7. Letter in DCM. George Macmillan has read the ms. 'with great interest' but his father, 'out of town for a few days', will write to Hardy after his return.
8. Hardy to John Blackwood, 9 June 1879 (National Library of Scotland: Blackwood Papers, ref.4391, folio 1). It is clear from earlier letters to Blackwood on 13 Feb, 12 Apr and 26 Apr 1877 (ref.4360, folios 168, 170, 172) that the earlier ms. was *The Return of the Native*. This means that the story had been rejected by *Blackwood's* before it was even offered to, and rejected by, Leslie Stephen at the *Cornhill*. There is no mention of the Blackwood's episode in Purdy, p.27, the standard bibliographical account of the novel.
9. Letter in DCM.
10. Letter in DCM.
11. A similar willingness to submit to editorial demands is shown in Hardy's 12 Apr 1877 letter to Blackwood submitting *The Return of the Native*: 'Should there accidentally occur any word or reflection not in harmony with the general tone of the magazine, you would be quite at liberty to stroke it out if you choose. I always mention this to my editors, as it simplifies matters.'
12. Draft of letter in DCM to Macleod's biographer, the Revd Sydney Smith (14 July 1925); the draft of Hardy's reply is written in his own hand on the back of a letter from Smith. Reproduced in Purdy, pp.32-3.
13. Cf. *Far from the Madding Crowd*, where the union of Bathsheba and Gabriel provides merely a conventional 'happy' ending. In *The Return of the Native* Hardy frankly regrets the marriage of Thomasin and Diggory Venn, forced on him by the exigencies of serial publication: see his footnote to Book Sixth, Chapter 3.
14. 'The Novels of Thomas Hardy', *Sewanee Review*, i (Nov 1892).

15. Carl J. Weber (ed.), *'Dearest Emmie': Thomas Hardy's Letters to his First Wife* (London, 1963) p.64. Emma's comment was recalled by Sir George Douglas.
16. Hardy to Blackwood, 9 June 1879 (National Library of Scotland).
17. 'What Kind of Fiction did Hardy Write?', op.cit., 308.
18. T.S. Eliot, *Four Quartets*, 'Burnt Norton', lines 1-3.
19. Letter (n.d. 1880) in DCM.
20. Hardy gives Anne some gently sobering reflections to temper her admiration for the soldiers: 'O yes, she liked soldiers, she said, especially when they came home from the wars covered with glory; though when she thought what doings had won them that glory, she did not like them quite so well.'
21. 'The Trumpet-Major/John Loveday/A Soldier in the War with Buonaparte/And/Robert His Brother/First Mate in the Merchant Service/A Tale.'
22. The weathervane is coloured for Bob (having earlier been coloured for John) and its variable currents are thus symbolically provided by Anne. The image of the weathervane persists throughout the novel. Anne inherits her indecisiveness from her mother, whom she takes to task in Chapter 10 for her changeable view of Festus: 'What a weathercock you are, mother!' Later her mother applies the epithet to Bob: 'It would so please me, my dear little girl, if you could get to like [John] better than that weathercock, Master Bob.' In complete contrast with the others, John displays in his firm and magnetic loyalty a 'determined steadfastness to his lodestar'.
23. Mr Garland had been a landscape painter, an impoverished but genteel occupation that renders his wife and daughter socially superior to Miller Loveday and his family: the miller is in commercial activity, John is an NCO and Bob an ordinary seaman. Mrs Garland, being 'so easy-minded, unambitious a woman', is unconcerned about 'the gradual levellings of social distinctions', and it is Anne who disparages the social standing of their neighbours and disdains the non-commissioned rank of trumpet-major.
24. In his '*Trumpet-Major* Notebook' Hardy lists over 30 plays of the period in which the story is set, mainly farces and comedies (see *Personal Notebooks*, pp.161-2). The theatrical terms in which the novel's lesser characters are conceived correspond to the conventions of many of these plays.
25. Cf. Captain Hardy's presentation in *The Dynasts*, Part First, Act V, Scenes 2 and 4.
26. Evelyn Waugh, *A Little Learning* (London, 1964; 1973 edn.) p.189.

Chapter 6: A Laodicean (1881)

1. Several extracts from Arnold's essays were copied out by Hardy in his commonplace book 'Literary Notes, ɪ' (DCM), which covers the years 1875-8. A number of these were copied in 1880, probably after Hardy met Arnold in February. Earlier references to Arnold include those on (page references to *Literary Notes*) p.13 (noted 1874-5), p.30 (noted in Apr 1876), p.104 (noted in Mar 1877), and especially pp.108-11 (from 'Heinrich Heine' and 'Pagan and Medieval Religious Sentiment', noted in Apr 1877;

cf. Arnold, *Essays in Criticism* (London, 1865), pp.156-93, 194-222). But it is the notes of 1879 and 1880 that evidence the most detailed reading of Arnold: pp.122-3 (from 'Wordsworth' in *Mixed Essays*: 'the noble and profound application of ideas to life is the most essential part of poetic greatness', 'poetry is at bottom a criticism of life', etc.), pp.126-8 (extensive quotations from 'Equality' in *Mixed Essays*), pp.131-5 (extensive quotations from *Essays in Criticism*: 'The Function of Criticism at the Present Time', 'The Literary Influence of Academies', 'Maurice de Guérin', 'Heinrich Heine', 'Pagan and Medieval Religious Sentiment', 'Joubert' and 'Marcus Aurelius'). See also Note 7 below.

2. Letter in DCM.

3. Letter in DCM.

4. See Purdy, pp.38-40. The proof-sheets are in the Library of Congress. (The original ms. was burned by Hardy.) Chapters 1-4 were in type by 3 Sep 1880 and 5-13 by 4 Oct. These represented serial instalments 1-3. The next instalment was in type by 6 Dec, the ms. of 5 was promised by 3 Jan 1881 and 6 was sent off on 5 Jan. Proof dates of subsequent instalments: 7, wanting; 8, 22 Mar; 9, 9 June; 10, 1 July; 11, n.d.; 12, 5 Aug; 13, n.d.

5. Letter in DCM.

6. During a conversation in 1900; W.L. Phelps, *Autobiography with Letters* (New York, 1939) p.390.

7. The movement of the story can be related to ideas in Arnold's essays, especially those which Hardy recorded in 1879-80 (see Note 1) just before writing *A Laodicean*, e.g. Hardy's paraphrase of a speculation in 'The Function of Criticism': 'Our material progress ... our railways, our business, & our fortune-making ... After he [man] has made himself perfectly comfortable [on these points] he may begin to remember that he has a mind, & that the mind may be made a source of great pleasure' (*Literary Notes*, pp.131-2). A main theme of *A Laodicean* (in which Paula's father is shown to have made his fortune in constructing railways) is precisely the investigation of the future of 'the mind' under stress of material progress and social evolution. The tentative form of Hardy's paraphrase, however, shows the danger of too-ready assumptions that he endorses all of Arnold's ideas. Neither in his note nor in the novel does he explicitly share the optimism of Arnold's original claim, which begins: 'In spite of all that is said about the absorbing and brutalising influence of our passionate material progress, it seems to me indisputable that this progress is likely, though not certain, to lead in the end to an apparition of intellectual life.' Arnold's ideas can often be more directly traced. But Hardy may simply have found a confirmation or an extension of what he already believed and of questionings in his own mind; to speak of Arnold's 'influence' could therefore be misleading. I have confined these suggestive correspondences, with one exception, to notes.

8. The theological uncertainty is one aspect of a larger conflict. The chapel scene images Paula's inability to choose. The verses that Mr Woodwell quotes from Revelation define Paula's spiritual condition: though 'rich and increased with goods' she is 'neither cold nor hot' and the story dramatises her quest for decisiveness. Hardy implicitly approves her rejection of the Nonconformist creed, as lifeless in its own way as the medievalism it seeks to replace, and champions Somerset's arguments against Mr Woodwell.

Hardy made some preliminary notes for this theological combat in the 'Trumpet-Major Notebook' (*Personal Notebooks*, pp.180-3).

9. Cf. 1895 Preface to *A Pair of Blue Eyes*. Sir William's attitude recalls the passage in Arnold's essay on Heine in which 'the modern spirit' is said to discern 'the sense of want of correspondence between the forms of modern Europe and its spirit, between the new wine of the eighteenth and nineteenth centuries, and the old bottles of the eleventh and twelfth centuries.' Hardy had copied out this passage and underlined it in red pencil (*Literary Notes*, p.109). More indications of the direction of Hardy's thought are suggested in the extracts he copied from Arnold's essay 'Equality' (*Literary Notes*, pp.127-8), detailing the now defunct role of the aristocracy.

10. Max Gate, which Hardy built for himself in 1883-5, invites enrolment as an example of 'mushroom modernism' and 'genuine roadside respectability'. In the sale catalogue of 16 Feb 1938 (after Florence Hardy's death) the house is described as 'most substantially built in a warm red brick, now mellowed and partially covered with jessamine and other creepers, with slate roof' (*Monographs on the Life, Times and Works of Thomas Hardy*, ed. J.S. Cox, No.66, 1970). Though modified by the 'jessamine and other creepers', the estate agent's description is ironically similar to Hardy's account of Mr Woodwell's austere dwelling.

11. Havill's anonymous letter to the newspaper is written along the same lines and protests against the possibility of the castle being made 'a complete ruin by the freaks of an irresponsible owner'.

12. Somerset chooses a method that is 'upon the face of it the true one' – a 'master-tradesman' responsible for each section of the work with Somerset as 'chief technicist' in overall design. But this is a pale imitation of the medieval ideal of the craftsman who was master of all trades himself. Morris laments the impossible lot of the 19th-century Gothic architect, forced 'to correct and oppose the habits of the mason, the joiner, the cabinet-maker, the carver, etc., and to get them to imitate painfully the habits of the 14th century workman, and to lay aside their own habits, formed not only from their personal daily practice, but from the inherited turn of mind and practice of body of more than two centuries' (May Morris (ed.), *The Collected Works of William Morris* (London, 1915), Vol.22, p.364).

13. Dare is its spokesman: 'We represent conditions of life that have had their day – especially me. Our one remaining chance was an alliance with new aristocrats; and we have failed. We are past and done for. Our line has had five hundred years of glory, and we ought to be content. *Enfin les renards se trouvent chez le pelletier.*'

14. *Essays in Criticism*, op.cit., p.220. The passage to which Paula's speech refers: 'The poetry of later paganism lived by the senses and understanding; the poetry of medieval Christianity lived by the heart and imagination. But the main element of the modern spirit's life is neither the senses and understanding, nor the heart and imagination; it is the imaginative reason.' The dilemma of the modern spirit, represented here by Paula, is defined in the essay on 'Heinrich Heine' (p.159): 'Modern times find themselves with an immense system of institutions, established facts, accredited dogmas, customs, rules, which have come to them from times not modern. In this system their life has to be carried forward; yet they

have a sense that this system is not of their own creation, that it by no means corresponds with the needs of their actual life, that, for them, it is customary, not rational. The awakening of this sense is the awakening of the modern spirit.' Arnold sees Heine as the exemplar of the modern spirit. Hardy copied both passages (*Literary Notes*, pp.109-10).

15. Somerset's becoming 'intently practical' is described without enthusiasm: 'It is an old story ... as has often been said, the light and the truth may be on the side of the dreamer: a far wider view than the wise ones have may be his at that recalcitrant time, and his reduction to common measure be nothing less than a tragic event.' This sentiment is emphasised in a moving simile describing the breaking of the haltered colt. That tragedy is implied in the subjugation of romanticism to common sense qualifies the hopefulness of the new society promised at the end; this is the price of progress. Both Somerset and Paula make concessions, but those later representatives of the 'modern spirit', Jude and Sue, refuse to submit to 'common measure' and meet with real tragedy. The novels in which these characters appear contain complementary approaches to the modern spirit, and identical assumptions underlie each story; while *A Laodicean* exhibits the victory of the realist, *Jude* describes the downfall of the dreamer.

16. Arthur MacDowall, op.cit., p.103.

17. J.I.M. Stewart, *Thomas Hardy: A Critical Biography* (London, 1971) p.154.

18. Shakespeare, *Love's Labour's Lost*, i.i.10.

19. 'Thomas Hardy: The Historian of Wessex', *Contemporary Review*, LVI (1889), 57.

20. See *Personal Notebooks*, p.57.

21. The note is a response to an entry made the previous day: 'After reading various philosophic systems, and being struck with their contradictions and futilities, I have come to this: Let every man make a philosophy for himself out of his own experience' (*L*, 310).

22. See J.O. Bailey, 'Hardy's "Mephistophelean Visitants"', op.cit., 1155-60.

23. Marcus Aurelius Antoninus, the Roman religious philosopher who taught that man's duty is to obey the laws of reason and accept suffering with equanimity. The quoted phrase recurs in *Tess*, Chapter 39: Angel shares the philosophy but finds it difficult to practise. Hardy's interest may have been inspired by Arnold's *Essays in Criticism*, where M. Aurelius is invoked both in 'Pagan and Medieval Religious Sentiment' and in a separate essay, 'Marcus Aurelius'. Arnold is interested in Aurelius since he too 'lived and acted in a society modern by its essential characteristics, in an epoch akin to our own' (*Essays in Criticism*, p.355). Though Aurelius generates a sense that man's burden is intolerable he urges 'man's cheerful acquiescence in whatever befalls him' (p.355).

24. David J. DeLaura, in '"The Ache of Modernism" in Hardy's Later Novels', *Journal of English Literary History*, XXXIV (Sep 1967) 380-99, gives an account of Hardy's intellectual response to the modern condition in the later novels.

Chapter 7: Two on a Tower (1882)

1. From 'Ode on the Pleasure arising from Vicissitude' (*L*, 149).

2. Hardy's 'scientific' letter, stating that he wished to ascertain the feasibility

of adapting 'an old tower, built in a plantation in the West of England for other objects, to the requirements of a telescopic study of the stars by a young man very ardent in that pursuit (this being the imagined situation in the proposed novel)', secured him permission to view the observatory, apparently in December. As Hardy must have learned, Swithin's tower would have been suitable. When a later Astronomer Royal decided 65 years afterwards to re-locate the Greenwich Observatory, several south coast sites were considered, and Herstmonceaux Castle, Sussex, was selected for meteorological reasons. The cloud cover in Dorset is substantially more than it is further east, otherwise a location in the area of Swithin's tower might have been chosen for the Royal Greenwich Observatory. I am most grateful to Professor Sir Martin Ryle, Astronomer Royal, and Dr Alan Hunter, former Director of the Royal Greenwich Observatory, for their cordial assistance.

3. Letter to Edmund Gosse, 4 Dec 1882; Purdy, p.44.
4. Letter to Edmund Gosse, 21 Jan 1883: 'The truth is that, though the plan of the story was carefully thought out, the actual writing was lamentably hurried ... it was printed without my first seeing the proofs' (Purdy, p.44).
5. There are explainable anomalies: *The Trumpet-Major*, although a 'lesser' novel, was written over seventeen months (some of which involved extensive research), while *Under the Greenwood Tree*, often accepted as a 'major' work despite its comparative slightness, took no longer than twelve weeks.
6. There were also some minor errors, notably a slip in styling Lady Constantine as Lady Helmsdale after her marriage to the bishop: this was quickly picked up by the *Saturday Review* and the *Athenaeum* (both 18 Nov 1882); cf. Purdy, p.46.
7. 'Thomas Hardy's Novels', *Westminster Review* (Apr 1883).
8. Before starting his next novel Hardy wrote only shorter works of fiction: 'The Romantic Adventures of a Milkmaid' and 'The Three Strangers' in autumn 1882 and 'Interlopers at the Knap' and 'Our Exploits at West Poley' in spring and summer 1883.
9. Hardy wrote this thirteen years after the novel's first publication, so the Preface gives a retrospective account of his intentions rather than his aims at the time of writing.
10. When Hardy had to draft an advertisement for the novel he described it as 'Being the story of the unforeseen relations into which a lady and a youth many years her junior were drawn by studying the stars together; of her desperate situation through generosity to him; and of the reckless *coup d'audace* by which she effected her deliverance' (Purdy, p.44). In other words, Hardy had to mask his serious intention behind a superficially entertaining one.
11. The Preface was written in July 1895, when Hardy was exasperated by readers' misconceptions about his work; some months earlier he had finished bowdlerizing *Jude* for serial publication.
12. Frye, *Anatomy of Criticism* (Princeton, 1957; New York, 1965) p.147.
13. Poem written in 1866. The reduction of earthly problems by contemplating the stars is also proposed by Swithin: 'Study astronomy at once. Your troubles will be reduced amazingly.' But Swithin proceeds to argue that 'your study will reduce them in a singular way, by reducing the importance

of everything', so that the sky will seem 'a juxtaposed nightmare'.

14. Written in 186- (probably referring to the eclipse of July 1860).

15. In a letter from Hardy to Gosse, 10 Dec 1882: 'I get most extraordinary criticisms of *Two on a Tower*. Eminent critics write and tell me in private that it is the most original thing I have done – that the affair of the Bishop is a triumph in tragi-comedy, &c., &c. While other eminent critics (I wonder if they are the same) *print* the most cutting rebukes that you can conceive – show me (to my amazement) that I am quite an immoral person: till I conclude that we are never again to be allowed to laugh and say with Launce – "it is a wise father that knows his own child"' (quoted in Purdy, pp.44-5). The only commendatory letter I have found among Hardy's papers is one from Charles Kegan Paul, who wrote on 12 Nov 1882 that the novel was 'very excellent' and who told Hardy: 'You introduce a marvellously comic touch in making the victim a Bishop' (DCM).

16. It is disturbing only to those whose attitude is strictly conventional – in other words most of Hardy's contemporary readers. Hardy's view, that it can hardly be said to matter how anyone is conceived, is made clear in his poetry. The marriage sacrament was, to him, simply the outward form of a civil contract. But in this novel, rather than saying explicitly what he believes (as he does later in his career) or using irony as cover for his attack, he is almost using it as a shield behind which to hide. In this he is by no means alone among Victorian novelists, but it dissipates the effectiveness of his satire.

17. J.C. Maxwell, 'Mrs Grundy and *Two on a Tower*', *Thomas Hardy Year Book*, No.2 (1971) 45-6.

18. 5 August 1920 (*One Rare Fair Woman*, p.192).

19. See J.O. Bailey, *The Poetry of Thomas Hardy* (Chapel Hill, 1970) pp.245-6.

20. Compare Stanza 7 with the description of Mrs Martin in an identical posture in Chapter 2.

21. Hardy's friendship with Mrs Martin, her kindness to him in his youth, their subsequent correspondence and meeting, is described in the *Life* (see pp. 18-20, 41, 101-2).

22. Quoted by Evelyn Hardy in *Thomas Hardy's Notebooks and Some Letters from Julia Augusta Martin* (London, 1955) p.129. Miss Hardy appends five letters from Mrs Martin to Hardy, sent between 1863 and 1887.

23. The unusual manner of Viviette's death probably derives from a notebook entry Hardy made between 30 Oct and Dec 1870: 'A man named Sherwood, a boxer, or as we now say, a pugilist. He used his wife roughly, left her, & went to America. She pined for him. At last he sent for her to come with the children. She died of joy at the news' (*Personal Notebooks*, p.7).

24. *Phoenix*, op.cit., p.438.

25. Letter dated 31 Oct 1920 (*One Rare Fair Woman*, p.193).

26. From the poem 'He Resolves to Say No More'.

Chapter 8: The Well-Beloved (1892, 1897)

1. C.C. Abbott (ed.), *The Letters of Gerard Manley Hopkins to Robert Bridges* (London, 1955) p. 238.

2. 'Candour in English Fiction' (1890), in *Personal Writings*, pp.128-9.
3. Ibid., p.132.
4. Hardy to Shorter, 29 Jan 1892, in Sotheby Sale Catalogue (29 May 1961) Lot 56.
5. Letters of 30 Dec 1896 and 24 Jan 1897 (*One Rare Fair Woman*, pp.58 and 60); subsequent letters of 27 Apr 1897 and 21 Dec 1905 (pp.64 and 125).
6. Letter of 25 Mar 1897 (National Library of Scotland, ms. file ref.8121).
7. Letter of 31 Mar 1897 (*One Rare Fair Woman*, p.63).
8. *The Revolt of Islam* (1818), Canto I, 1.363, and Canto VIII, 1.3276. Shelley's Platonic doctrine of love is best described in 'Epipsychidion' ['A soul that is complementary to a soul'] (1821), which exemplifies the search to which Jocelyn is made subject: 'In many mortal forms I rashly sought/ The shadow of that idol of my thought' (11. 267-8).
9. *Phoenix*, op.cit., p.480.
10. From Richard Crashaw (1612?-49), 'Wishes to His (Supposed) Mistress.' Hardy quotes: 'Now, if Time knows/That her, whose radiant brows/ Weave them a garland of my vows;/... Her that dares be/What these lines wish to see:/I seek no further, it is She.'
11. All 'omitted' passages are quoted from the serial version, 'The Pursuit of the Well-Beloved', in *Illustrated London News*, CI (July–Dec 1892), issues 1 Oct–17 Dec. (In the serial Jocelyn's surname is spelt 'Pearston'.) This phrase appears in the 8 Oct issue (serial p.458).
12. 15 Oct issue (serial p.481).
13. Ibid.; cf. *Jude the Obscure*, Part First, Chapters 9 and 11; Part Fourth, Chapters 2 and 4; Part Fifth, Chapter 3; Part Sixth, Chapter 8.
14 and 15. Ibid.; cf. *Jude the Obscure*, Part Fourth, Chapter 2; Part Fifth, Chapter 4.
16. 3 Dec issue (serial p.711). There is no corresponding passage in the book since the serial version was virtually discarded after Chapter 27 (corresponding to the end of Part Third, Chapter 4 and part of Chapter 5). Part Third, Chapters 6 to 8, were newly written. Compare this passage with *Jude the Obscure*, Part Fourth, Chapter 4.
17. 10 Dec issue (serial p.743). Cf. Phillotson, who 'did not see how an act of natural charity could injure morals' (*Jude the Obscure*, Part Fourth, Chapter 6). Also cf. Hardy's poem 'The Burghers', written about the time of this novel and *Jude*: 'And I may husband her, yet what am I/But licensed tyrant to this bonded pair?/Says Charity, Do as ye would be done by.'
18. 17 Dec issue (serial p.774). Jocelyn has already convinced himself that 'whatever the rights with which the civil law had empowered him, by no law of nature, of reason, had he any right to partnership with Avice against her evident will' (10 Dec issue); Phillotson declares himself 'more and more convinced every day that in the sight of Heaven and by all natural, straightforward humanity, I have acted rightly' (*Jude the Obscure*, Part Fourth, Chapter 6). Cf. also *Jude the Obscure*, Part Fourth, Chapter 4, in which Jocelyn's quoted speech is virtually reproduced.
19. In the serial, after Jocelyn has made an unsuccessful attempt at suicide, Marcia reappears by his bedside, her presence nullifying his marriage with Avice. The story concludes with Jocelyn in a fit of ghastly laughter.
20. May O'Rourke, *Thomas Hardy: His Secretary Remembers* (Beaminster, 1965) p.8.

21. 15 Oct issue (serial p.481).
22. 'The Voice'. In a note of July 1926 Hardy remarked that the theory exhibited in this novel had later been developed by Proust, and he quotes from *À la recherche du temps perdu*: 'Le désir s'élève, se satisfait, disparaît – et c'est tout. Ainsi, la jeune fille qu'on épouse n'est pas celle dont on est tombé amoureux' (*L*, 432).
23. 15 Oct issue (serial p.481).
24. 1 Oct issue (serial p.425); cf. 'The Photograph'.
25. 1 Mar 1888 (*L*, 206).
26. 1 Oct issue (serial p.426).
27. Cf. for example Hardy's letter to Sir George Douglas many years later: 'I have not been doing much – mainly destroying papers of the last 30 or 40 years, & they raise ghosts' (7 May 1919; National Library of Scotland, file ref. 8121).
28. Letter to A.C. Swinburne, 1897 (*L*, 28).
29. Helmut E. Gerber, 'Hardy's *The Well-Beloved* as a comment on the Well-Despised', *English Language Notes*, I (1963) 48-53.
30. For example those on serial pp.514, 578 (three passages), 642, corresponding to Part Second, Chapter 3; Part Second, Chapters 8 (two passages) and 9 (one passage); Part Second, Chapter 12.
31. Letter to Sir George Douglas, 25 Mar 1897 (see Note 6).
32. 17 Dec issue (serial p.775).
33. The internal torture of being misunderstood, a feeling familiar to Hardy, persists in his final association with Avice the third: 'He would fain have removed the misapprehensions on which [ridicule] would be based. That, however, was impossible. Nobody would ever know the truth about him; *what* it was he had sought ... His attraction to the third Avice would be regarded by the world as the selfish designs of an elderly man on a maid.'
34. Hardy's letter to the *Academy* (3 Apr 1897).
35. Ibid., where Hardy writes: '"Caro" (like all the other surnames) is an imitation of a local name which will occur to everybody who knows the place – this particular modification having been adopted because of its resemblance to the Italian for "dear".'

Chapter 9: Conclusion

1. Leonard Woolf (ed.), *Virginia Woolf: Collected Essays* (London, 1966) p.258.
2. 'General Preface to the Novels and Poems' (Wessex Edition, 1912).
3. Woolf, op.cit., pp.256-7.
4. *Under the Greenwood Tree* (1872), *Far from the Madding Crowd* (1874), *The Return of the Native* (1876), *The Mayor of Casterbridge* (1886), *The Woodlanders* (1887), *Tess of the d'Urbervilles* (1891), *Jude the Obscure* (1895).
5. *A Pair of Blue Eyes* and *Desperate Remedies* are also contemporary stories, though contemporaneity is less important in the theme of the former and irrelevant to that of the latter.
6. 'The Profitable Reading of Fiction' (1888), in *Personal Writings*, p.115.

Index